Nation, Society and Culture in North Africa

Edited by James McDougall

FRANK CASS
LONDON • PORTLAND, OR

306.0961
NAT

First published in 2003 in Great Britain by
FRANK CASS PUBLISHERS
Crown House, 47 Chase Side, London N14 5BP

and in the United States of America by
FRANK CASS PUBLISHERS
c/o ISBS, 920 NE 58th Avenue, Suite 300
Portland, Oregon 97213-3786

Website www.frankcass.com

Copyright © 2003 Frank Cass & Co. Ltd.

British Library Cataloguing in Publication Data

Nation, society and culture in North Africa. – (Cass
 series. History and society in the Islamic world; 6)
 1. Nationalism – Africa, North 2. Popular culture – Africa,
 North 3. Politics and culture – Africa, North 4. Africa,
 North – Civilization 5. Africa, North – Social life and
 customs
 I.McDougall, James
 306'.0961

ISBN 0 7146 5409 4 (cloth)
ISBN 0 7146 8337 X (paper)
ISSN 1466 9390

Library of Congress Cataloging-in-Publication Data:

Nation, society and culture in North Africa / edited by James McDougall
 p. cm. – (Cass series–history and society in the Islamic
world, ISSN 1466-9390)
Includes bibliographical references and index
 ISBN 0-7146-5409-4 – ISBN 0-7146-8337-X (pbk.)
 1. Africa, North–Politics and government–20th century. 2.Africa,
North–Civilization–20th century. 3. National state–Africa, North.
I. McDougall, James, 1974- II. Series.
 DT176.N38 2003
 961'.03–dc21

2002155478

This group of studies first appeared in a Special Issue on 'Nation, Society and Culture in North
Africa' of *The Journal of North African Studies* (ISSN 1362-9387) 8/1 (Spring 2003).

Printed in Great Britain by Antony Rowe Ltd., Chippenham, Wiltshire

Contents

MAP OF NORTH AFRICA

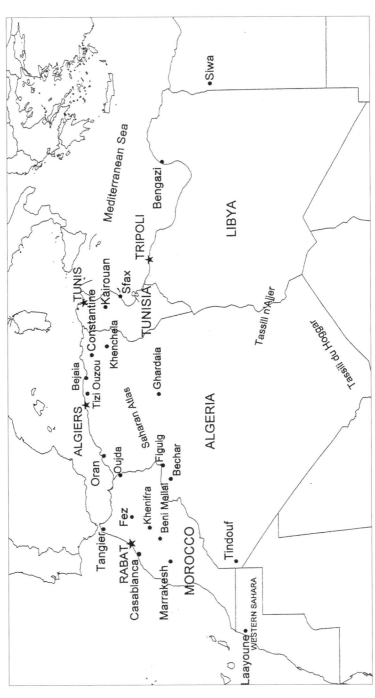

Foreword

It is with pride and honour that I introduce this volume on *Nation, Society and Culture in North Africa* edited by James McDougall which appears both as a book and as a special issue of *The Journal of North African Studies* that I edit with my colleague George Joffé. The study of North Africa or the Maghrib in the English-speaking world has expanded rapidly in recent years as reflected by the quality and quantity of original scholarship being produced, so well represented by the contributors to this collection.

History, geography, politics, and economics have long combined to explain the domination of French-language research and writing on the Maghrib. Yet, even during the most active period of Francophone scholarly production, English-language writers published some of the most intellectually stimulating, theoretically innovative, and empirically enriching scholarship ever produced which continues to inspire the work of younger researchers. Select representatives of these earlier writings are such distinguished intellectual path-breakers as Ernest Gellner, Clifford Geertz, David Hart, John Waterbury, Carl Brown, Charles Micaud, Bill Zartman, Charles Gallagher, John Ruedy, Clem Moore Henry, and Terry Burke, among others.

This is not at all to suggest that separate disciplinary traditions were being pursued, ones which divided Francophone scholars from their Anglophone counterparts. Indeed, from the outset there was an extensive cross-fertilisation of ideas and frameworks of analysis between French, British and American academics each using the others' language along with that of Arabic and Berber to deepen and extend the understanding of the North African state, culture, and society. James McDougall and his colleagues represent the best in this cross-over tradition integrating as they do different generational cohorts and disciplinary perspectives. What is particularly enlightening in this collection is the strong representation of women's scholarship with six of the nine substantive articles being written by female scholars.

While the first generation of modern English-writing on the Maghrib was dominated by men, subsequent generations have included a plethora of highly productive female writers within and outside North Africa including both senior and junior authors like Lisa Anderson, Melanie Cammett, Emma Murphy, Julia Clancy-Smith, Claire Spencer, Mounira Charrad, Boutheina Cheriet, Elaine Combs-Schilling, Laurie Brand, Eva Bellin, Susan Slyomovics, Alison Pargeter, Marnia Lazreg, and Susan Ossman.

This collection also continues in an impressive intellectual tradition of multi-authored volumes covering a wide-ranging cross-disciplinary landscape first initiated by Carl Brown at the time of North African independence (Leon Carl Brown (ed.), *State and Society in Independent North Africa*, 1966) and then continued by Bill Zartman covering the post-independence periods (I. William Zartman (ed.), *Man, State, and Society in the Contemporary Maghrib*, 1973 and I. William Zartman and William Mark Habeeb (eds.), *Polity and Society in Contemporary North Africa*, 1993).

The volume's lasting contribution, however, lies in the methodological rigour, theoretical focus, and sharp empirical insights provided by this impressive amalgam of multinational researchers directing their attention towards the Maghrib's representation of nationhood. In an age and in a region where political violence, civil unrest, and economic hardships occupy the headlines, close and careful attention to the historic roots of identity-formation, nation-building, and cultural construction as understood and lived by the people themselves are too often lost, ignored, or bypassed. The authors of this volume refocus our attention to the ways in which Maghribis have sought to define their existences through culturally-specific frameworks of analysis that transcend the bounds of colonialist constructions and imperialist designs. It is this shared concern of all the contributors with the 'lived realities of North Africans' contemporary historical experiences' that so impresses the reader of these chapters.

James McDougall must be given exceptional credit for initiating this scholarly enterprise and gathering such an impressive array of established and younger scholars across different disciplines. Specialists and lay readers alike will benefit greatly from this effort which brings knowledge about the nation, society and culture of North Africa to the English-speaking world at a time of great global anxiety and uncertainty. The timing of this publication is fortuitous as is the careful selection of topics and scholars.

John P. Entelis
Fordham University, New York
January, 2003

Introduction:
History/Culture/Politics of the Nation

JAMES MCDOUGALL

Studies focused around the concept of nationhood perhaps have a natural tendency towards homogenisation. The point of departure for discussions of social movements and political formations operating under the 'nation' rubric has often been some version of Renan's question, posed as long ago as 1882, 'what is a nation?'[1] The presuppositions involved in such questioning should be only too obvious – what is sought is a substantial entity, a *thing* which can be described, a sociographic form of being to which the name 'nation' can be satisfactorily (even 'scientifically') affixed. Influential variations on this theme have been contributed by figures as diverse as Josef Stalin and Ernest Gellner, without ever breaking out of the mould of thinking that has sought 'nation' in unifying forces of *identity*, that is in a shared *sameness* of historical experience, cultural world and political belonging. Whether emphasis is laid on the sites of language, 'universal high culture', or myth and memory; whether the key processes invoked are the shift from agrarian to industrial production, and from 'mechanical' to 'organic' solidarity, or the persistence of pre-modern '*ethnie*' and its transformation into the modern 'nation', or again, the centralising and integrating power of a strong, state-led political project,[2] such identity/sameness, and its function as the basis of a group identification on which legitimate political organisation in the modern world is held to be founded, has been a central focus of scholarly attention, particularly in recent years.

    With regard to what used to be called the 'new states' of the decolonised and developing world, the location of these factors of identity, and the means by which they might be seen to contribute to the development of stable 'nations' (by which has been meant, stable states governing stable societies), has been a predominant goal of much work in the humanities and social sciences since at least the mid-1960s. Conflict and instability between and within these societies, legitimacy deficits and alienation in the relations between societies and state-elites, failed efforts at partnership and union among states and threats of disintegration and fragmentation within their borders (almost always qualified in these instances as 'artificial' borders – as though there were any other kind), have very often been accounted for in terms of the same logic – the nation does not 'fit' the state, or there are too many nations, or not enough of a nation (it is too young, 'immature', not 'fully-formed'), or the nation 'does not really know what it is', there is an 'identity crisis', and so on. In the case of contemporary North Africa, a great deal of ink has been spilled on these same questions, in identifying processes of 'nation-formation', on analytic agendas which have sought to observe how Maghribi states and societies have overcome – or have continued to suffer from – their inherited conflicts and divisions,[3] how they have shaped themselves and their place in the world, how they have approached, and fared in, the struggle to 'modernise'.

It is above all the nation, its 'birth' or 'rebirth', its origins and development, that has provided the organising principle, the guiding sign of this now very substantial literature,[4] and 'recovered' or 'reasserted' national identities, as cultural–historical *continuities* imagining the present community in its sameness with the ancestral past ('who/what we *are*' as fundamentally explicable in terms of who/what our forefathers *were*) are everywhere invoked as having a crucial, constitutive role in these processes, even as having been, in the colonial period, the central social facts of cohesion which 'justified and legitimised [...] emancipation'.[5] This central role attributed to the nation and its identity sits, however, in implicit but striking unease with the remarkable elusiveness of both terms themselves. Attempts to directly address the category 'identity', in particular, when it is not taken simply as a given (as it is in a great many of the major works on contemporary North Africa[6]) are either spectacularly uncritical or else show up, by their very lack of resolution (and the often heated emotional debate which they occasion), the at once protean intangibility and dense affectivity of the object pursued. Attempts at definition, searching to answer the question 'what is a [North African] nation?', either run up against a blank, bland façade of officially sanctioned verities or exhaust themselves in chasing the wind.

It is, perhaps, more useful, since the 'nation' is inescapably central to our preoccupations, to ask instead *how 'it' works*, rather than what 'it' is.[7] The point of this shift is to focus our attention directly on the problematic modality of the nation's existence, rather than presuming that existence, as a *thing* with strong ontological status, to be satisfactorily proven and merely a matter of traceable historical development, through the chronology of 'awakening' or 'self-realisation' and the cultural–political process of institutionalising 'identity'. If we are to address questions of the history and culture of nationhood, the particular form taken by the intersection of contemporary history, culture and politics which manifestly *is* a crucial question for the recent experiences of most of the world's population, we ought similarly to

consider not *what* 'identity' is – that is, what supposedly authoritative characterisations of 'the people' declare them to be – but *how* actual, specific
socially and historically located people, and groups of people, themselves
articulate their self-conceptions, their historical experiences and their place in
society, how it is that they conceive of themselves, and the society within
which they live, think and act, as constituting a nation. In other (more concise)
words, we should 'abandon the nation as a category of analysis and treat it,
instead, as a category of *practice*'.[8] It is to this kind of enquiry that, I suggest,
the articles in this volume most effectively contribute.

It might be as well to point out at once that not all the authors assembled
here (perhaps none of them) will necessarily agree with what I am here
advancing as a suitable method of reading their various contributions. Each of
these articles pursues its own line of argument, following the different,
ongoing, research interests of their individual authors. The intention of this
collection has in no sense been to present a unified body of research all
tending in one direction, driven by a single theoretical or methodological
orientation or a focus on a single body of subject matter. On the contrary, the
aim has been to present a highly varied array of new research by a diverse
group of scholars from across a range of backgrounds and disciplines, and at
very different stages in their academic careers. The work drawn together here
is by doctoral students and junior researchers, by well established scholars,
and by distinguished and internationally recognised authorities on their
subjects, from France, Italy, North Africa, Britain and the USA. Collectively,
we have not sought to work in consensus and we draw no definitive
conclusions, but rather pursue a self-conscious multiplicity of enquiries and
indicate a number of possible directions that future work might take. The
articles address intellectual history, international relations, the politics of exile
and liberation, modern art, cinema, ethnicity, historiography, subalternity;
methodologies and sources drawn upon range from oral history to archives,
newspapers to postcards, corporate offices to desert frontiers. The point is not
eclecticism (or evasion of due rigour) but the illustration of the immense
diversity possible within the study of North African history, culture and
politics, and the potential of greatly varied approaches and focal points to
illuminate our understanding, with – I believe – far greater heuristic results
than are attainable in chasing after stable, reified (and actually non-existent)
definitions of nation, self and society.

What all the contributions have in common is a focus on the representation
of nationhood in the different societies considered – Morocco, Algeria,
Tunisia and Libya. The object pursued in each of these articles is the many
ways in which specific groups, individuals and organisations, from exiled
Tripolitanian civil servants in the 1930s through berberophone Moroccan

footsoldiers of the French army in the 1940s and 1950s to film makers, figurative artists and financiers in the late 1990s, and a host of others, have imagined, envisaged, related to – fitted in with or become marginalised from – struggled for, disputed or challenged different representations of 'the nation'; that is, how, for each of these groups of people, whether 'from above' or 'from below', the nation has 'worked'.

The cases examined are by no means exhaustive, and in several instances the work presented here is new and in progress, indicating not completed investigations but ongoing directions of enquiry – this too is deliberate, as what we have tried to show is the variety of some of the very latest work in this area, and the possibilities for its future development. There is, then, no pretension here to a comprehensive survey of the complexities of North African nationhood and the multiplicity and vitality of the many social actors involved in its continuous reconstruction and transformation. There is very little here on youth, and nothing on children; nothing on labour movements and workers, the unemployed or the parallel economy; as in (too) many studies of the region, the greater part of its actual geographical territory – the *grand sud* and its populations – go unmentioned, and (this time in contrast to much of the existing recent literature) there are only passing references to Islamism and Islamists. It is to be hoped that what *is* presented here is suggestive of avenues of approach that might be taken to these, and many other, questions. In addition, the very uneven coverage of the area, with a pronounced imbalance in favour of Morocco and Algeria (with Morocco more visible overall), less on Tunisia and a single article on Libya (and no mention, save one in passing, of Mauritania) is probably a more or less faithful reflection of the state of current research (at least in English) and its preoccupations and possibilities; in this, too, this volume is intended to illustrate a range of work that is currently being pursued. It is to be hoped that the cases afforded less attention here will also become progressively more visible in the scholarly literature available in English.

If an older-established approach to the history, culture and politics of nationhood stressed processes of homogenisation, cohesiveness and a posited 'identity' (sameness) at its base (as nationalist politics, official culture and history themselves, of course, did), these articles demonstrate how much there is to be said for both a fragmentation of the focus on totality, to enable a close reading of small details, individual persons and local particularities, and a widening out of the angle of view, to resituate the territorial nation states (concentration on which, it has rightly been pointed out, is 'an aberration from longer-term patterns in the Maghreb'[9]) and their region within their multiple, overlapping and, throughout history, continually, changeably interconnected contexts – African, Mediterranean, Middle Eastern, European and Atlantic.

This latter agenda is one which has recently, and again quite rightly, been much promoted,[10] and these articles all share in the growing tendency to open up the study of North Africa to the realities of the several interlinked worlds which its people have, over the past century, inhabited. The importance of both Europe and the Middle East is particularly visible, but more distant connections – to Latin America and the former Soviet Union, the United States and Southeast Asia – are also touched upon. Experiences of the nation's forcible integration into, and negotiation of positions within, different regional and global systems, from the colonial empires of the first two-thirds of the twentieth century to the globalised, neoliberal financial markets of the last two decades are also addressed.

The dominance of these systems, however, has not been exclusive. These articles also show how North Africans have continued to think and act within other frameworks, too, whether those beyond the dominant boundaries, centred on the late Ottoman state and emergent Turkey in the early 1920s, nationalist Egypt and Syria a decade later, or closer to home, within the national frontiers, where relations of domination between men and women, the affluent and the impoverished, the legitimate mainstream and the suspect periphery, have shaped the social landscape of struggles over the ownership of, and participation in the production of, narratives and institutions of nationhood. If there is one unifying feature running through all these articles, it is the concern shared by all the authors with the lived realities of North Africans' contemporary historical experiences, with the ways in which specific, socially and historically located people have sought to shape the intersection of history, culture and politics where the 'nation', as the dominant legitimate category of community and its political organisation, is constantly and creatively reproduced in processes of struggle and self-assertion, in battles over authority, recognition, and social change.

The first article, by Benjamin Stora, gives an overview of 40 years of relations between Algeria and Morocco, considering the often turbulent relationship of North Africa's two largest states in terms not only of political process, territorial rivalries and geopolitical alignments, but also with regard to the imaginaries of nationhood and history predominant in the two societies.

Different relationships to the past, particularly to the recent history of colonialism and decolonisation, he argues, as well as to national space and the symbolic centres of the state, have structured the relationship between Algeria and Morocco in particular ways, intersecting with more readily visible ideological and territorial differences, as well as with the many factors held in common and which plead for viable partnership. We are given an account of the military and diplomatic confrontations which have pitted the two states against each other, from the brief War of the Sands in 1963 through the

Western Sahara question to the most recent public vituperations of one country by the other, but this history is set against a broad-brush discussion of more subtle divergences. The 'federative discourse' of fraternal anticolonialism, in which ritual declarations of solidarity and alliance are often couched, disguises major differences in the development of each country's nationalism and attempts to find grounds for building a more stable, productive relationship between the two by aligning both against their common former coloniser. This, though, cannot efface the complexities of the triangular relationship between Morocco, Algeria and France, still present not only in the use of the French language and the pull of emigration to the former metropole, but in the two brother-nationalisms' very different conceptions of themselves, which can be seen as having been powerfully influenced by idioms drawn from French history and, of course, by the practices of colonialism itself which had such massive impact in both countries. There is also the ironic importance of France as a place of meeting and transit between Algeria and Morocco – with borders still closed and visa requirements imposed, important processes of exchange and acquaintance occur in the immigrant community in the ex-metropole. In fact, while for many reasons – among which domestic political expediency is not the least – the states continue to find it difficult not to 'kick each other's shins', processes of convergence and rapprochement are occurring, Stora argues, on the level of the two countries' expanding, young and dynamic civil societies. Shared problems and concerns as well as the international demands of Euro–Mediterranean construction and open markets are insistent reasons for a working partnership to be finally established.

Kmar Bendana shifts the focus entirely, to Tunisia and to cultural production. In an accomplished critical sweep, she takes us through the first 40 years of independent Tunisia's film industry to explore the various ways in which film makers have constructed images of the nation and of what it means to be Tunisian. Recent historical experiences, whether narrated according to official text-book 'vulgate' or in a more revisionist vein, have been consistently concerned with the totalising story of 'the national movement', a structure dominating the representation of Tunisian history, culture and politics through fixed chronology and stock characters. More innovative work has sought to explore lost social and cultural worlds, finding a specifically 'Tunisian' aesthetic and identity in a 'nostalgic' cinema focused on the old city of Tunis or, alternatively, on the (somewhat romanticised) fragile and disappearing worlds of the countryside.

Yet other directors have explored cultural plurality, or the difficulties of urbanisation and economic change, and have been able to transcend stereotyped characterisation and unanimist plots, portraying Tunisians and

Tunisia in local specificity. An opposite tendency, in contrast, has sought access to a crowded and competitive market-place by resorting to allegorical stories in indeterminate settings, told in foreign languages or literary Arabic. These two diametrically opposed approaches may be taken to summarise the range of possibilities explored in Tunisian cinema for expressing a contemporary culture of nationhood – while 'Tunisian-ness' remains incompletely embodied in each partial attempt to convey its texture and meaning, 'Tunisian cinema' may eventually mean nothing more than the inescapable requirement to organise artistic expression in 'national' terms, in a market dominated by a single, 'transnational' producer – the USA – and in which other creative forces must compete for their own parcels of territory and audience.

The following four articles may usefully be read together as explorations of different North Africans' relationships to their own homes and homelands through their experiences and perceptions of other spaces and places, within wider regional and global contexts. Moshe Gershovich's series of war veterans' oral histories, collected along the road that runs from Fez to Marrakesh through the berberophone Middle Atlas of Morocco, is itself a kind of travelogue that also takes us on further journeys beyond the mountains into the cities and from there to the Western Front in First World War France, Germany and Italy in the 1940s, and Vietnam in the 1950s. His article not only highlights the narratives of a group of individuals – Moroccan veterans of France's colonial army – generally inaudible in the historical record, charting their travels and the ways in which they negotiated their impoverished subaltern position in the colonial order, it also explores the complexities of 'fitting in' such particular, and discrepant, historical experiences with dominant notions of national history and politics, whether in Morocco as a whole, in France, or in the local communities to which these men returned from years of arduous and sometimes crippling service.

Odile Moreau and Anna Baldinetti both present work in progress, drawing on a large body of primary archival and other research to illustrate Middle Eastern influences on the development of conceptions of North African political nationhood, and action for their realisation. Both advance revisions of received histories of nationalism, with Moreau's study arguing for greater attention to be paid to events in the 1920s, and to the still pertinent links at this time between the Maghrib and the eastern Mediterranean, and Baldinetti's work focusing on the political activities in exile of groups of refugees from Italy's colonisation of Libya.

Moreau's reading of the responses of colonial officials, religious dignitaries, young modernist activists and monarchs to the tumultuous events that marked the final dissolution of the Ottoman empire and the emergence of the Turkish republic, in 1919–24, illustrates the ways in which the only decisive nationalist liberation victories to be won at this time of high colonialism created images and ideas that were received with enthusiasm in the Maghrib. While both imperial France and her opponents in colonial North Africa hoped to reap symbolic benefits from events in Anatolia, Turkey's war of liberation only briefly provided material for concern, on one side, and, for inspiration, on the other. With the abolition of the caliphate, the last remaining symbolic site of sovereignty available to be held by North Africans (particularly in Tunisia) outside the imposed frame of the French empire was lost, enthusiasm for Kemalist radicalism waned, and a potential platform for expression by Maghribi nationalists disappeared.

At almost exactly the same time, in contrast, in the mid-1920s, the first associative groups were being founded by Libyans who had fled Italian colonisation and settled in Syria and Egypt. These groups, Anna Baldinetti suggests, were precursors of the political parties that would eventually emerge in Libya itself after the expulsion of the Italians by the (in this sense) incidental intervention of the Second World War. It was the communities of exiles who first began making plans for a united and independent Libyan nationhood, some of them, of course, in terms quite different from those which would eventually be implemented with the establishment of the monarchical state under Idris at independence. Egyptian national ambitions framed in terms of an Egypt-led Arabism were also involved, with notable figures such as 'Abd al-Rahman 'Azzam reportedly dreaming of a governorate or principality in Libya under Egyptian tutelage. Both articles contribute important insights regarding the regional imbrications of North African nationalism in the colonial period.

Paul Silverstein's study complements these with a consideration of contemporary Kabyle politics in an even wider world of networks and movements, as he charts its ethnic, national and transnational dimensions. Silverstein's article sets the particular experiences of Kabylia and its diaspora in the civil war of the 1990s within the longer timeframe of the complex negotiations and struggles that have marked the relationship of this region to a wider Algeria, to France and to other places of emigration and activism (Belgium, the USA, Canada) since the War of Independence. The dynamic tensions of Kabyle political life and community organisation – whether in explicitly political platforms and party apparatuses, more diffuse cultural orientations and demands, or, yet more broadly, the imagination and enactment of Kabyle community itself – are explored in three arenas: the local, national, and transnational, whose complex interrelationships are delineated.

Drawing on a range of sources – the activities of community associations, political groups, sports teams, the media and cultural producers – the expression of Kabyle aspirations, and the place of these aspirations within the French and Algerian nations, are examined through the changing image of the martyr-patriot. This figure, a densely emotive and politically-charged symbol anchored in memories of recent history and re-actualised through successive moments of struggle, from the revolution through to the 'Black Spring' of 2001, serves as a central focus around which narratives of *amazigh* selfhood, history, politics and culture are articulated. The recent violence and the accompanying socio-economic crisis in Algeria, however, have drawn Kabyle politics in two important, and potentially conflicting, directions. While forms and networks of political organisation have become increasingly vocal and transnational, the war has also created a deep gulf, dividing the ideologies and practices of the movements claiming to represent Kabylia and its hopes from the everyday realities of life in Kabylia itself.

The last three articles in the collection can also be read alongside one another, as their authors present new and highly insightful discussions of the cultural politics, and political culture, of Morocco and Algeria. Feminist journalists, contemporary artists, corporate financiers, and intellectuals of widely differing persuasions are the focus of these three articles which deal, each in a distinct way, with some of the most recent, and some of the most deep-rooted, struggles in North Africa over the expression of national history, culture, and the political framework within which history and culture are formed, and which history and culture themselves help to form and justify as 'legitimate'.

Liat Kozma's account of the struggle over the historiography of Morocco's national liberation adopts a perspective drawing both on Hayden White's tropology of historical narrative and a Gramscian approach to hegemony mediated through the (now much neglected[11]) critique of Raymond Williams. She employs this considerable theoretical armoury critically to investigate the emergence in the 1980s and 1990s of a highly articulate feminist movement into the scene of contemporary Moroccan society and politics, spheres where women's rights have been curtailed by personal status legislation and predominantly patriarchal forms of authority. Kozma shows how, in their battle for recognition and social change, Moroccan women engaged with dominant historiography to reclaim a place for women in the central historical narrative of contemporary Moroccan nationhood, that is, the history of the anticolonial struggle for national liberation.

In order to legitimate progressive, feminist-driven change in Moroccan society and politics, it seemed necessary for the women's movement to find 'authentic' grounds for their claims to recognition in the recognised central sites of Moroccan culture and history. Thus, the role of women in the anticolonial liberation struggle, a neglected aspect of dominant historiography, was sought out and exalted to demonstrate that, while independence had not brought liberation to Morocco's women, they had nonetheless played to the full a part in the struggle for sovereign nationhood, and were thus due their share of the freedom that struggle was supposed to obtain. In ultimately achieving the recognition they sought in history, however, Moroccan women were carving out a place within the dominant, total structures of national power, not challenging those structures themselves. In shifting to accommodate the demands for women's inclusion in narratives of national liberation, the dominant forms of national history and politics incorporated 'women' as a totalised group within its purview, a group now visible where before they were absent, but nonetheless appropriated into the workings of a fundamentally unaltered hegemonic system. The consequence of this shift was the appropriation of demands stemming from the women's movement into programmes of – ultimately much more modest – reform led by the institutions of the state, and the presentation of an independent feminist movement as a redundant irrelevance.

Staying with Morocco, Katarzyna Pieprzak turns to the staging of Moroccan nationhood through museums, and to the question, almost completely ignored by state museum collections, of contemporary art. Despite pressure from artists and intellectuals, and the predominance of a modernist elite, calls for a state-sponsored museum of modern art for Morocco have gone unheeded since independence. Pieprzak focuses on the appearance, in 1988, of a gallery space devoted to modern art in the foyer of the corporate headquarters of one of Morocco's major commercial banks, and offers a highly sophisticated and incisive account of the rhetoric, the cultural values, and the political and social significance of this meeting of cultural production and international capital.

While proclaiming its identity as a transnational, modern citizen of a global community of competitive investment capitalism, the bank's patronage of art is also framed to set the institution in its specific location as part of a Moroccan nation under the King. The social roles of subject and citizen, the explicit orientation to 'modernisation' and the global market set resolutely within the context of nation and monarchy, the association of the state and its dominant institutions with the pursuit of capitalist free enterprise, are all negotiated and mediated through the way in which the bank sets itself up as a stage for the display of culture. The art on display to a limited public formed by Casablanca's bourgeoisie and international investors serves to establish the credentials of the bank as in tune with international trends in corporate patronage, a reliable institution as well aligned with international (that is, Western) financial practices as its collection is with international (that is, Western) taste in pictorial art. Pieprzak's article shows how, where narratives of Moroccan nationhood staged in museum collections exalt a long and continuous past, the new narratives conjured up by the bank's displays of art serve to orient conceptions of a contemporary nation turned towards the future. Exactly who might have ownership of this nationhood, and its symbols of culture and history, or be permitted access to it and its expression, remains an issue of some doubt.

In the final article of the collection, Fanny Colonna offers an exploration of the crucial cultural and political aspect of contemporary Algeria constituted by the occultation of 'the local, the particular, the singular'. Her article examines, through three emblematic intellectual figures – Mostefa Lacheraf, Mouloud Mammeri and Abu 'l-Qasim Sa'adallah – the conditions of the impossibility of a shared, unified-yet-plural Algerian patrimony, one assumed by all Algerians, while expressing the realities of locally rooted, specific historical and cultural experience.

Through a rigorous analysis drawing on her own personal and professional experience as well as on a range of recent literature from *Subaltern Studies* to Rancière and Ricoeur, Colonna presents a searching examination of the cultural 'segmentarity' of contemporary Algeria, of the lack of Algerians' intellectual and cultural autonomy in the face of the political, and of the persistent difficulty of articulating a serene, self-accepting and democratic conception of the meaning of 'being Algerian'. Her consideration of the respective contributions that three outstanding figures have made to conceptions of Algerian patrimony, particularly through the various, local 'voices from below' that they have brought to light and celebrated (respectively, village cultures, Kabyle poetry and peripheral scriptural authors and traditions), demonstrates how, despite these major thinkers, their own experiences beyond Algeria and their own very significant works, local particularity has remained submerged, in dominant political culture and in the politics of culture, by unanimism and utopianism. Her article concludes with an indication of the kind of work now needed to begin to remedy some of the problems identified, in particular the need for 'a renunciation of totalisations, of syntheses and of any overarching, commanding view of "culture", "society", or "religion", and *a fortiori* of "the state" or "Algeria"', with the aim of making acceptable 'work on the fragmentary, the discontinuous' and the particular.

This, I think, recalls the point with which we began, with the need to get away from, or at least to problematise, the homogenising totalities of 'nation' and 'identity', and to look instead at *particularly situated practices* of producing, institutionalising and contesting representations of 'the nation', with a critical eye to the means and relations of that production, the material forces in play in the 'market of symbolic goods' (to borrow from Bourdieu) where the history, culture and politics of nationhood meet.[12]

Colonna concludes with a distinction drawn between 'personality', the experience of historicity that makes one what one becomes, and 'the carry-all concept of "identity"', a distinction which can be applied as usefully to communities as to individuals. The ubiquitous notion of 'identity' with which we began, identity in the mathematical sense, as *sameness*, or what Paul Ricoeur calls *mêmeté, Gleichheit*, is thus distinguished from 'personality' – Ricoeur would say, *ipséité, Selbstheit,* that is, *'selfhood'*.[13] In searching for a more adequate understanding of the nature of nationhood, which must, indeed, remain a crucial focus of enquiry into contemporary history, culture and politics in the twentieth and twenty-first centuries, it is to the specificities of historical experience and the changing structures of social relations, which together influence the conditions of the production of 'self', that we should look. It is my hope that the articles collected here might be read so as to provide suggestive avenues of further exploration of these issues, in respect of the societies of North Africa and the many and varied people who live in them.

ACKNOWLEDGMENTS

This collection of studies began as a panel presented under the title 'The Nation and its Representations in North Africa' at the 2001 annual meeting of the Middle East Studies Association in San Francisco, CA. Some of the papers presented there do not appear here, and three of the articles in this collection were not presented at the original meeting. I should like to thank everyone who participated in the two sessions, Mark Tessler for his support and encouragement in the organisation of the panel, and John Entelis whose original idea it was to publish the papers. Particular thanks to Julia Clancy-Smith who stepped in at the last moment to chair one of the sessions, to Eugene Rogan whose advice was, as always, invaluable, to Michael Middeke at Frank Cass, to all the contributors who kept to unreasonably stringent deadlines – and to Anna, who helped with everything.

NOTES

I had intended to contribute my own paper from the San Francisco meeting to this collection, but before the appearance of this volume was finalised it was published in *Radical History Review* 86 ('National Myths in the Middle East'). Instead I ended up translating the four contributions by Stora, Bendana, Moreau and Colonna, which were originally presented in French; I would like to thank the authors concerned for permission to translate their work. I own responsibility for any errors that may have occurred in this process, and I thank the reader for exercising the additional patience required by a longer introductory essay than would otherwise have appeared.

1. Ernest Renan, 'Qu'est-ce qu'une nation?', lecture delivered at the Sorbonne, 11 March 1882 (Paris: C. Lévy 1882).
2. For high culture, agrarian–industrial transformation and Durkheimian schemes of solidarity, see Ernest Gellner, *Nations and Nationalism* (Oxford: Blackwell 1983); for *'ethnie'*, Gellner's student Anthony D. Smith, 'Ethnic Persistence and National Transformation', *British Journal of Sociology* 35/3 (Sept. 1984) pp.452–61; *The Ethnic Origins of Nations* (Oxford: Blackwell 1986); *National Identity* (London: Penguin 1991); 'The Resurgence of Nationalism? Myth and Memory in the Renewal of Nations', *British Journal of Sociology* 47/4 (Dec. 1996) pp.575–98; 'The Golden Age and National Renewal', in Geoffrey Hosking

and George Schöpflin (eds.), *Myths and Nationhood* (London: Hurst 1997) pp.36–59; for the state, John Breuilly, *Nationalism and the State* (Manchester: Manchester UP 1982).

3. L. Carl Brown 'Introduction' in C. Brown (ed.), *State and Nation in Independent North Africa* (Washington DC: Middle East Institute 1966).

4. Among the most indispensable examples, taking only Algeria: John Ruedy, *Modern Algeria, the Origins and Development of a Nation* (Bloomington and Indianapolis: Indiana UP 1992); Ahmed Koulakssis and Gilbert Meynier, *L'Émir Khaled, Premier Za'im? Identité algérienne et colonialisme français* (Paris: L'Harmattan, 1987), especially the introduction; Pierre Vidal-Naquet, Preface in Gilbert Meynier, *L'Algérie Révélée: la Guerre de 1914–1918 et le Premier Quart du XXème siècle* (Geneva: Droz 1981).

5. Houari Touati, 'Algerian Historiography in the Nineteenth and Twentieth Centuries: from Chronicle to History' in Michel Le Gall and Kenneth Perkins (eds.), *The Maghrib in Question. Essays in History and Historiography* (Austin: University of Texas Press 1997) pp.89–94, quote p.93.

6. See for example Mahfoud Kaddache, *Histoire du Nationalisme Algérien. Question Nationale et Politique Algérienne, 1919–1951*, 2 vols., (Algiers: ENAL 1993 [2nd edn.]).

7. cf. Michel-Rolph Trouillot, *Silencing the Past. Power and the Production of History* (Boston: Beacon Press 1995) writing on the historiography of the Haitian revolution.

8. Nadia Abu El-Haj, 'The Problem with Memory. On the Articulation of Archaeology, Nationhood and Settlement', paper presented to the workshop *Memory and Violence in the Middle East and North Africa*, Rice University, Houston TX, 23–25 March 2001.

9. 'The Maghreb Review: a Manifesto for the Twenty-First Century', *The Maghreb Review* 25/3–4 (2000) pp.355–6, quote p.355.

10. Ibid.; Julia Clancy-Smith, 'The Maghrib and the Mediterranean World in the Nineteenth Century: Illicit Exchanges, Migrants, and Social Marginals' in Le Gall and Perkins (eds.), (note 5) pp.222–49; also her 'Introduction' to *North Africa, Islam and the Mediterranean World from the Almoravids to the Algerian War* (London and Portland OR: Frank Cass 2001); and Allan Christelow, 'Re-envisioning Algerian Cultural History in the Imperial Age', *The Maghreb Review* 24/3–4 (1999) pp.108–15.

11. See Perry Anderson's comment on the disappearance from the view of most students (of my own and Miss Kozma's generation) of an 'entire horizon of reference', from Jaurès or Lukács to Raymond Williams, who 'has been put out of court', 'Renewals', Editorial, *New Left Review* n.s. 1 (Jan.–Feb. 2000) p.18).

12. For excellent examples of work in this vein, see Prasenjit Duara, *Rescuing History from the Nation. Questioning Narratives of Modern China* (Chicago: Chicago UP 1995); Andrew J. Shryock, *Nationalism and the Genealogical Imagination. Oral History and Textual Authority in Tribal Jordan* (Berkeley and Los Angeles: California UP 1997); James L. Gelvin, *Divided Loyalties. Nationalism and Mass Politics in Syria at the Close of Empire* (Berkeley and Los Angeles: California UP 1998). Very suggestive applications of not dissimilar theoretical concerns can also be found, for example, in Gilbert Joseph and Daniel Nugent (eds.), *Everyday Forms of State Formation. Revolution and the Negotiation of Rule in Modern Mexico* (Durham NC: Duke UP 1994) and Mary Kay Vaughan *Cultural Politics in Revolution. Teachers, Peasants and Schools in Mexico, 1930–1940* (Tucson: Arizona UP 1997).

13. Paul Ricoeur, *Soi-même comme un autre* (Paris: Seuil 1990), esp. p.140 ff; see also his essay 'Narrative Identity' in David Wood (ed.), *On Paul Ricoeur. Narrative and Interpretation* (London: Routledge 1991) ch.2. Notions such as 'national self', 'collective self', or 'national personality' and the like (*'la personnalité algérienne'* is a constant of Algerian national historiography, for example) have often been collapsed into 'national identity' and 'collective identity' in the literature, which, faced with such strident categories, has sometimes suffered from a wholesale failure of critical nerve, and had panicky recourse to mystical notions of 'genius' or *nafs*, to metaphors of geology ('deep reality' and 'bedrock'), or to distinctly Romantic sensibilities ('emotive resonance', 'the hearts of the people', *'les forces vives de la nation'*).

13

Algeria/Morocco: The Passions of the Past. Representations of the Nation that Unite and Divide

BENJAMIN STORA

Algeria and Morocco are the two principal states of the Maghrib, in terms of geographical extent and population size (*circa* 30 million inhabitants in each of the two countries). An Algero–Moroccan partnership has the greatest potential as the motor of dynamic economic and political development for the whole region. These two states share linguistic, religious, ethnic and historical elements (the Arabic language, Islam, a numerous berberophone minority, a heritage of harsh struggle for independence from the same colonial power). On 17 February 1989, the constitutive summit of the *Union du Maghreb Arabe* (UMA) was held in Marrakesh. In the summit's final declaration, the five states present (Algeria, Libya, Morocco, Mauritania, Tunisia) pledged themselves to create a free trade zone, to facilitate the free circulation of goods and persons, and to establish a customs union. However, at the beginning of the twenty-first century, the UMA's development process is impassably blocked, principally due to the *impasse* in Algero–Moroccan relations, the stalled motor of North African dynamics. I shall examine in this article how the question of the Western Sahara, from the 'war of the sands' in 1963 through the Green March (November 1975) and Algerian support for the POLISARIO Front, weighs heavily on relations between Algeria and Morocco. Beyond the – fundamental – Sahara dispute, however, lie other factors: differential contemporary relationships to space and to history, which also require consideration.

Two Legitimations of the Nation

Algerians and Moroccans are not fundamentally divided over the concept of 'nation', which for the people of both countries is basically construed as a form of the constitution in community of a majority group of believers – Islam is the religion of state in both countries. Other shared elements of collective self-definition might also be considered apposite: common

14

elements of language and culture, the experience of a common colonial (or rather, *anti*-colonial) history, a shared general geographical region, the (at least declared) 'wish for men to live together', as suggested by the aspirations embodied in the *Union du Maghreb Arabe* (Arab Maghrib Union). Between Algerians and Moroccans, the key difference in representations of the nation is to be found in the historical experience of the nation state, that is, in different experiences, or constructions, of temporality.[1] The dominant conception of Moroccan nationhood traces itself back over centuries, identifying the nation with the multi-secular continuity of a state. Algeria, on the other hand, is self-consciously a 'late-coming nation', issued in its modern form from the long war of independence fought against France. The contestability (instability?) of this brief and unfinished national self-conception may go some way towards explaining why an ongoing work of national self-definition has been pursued in so difficult, so tragic a fashion during the 1990s.[2]

In Algeria, the construction of nationhood was manifestly the work of the independent state; the state created the nation, affirming and confirming its existence (and conversely, the crisis of the state's legitimacy since the late 1980s has led to the fragmentation of 'the nation' itself, with a real threat of regional dislocation). This model of an authoritarian, centralised state was independent Algeria's inheritance from the Jacobinism of the French colonial presence. Morocco's situation, on the other hand, is quite different. Here, whereas the nation's longevity is identified with that of the sultanate, the two were not always congruent – state and nation are imagined as having historically covered overlapping but distinct spaces, in the geographical distinction traditionally simplified into the division between *bled al-makhzen* and *bled al-siba*. At the end of the nineteenth century, the sultan's effective authority, exercised through the apparatus of the *makhzen* and the *mahalla*, extended through a significant part of the territory, but still had to be asserted against the 'dissidence' of parts of the countryside.[3] A common belonging to the modern nation unified both, at independence in 1956, around the sovereign institution of the monarchy.

For Algerians, national territory does not pre-exist national history as a kind of natural framework, cut out and defined in advance. Rather, it is history (colonial/anticolonial – the administrative division and political incorporation of territory by the French, and the histories of regional and local resistance, or of the different *wilayas* of the war of independence) which creates territory. History draws the borders, effacing the 'natural' marks of geography. But after independence, it is a national geography which asserts itself most powerfully in the celebration of the triumph of anticolonial history. The immensity of the territory bequeathed (or, rather, seized), and the vastness of its natural resources, come to the fore, consigning to the background the more obscure aspects of an Algerian history crosscut by successive foreign occupations. For Morocco, in contrast, the shape of the nation is not thought so arbitrary, but instead is conceived as the expression of the historical development of the land. The centre of the nation (institutionally and symbolically) is not defined by the arbitrary lines of frontiers, but is located in the monarchy, which functions as the centre of contact and exchange between the different provinces of the kingdom.

These different perceptions underlie two different forms of the legitimation of the nation state – particularly through a long history, and the continuous existence of the monarchy, in Morocco, and by geographical weight and the wealth of natural resources in Algeria. These two major states of North Africa, similar and divided by so many things held in common, must seek in their recent history the means of a *rapprochement*. Thus resurfaces the invocation of anticolonialism, and of the struggle against the French colonial presence.

A Federative Discourse: The Ritual Invocation of Anticolonialism

From the 1930s through to the 1960s, the political, cultural and religious elites of Morocco and Algeria shared crucial experiences of anticolonialism. After independence, relations between the two countries, and with France, were necessarily informed by the accumulated experiences of each in respect of the others. In expressions of Algero–Moroccan relations, the complex relationship of each with the former colonial power is often invoked to emphasise moments of common history, powerful images which constitute epic, mythologised narratives of a fraternal nationalist Maghrib. The anticolonial discourse is federative. This obvious, almost self-evident, point – the obsessive reference to a common history of anticolonialism – does not, however, lessen the persistence of a mysterious fact – the massive use of the French language, which is still today audible and visible in the streets of both countries, finds expression in a highly developed francophone Maghribi literature and in North Africa's widely circulated francophone press. In Algeria, the francophone newspapers *El Watan* and *Liberté* are printed at the rate of 80,000–100,000 copies every day. This 'mystery' of persistent francophony doubtless derives from the unusually long colonial period which linked France to the Maghrib (132 years in the Algerian case, although 'only' 43 for Morocco), as well as to the persistent density of physical and affective relationships between the three countries, and the presence in France of a large community issued from Maghribi immigration (estimated at some three million persons). This persistence of French and of France in the everyday life of the contemporary Maghrib contrasts brutally with the violence of the denunciations which occur in discourses on history, particularly in the evocation of decolonisation. The Moroccan daily *Le Matin du Sahara et du Maghreb* underlined, in an editorial published in May 1999, the possibility of convergence and partnership between Morocco and Algeria, thus:

> Our two countries have sometimes been joined in a common relationship. They faced the same coloniser and fought the same battle for independence in the name of the same ideals. They set up solidarity, understanding and brotherhood-in-arms as a common symbol. [...] When French colonisation began with the landing at Sidi Fredj in 1830,[4] Morocco at once aligned itself alongside its brother country and gave evidence of an active solidarity which never ceased until liberation in 1962. One can never sufficiently emphasise the fact that Morocco and Algeria have faced common distress and that in the darkest hours, Morocco, mobilised entirely behind her King, stood at the side of valorous Algeria.[5]

In April 1999 King Hassan II sent a long congratulatory message to Algeria's new President, Abdelaziz Bouteflika, in which he wrote that 'relations between Morocco and Algeria extend far back in history, and were reinforced during the war of national liberation.' In his reply, the Algerian President similarly referred to the common struggle against France as the foundation of a possible unity of the two countries:

> It is hardly fortuitous that Algeria and Morocco celebrate together the anniversary of 20 August 1953,[6] the day which marks the battles and epic struggles undertaken by Algerian *mujahidin* in solidarity with their brothers, the Moroccan people, who on that day lived through the exile of its symbol, your late father His Majesty King Muhammed V, and of yourself, an exile which led you far from your fatherland, but which affirmed your patriotism and your spirit of sacrifice for the independence of Morocco and for the dignity of its great people, thereby contributing to the complete liberation of our great Arab Maghrib.[7]

From behind this now ritual invocation, a practice of defining the nation in its rejection of colonialism, other relationships with France nonetheless emerge, different attitudes in which the singularities of each country's political culture may be traced.

The Illusory Twins of Maghribi Nationalism

Anticolonial struggles forged representations of nationhood, history and society held in common, common refrains which recur, as we have seen, in the chronologies of nationalist history. It is true that the 'Young Moroccan' movement of Allal al Fasi and Ahmed Belafredj, and the 'Young Algerians' of the generation of Ferhat Abbas, entered political life at the same moment, at the turning-point of the early 1930s, and that the radical, armed struggles for independence also began, in Morocco and Algeria, at around the same time, in 1953–54. And yet the two countries are only illusory twins. The congruence of the two chronological sequences does not make for two synonymous trajectories. A common plot structure – the decolonisation struggle – and a dominant idiom of expression – the community of Islam – do not make one story the copy of the other. Rather, within the same, shared historical framework, different mechanisms were set up. The divergence of one from the other was governed by multiple factors: the two societies' different political situations, personalities, and above all, the stakes being played for. Analysis of the contrasts between these two nationalisms is more illuminating than is the notion of family unity suggested by today's political actors and by simple comparative chronology.

Although the two countries' acquisition of independence may have made substantially the same break with the past (with the colonial system), they initiated two very different projects for the construction of the future, of different states – and different relationships between the nation and its history. Whereas the political culture of Algerian independence was framed as the reconquest of national sovereignty, as it were, on a clean slate, Morocco saw its independence as the recovery of its long and continuous past. Revolutionary Algeria refused to recognise its own birthplace, in Algeria's long and recent colonial history, and – despite all the declarations about the reconquest of a lost identity – it remained suspicious, too, of its distant, Latin, Berber, and Islamic, past, a history altogether too complex, too mixed and plural. While a Minister under President Boumedièenne, Ahmed Taleb Ibrahimi could thus write:

> In reading all that has been written about Arabs and Berbers in Algeria, one realises that a deliberate work of subversion has been undertaken to divide the Algerian people. To suggest, for example, that the population of Algeria is composed of Arabs and Berbers is historically false. The first Arabs to settle in Algeria, in the seventh century, married local women and their blood became mixed (and the religion which the Arabs and their descendants brought would become a cement, a catalyst, a rampart). In consequence, Algeria is not (contrary to what one often hears) a juxtaposition of Arabs and Berbers but an Arab–Berber fusion which, embracing the same faith and adhering to the same system of values, is animated by a love of the same land.[8]

Such a historiography eliminates all traces of the conflicts which arose within political nationalism, determining the monolithic unity of a movement which is presented as having been founded exclusively on Islam and Arabism.

Algerian nationalists imagine the colonial period exclusively in the univocal register of a long oppression. In various official writings since independence, the colonial past is transformed, in its entirety, into a *passé-repoussoir*, a period of unrelieved blackness serving exclusively as a contrast to the present, legitimating the self-justifications of the contemporary social order. All that, but only what this history contains that was precarious, sordid, pitiless in its relation to human life and work is readily evoked. The 132 years of French presence are a mere parenthesis. Thus, the dominant, official historical mindset has come to oppose a colonial pre-war darkness (in short, an 'Ancien Régime') to a constantly reiterated and ever-present glorious war and its hope of a radiant future. This perception of the colonial experience pervaded the whole Algerian political spectrum; Ferhat Abbas, the liberal, francophone leader and a republican in the '1789' sense of the word, would write of 'the colonial night'[9] in evoking the French presence (from which he had, earlier in life, hoped for so much[10]). In cutting themselves off from their recent history in such a way, without making more searching analyses (or even making an inventory of the 'good' and the 'bad') Algerians risk leaving themselves with nothing but an abstract universalism. In so doing, they would, ironically, parallel that very French conception of history which sees the origins of the nation in its radical separation from the Ancien Régime. At the same time, the hypercritical relationship to the real and recent past enables a reappropriation of the most apparently archaising forms of historical imagination.

In the political traditions of contemporary Morocco, a different relationship to independence, and the history of the pre-independence period, may be observed. If, in Algeria, the continuity of historical time is smashed by a rupture and an advent (war and the independent state), in Morocco, independence seems to mark the return to a system of state which was always present and only (if for too long) held in subjection. One only has to consider the role of the monarchy in the early development of Moroccan nationalism to observe as much. When, on 16 May 1930, the young sultan, Si Muhammad, not yet three years on the throne, signed the 'Berber *dahir*' (a measure for the institutionalisation of 'customary law' in berberophone areas, designed to facilitate French control), massive protests were sparked. But the sovereignty of the sultan himself, however dependent he might be on the French authorities, was never in question. Morocco's nationalists instead began, as of 1933, to celebrate each year the anniversary of Sidi Muhammad's accession, thus beating the French protectorate at its own game – immune to the charge of threatening the stability of Moroccan tradition, incarnated by the sultan, they set themselves up, on the contrary, as its staunchest protectors. Their struggle for national liberation would operate through the preservation of the monarchy. The monarchy, in fact, was held up as the nationalists' own most powerful symbol. After the deposition of the same sultan, 20 years later, Allal al-Fasi, leader of the Istiqlal party, protested:

> The French forces have executed this design without considering that the true throne of Muhammad V is more majestic than that throne which, as they see, was offered him by a foreign protectorate. [...] France has oppressed and mistreated, in the person of Muhammad V, not only all Moroccans but all Muslims and all Arabs of the world, for His Majesty Muhammad V incarnates the honour of the believing Muslim, the strength of those who struggle and the nobility of the Arab.[11]

For Moroccans, the monarchy remained an institution whose meaning could be seen as having remained intact, and which could therefore be reappropriated and proposed anew as a model. A kind of deliberate archaism, a passion for the past, is thus the articulation of Moroccan nationalism, re-establishing its imagined historical continuities. For Algerians, on the other hand, the new model of sovereignty in the independent state would promote a vigorous, passionate rejection of the immediate past, a 'vital forgetfulness' which would open up the future. Revolutionary Algerian nationalism would be led to forget its own founding figures. Messali Hadj, inspirational leader of the first Algerian independence movements, the Étoile Nord-Africaine (ENA, founded in 1926) and the Parti du Peuple Algérien (PPA, founded in 1937) was violently pushed aside by his 'sons', the initiators of the insurrection of November 1954. The young avant-garde of the PPA, Ahmed Ben Bella and Mohamed Boudiaf, desired only to make an end of a 'father' who had become cumbersome. Like its illustrious predecessor of 1789 (or rather, 1793), the Algerian revolution too carried the conviction that its accomplishment could only be achieved by the elimination of those elements judged too 'lukewarm'. The father of Algeria's nationalism was devoured first – the children of its revolution would come later... A similar fate awaited Ferhat Abbas, the man who wished to preserve the republican principles introduced (however ambiguously) by colonial France, while remaining faithful to the traditions of an Islamic culture. He more than anyone else incarnated the 'French rebellion' in the Algerian revolution. But the activist core which held the real power in the FLN wanted nothing of this vision, preferring a unanimist conception of a nation arising as one, untouched by external influence.

These two distinct, but equally passionate, relationships to the past carry us into a world of implicit references, fashioned, in part, in both cases by a very French fancy – the centrality of the state, patiently forged by a monarchy over the centuries; the advent of the nation in revolutionary rupture. These two faces of history illuminate aspects of contemporary political culture in each of Algeria and Morocco.

A Single Field of Reference for Two Nationalisms

As I began by pointing out, Algeria and Morocco were for a long time, as it were, out of phase with one another in geopolitical terms: differential factors which ought to be borne in mind include the Ottoman presence in Algeria and its absence from Morocco, the colonial fracture occurring earlier in Algeria, and lasting longer, the occurrence of decolonisation at staggered intervals and in quite different forms. Nonetheless, modern Algerian and Moroccan nationalisms appeared together in the 1930s and were both rooted in a social landscape profoundly worked over by colonial structures: an unfinished social differentiation had resulted in the maintenance of an 'underclass people', an almost non-existent urban proletariat, massive inequality in development between different regions of each country, a famished bourgeoisie with no real project of modernisation, an immense peasantry within which very different social relations were juxtaposed. A single referential field, such as 'identititarian' struggles for self-preservation and the defence of Islam – could have served to structure them. In fact, although in Morocco political nationalism was indeed structured, from the moment of the Berber *dahir* in 1933 onwards, around the first leadership's call to *salafiyya*,[12] the radical current in Algeria emerged in the milieux of proletarian emigration to industrial France. These very different origins of the two nationalisms were for a long time masked by the high profile allowed to the movement of the *'ulama* in Algeria, founded and initially led by 'Abd al-Hamid Ben Badis.[13] This patrician from Constantine, and his struggle for the preservation of Arabic and Islam, was certainly better known in Fez or Marrakesh than was Messali Hadj, the standard bearer of a political project of separation from France. The interwar cultural–religious campaign of the Algerian *'ulama* in the name of Islam in no way foresaw the political independence of Algeria. At the 1936 Muslim Congress in Algiers, the *'ulama* did not hesitate to endorse the famous article calling for 'the *rattachement* (administrative and judicial integration) of Algeria with France'.[14]

Despite the different origins of the two nationalisms – urban and bourgeois in Morocco, rural–metropolitan émigré and proletarian in Algeria – Algerians and Moroccans after independence nevertheless forged themselves a common system of nationalist representations. Both nations are predominantly seen as the outcome of struggles for the definition of an

Arab–Muslim national personality, effacing Berbers and all the other various influences which have historically interacted to shape their societies. The Moroccan scholar El Khatir Aboulkacem has written, referring to the birth of Moroccan nationalism in the 1930s with the protests over the Berber *dahir* which the colonial system tried to impose, that:

> With this event, the *amazigh*[15] found him/herself, in this moment of the constitution of a national consciousness, identified with colonial policy and with the antithesis of nationalism. S/he is thus condemned to a loss of status at the very moment when the urban élite established itself as the group best placed to lead, best placed to build an age of nationalism. This, thereafter, contributed to the negation of the *amazigh* in the project of nation building, a project envisaged within the monolithic framework of Arabo–Islamism.[16]

Each nation thus constructed a representation of itself which would be exploited, after independence, by 'conservatives', Ba'thists and Islamists, to evoke an 'identity in danger'. This representation establishes a kind of eternal harmony, tying the contemporary nation (across the abyss of the immediate, colonial past) to precolonial times. But still, and even before political independence, distinctions in terms of geopolitical opposition were emerging between Algeria and Morocco. Since the 1960s, and up to the beginning of the twentieth century, these oppositions have never ceased to intensify.

Postcolonial Separations: Lines in the Sand

The statist, centralising control which marked the final years of the reign of Muhammad V in Morocco was contemporaneous with the experience of *autogestion* (agricultural workers' self-management) in Ben Bella's Algeria. When Morocco began to develop its agricultural sector, privileging the economy of the plains region which was turned towards exports to Europe, Algeria under Houari Boumediènne engaged itself in an almost neo-Stalinist programme of *industries industrialisantes* and the collectivisation of land. At the same moment that the sherifian kingdom, after the assassination of Mehdi Ben Barka in 1965, realigned its foreign policy towards the United States and Israel, Boumediènne's republic profited from the decline of Nasser's Egypt to make Algiers the long-range artillery platform of revolutionary third-worldism. The two states, with so much history and culture shared in common but such rigorously oppositional social and political maxims, were perhaps bound to end in open conflict. The Sahara was in a sense a pretext – and a field sufficiently distant from both sides' major population centres – for the brother enemies to permit themselves a war.

From independence in 1956, Morocco laid claim to Saharan territories still part of French Algeria, in particular the towns of Tindouf and Béchar as well as part of the Algerian Sahara. When, in 1959, the French made overtures towards negotiation on these territories, (with the obvious ulterior motive of a cessation of Moroccan aid to the Algerian rebellion) Muhammad V preferred to decline the offer, since 'any negotiations entered into with the French government at this time concerning Moroccan claims and rights would be considered a stab in the back of our combatant Algerian friends'; the King would prefer 'to wait until the independence of Algeria might give us an opportunity to lay the question of borders before our Algerian brothers.' Morocco hoped, indeed, that after Algeria's independence, the Saharan frontier, drawn by the French in the early years of the twentieth century, would be adjusted in its favour. The expectation was all the stronger since the Algerian Provisional Government (GPRA) had signed, on 6 July 1961, a secret agreement with Muhammad V which foresaw the creation of an 'Algero–Moroccan commission' intended to resolve the dispute: the 'territorial problem, created by the arbitrary imposition of a delimitation between the two countries by France, will find its solution though negotiation between the government of the Kingdom of Morocco and that of independent Algeria.'

But by 1963, things in Algeria had changed. The GPRA had been removed, during the crisis of the summer of 1962, and Ben Bella's government did not consider itself bound to engagements contracted by a defunct entity. Algiers referred the Moroccans instead to the principle of the non-negotiability of frontiers inherited from the colonial period, a principle which would be adopted by the Organisation of African Unity in May 1963. Finally, Algeria's leaders pointed out that independence had been delayed precisely because of the question of the Sahara (on which negotiations with the French had repeatedly foundered, the FLN insisting on complete territorial integrity), and that there could be no question of abandoning the smallest part of national territory 'for which the sufferings of the Algerian people were prolonged'. Algiers, then, refused to negotiate, and as for the people living in the disputed border zone, the prospect of more upheaval could only be considered as an aggression – this time on the part of the Moroccans – by a population hardly yet recovered from seven and a half years of war. Ben Bella was thus able to benefit from a closing of ranks around his position, one all the more important in the face of other problems, notably Hocine Aït Ahmed's insurrection in Kabylia. Relations with Morocco thus became a factor on Algeria's internal political scene.

On the Moroccan side, the situation was somewhat comparable. Algeria's intransigence was received with all the more bitterness since Morocco had served as a base for the revolutionary ALN (Armée de Libération Nationale):

a significant fraction of Morocco's political class was sure that Algiers would 'make a gesture'. At the same time, Hassan II was himself facing down a major political challenge from the left under Mehdi Ben Barka, and the 'War of the Sands' enabled a consolidation around the throne of the Moroccan opposition (indeed, the 'opposition' has always, in any case, been intractable on questions of territorial integrity, never ceasing to demand the restitution of territory identified as having belonged to Morocco, whether the Western Sahara or the Spanish coastal enclaves in the North). Conditions in both countries thus converged towards the likelihood of confrontation.

A long period of tension followed the public announcement, in the early summer of 1963, of Moroccan claims to sovereignty over part of the Algerian Sahara. In July, both countries began military build-ups in the region of Tindouf. On 8 October, Moroccan and Algerian troops engaged one another in brief but intense skirmishes along the Saharan frontier. That evening, King Hassan II sent an emissary to Algiers, but the fighting continued and increased in intensity from 10 October onwards. In Algeria, the general mobilisation of ALN veterans was announced. The escalation threatened to engulf the whole region, pitting against each other two armies with no previous experience of fighting from fixed positions. The conflict was halted thanks to the mediation of several African and Arab states. The intervention of the Ethiopian ruler, Haile Selassie, at the Bamako conference of 29–30 October resulted in a ceasefire agreement signed on 2 November. (Fighting nonetheless continued in the area of Figuig, north of Tindouf, until 5 November.) The War of the Sands crushed the hopes of anyone who had hoped that Algerian independence would signal an effective Maghribi union. Worse, this brief war would find a more serious, and long-running, prolongation in the Western Sahara, 12 years later.

In May, 1975, a UN mission recommended the application of the principle of self-determination for the former Spanish Sahara, having been impressed by the mass demonstrations organised by the Polisario.[17] In October of the same year, the International Court of Justice at the Hague followed suit, while also recognising 'the existence, at the time of Spanish colonisation, of juridical ties of allegiance between the Sultan of Morocco and certain tribes living in the territory of the Western Sahara' – and at the same time noted that similar ties had also existed 'with certain Mauretanian authorities.' This evidently satisfied none of the parties, just as it failed to give a satisfactory answer to the question of whether the Western Sahara could be considered as having been a *terra nullius* (a land belonging to no-one) at the moment of its colonial occupation.

Events were not slow to develop. On 16 October 1975, Hassan II called for a peaceful march for the reconquest of the Southern Provinces – 'the

Green March'. With the exception of the far left, the kingdom was united in total consensus and the Spanish army stood by while the impressive cortège passed the frontier. But, as Khadija Mohsen-Finan has pointed out, if the march, with its 350,000 participants, did in fact pass off peacefully, it nonetheless assumed the symbolic and traditional aspect of a punitive expedition sent to cow tribes who had defied royal authority.[18] The Spanish authorities, at least, were convinced, and completed a rapid withdrawal. On 14 November 1975, the Madrid Accord decided the partition of the Sahara between Morocco and Mauretania. On 11 December, 4000 Moroccan soldiers entered La'youn.

Algeria's President, Houari Boumediènne, hesitated before two options. The first, advanced by his Foreign Minister, Abdelaziz Bouteflika, aimed at a compromise with Morocco. The supporters of this option argued for acceptance of the Moroccan occupation of the Western Sahara in exchange for Morocco's definitive recognition of Algerian sovereignty over Tindouf (by ratifying the 1969 treaty of Ifrane). The second option was championed by the army, some of whose chiefs had nursed hopes of *revanche* since 1963, and by the Minister for Industry, Belaïd Abdesslam, who had come into conflict with the Moroccan authorities at the very moment of independence in 1962, in his role as the FLN's representative in the region of Bechar and Tindouf. This second group pleaded for Algerian military intervention to counter the Moroccan action and 'offer' the Sahraouis their independence. The prospect of obtaining control of a corridor to the Atlantic, and ultimately of control over the Western Sahara's rich natural resources, can hardly have been absent from their minds. Boumediènne decided in favour of the latter option.

The second Algero–Moroccan war broke out. From 27 January to 15 February 1976, violent engagements took place between the two armies at Amgala. Algiers and Rabat traded accusations of 'expansionism' and 'hegemonic ambitions'. The press of each country set about the other in virulent media campaigns, and ambassadors were recalled – diplomatic relations were broken off in March. Several thousand Moroccans living in Oranie (north-western Algeria) were expelled. On 26 February, the remaining Spanish authorities, wanting no part in a regional conflict, announced their decision to quit the territory definitively. The fighting between the regular armies stopped in the same month, but on 28 February Polisario proclaimed the Saharan Arab Democratic Republic. Having set up refugee camps across the Algerian border the Front began years of guerrilla warfare, with Algerian military support. Twenty years later, with the exhaustion of a war that cost thousands of dead, wounded and 'disappeared', Morocco and Algeria would again have to try to find common points of contact in their shared history.

The 1990s: Ideological and Societal Convergences

Since the late 1980s, Morocco and Algeria seem, for the first time since independence, to have recovered a degree of social and political development in parallel, as both countries have moved towards political and ideological pluralism. If it is possible, now, to lay good odds on the possibility of some kind of political rapprochement between the two countries, this has not come about by the will of the respective states, in a deliberate and organised manner from above, but through the political movements of two societies towards greater pluralism. It is this societal movement that might be expected to result in greater convergence.

It is self-evident that Algeria, coming through the terrible civil war that has racked the country and which is now pursued in the form of political and familial acts of vengeance, cannot escape questions of public freedoms, multi-party politics, the end of a centralised economy and the existence of a civil society. Morocco has been confronted for several years now with issues of political pluralism and *alternance* – the institutionalised transition of executive power – the freedom of the press, and the emergence of a society of citizens. In both countries, questions must be asked regarding the position of women, the *movement citoyen* which constitutes the visible expression of civil society, and of claims made in the name of 'Berber-ness' (*l'amazighité*).[19] Foreign partners, whether European countries or the United States, are obliged to take an interest in Morocco and Algeria, and their new – younger, educated, urbanised, dynamic – societies. Europe and the USA have to deal with societies in a stage of advancement, and can no longer play on oppositions (which were already real enough) between one country and the other. This, in terms of international political and economic alignments, marks a major change. In the 1960s and 1970s, Morocco displayed a manifestly pro-Western stance, while Algeria held to a more Arab nationalist and Third Worldist role. The 'Arab identity' proudly brandished by both paradoxically signified the divergence of the two brother countries, placing them in different ideological constellations: Algeria, the 'first-born daughter' of Nasser's Egypt, was a natural ally of populist, radical nationalisms in the Mashriq, and of the PLO, while Morocco took up its place at an equal distance from the Hashemites and Saudis at the front of 'pro-American' Arab monarchies. Since the fall of the Berlin wall, this bipolar ideological distinction between an Algeria on the 'Arab left' and a 'pro-Western' Morocco no longer holds water. Equally, of course, with the Bosnian and Chechen wars, the notion of Russia as an ally of the Muslim world against Israel has more or less evaporated. The Maghrib is less and less dominated, in its cultural–political self-definitions, by the singular notion of Arab-ness (*arabité, 'uruba*), whose hegemony has been challenged by political Islam and politicised *berberité*, both of which are also rooted in the *longue durée* of history.

26

In both countries, Islamist movements have been developments of national histories, connecting more with national singularities than with a transnational *umma* (community of faith). The individuality and the strength of the FIS (Front Islamique du Salut, Islamic Salvation Front) can be understood in its populism, a mantle it appropriated from the FLN. In the same way, the movement of Shaykh Yasin in Morocco (*al-'adl wa 'l-ihsan*, the Justice and Charity movement) is rooted in national specificities. In both countries, the Islamists have engaged themselves in the existing political games. Islamism, too, must develop or risk marginalisation. The condition of society in the Maghrib has changed since the emergence of Islamist movements in the late 1970s and early 1980s. The major questions with which they are faced are those of individualisation and emigration/exile, not those of communitarian retrenchment. The appeal of religious and 'identity' discourses, while it remains substantial, does not necessarily offer a political solution to the Maghrib's problems which can be espoused by the whole of society. To the often violent crises of family and community life affecting North Africa, political Islamism can only offer ancient remedies couched in terms of comforting communitarianism.

Another important factor is the tendency of Algerian and Moroccan immigrant communities, principally in France, to mix, to forge links of acquaintance, and the weight of these groups is felt in North Africa, among the intelligentsia and in civil society. They tend, too, to maintain and reintroduce multilingualism. Intellectuals of both countries, arabophone or francophone, religious or secular, are increasingly aware – as are their counterparts in Turkey – of the proximity of their countries and societies to Europe. At the same time, academics and technocrats are rediscovering an interest in Maghribi unity. This convergence in social, political and cultural terms, irrespective of the intentions of the states' leaders, and even if Algeria refuses to open the border with its western neighbour,[20] signals a movement of each society towards openness and circulation. Despite archaic survivals and old themes repeatedly rehearsed in official rhetoric, the important dynamics move through consumerism and citizenship.

On the other hand, transversal exchange between the two countries at the level of intellectual, political and economic elites remains weak. The obligation to make a detour via Europe in order to reach one another, understand one another, to allow information to circulate, complicates and slows rapprochement. And the level of economic exchange and investment between – and within – the principal countries of the Maghrib sits at an extraordinarily low level. If the two nations' people are engaged in identical movements, on the political level there remains a generation problem. The older generation grew up in the ideology of a unifying Maghribi nationalism,

27

a vision broken at independence by the primacy and rivalry of very different kinds of nation states. New generations now acceding to positions of responsibility do not share this history. For them, as they take up the reins of politics and the economy, the societal convergence occurring on the level of civil society provides an incentive to reappropriate a shared historical memory. However, if there are evident desires for rapprochement in Algero–Moroccan relations, they have remained subject to frustration. As before, the perpetual degradation of each effort at unity occurs on the borders. At Bechar, right on the frontier, a horrific massacre of civilians was committed on 15 August 1999 by armed groups identifying themselves with Islamism. The incident immediately scuttled possibilities of concord between Algiers and Rabat. A glance at the official declarations made during the summer of 1999 reveals both the possibilities and the disappointments of relations between the two countries.

Summer 1999 – a Handshake and a Massacre

On Sunday, 25 July 1999, after the funeral of Hassan II, there was a remarkably warm atmosphere between the new Algerian President, Abdelaziz Bouteflika, and the young Moroccan King Muhammad VI. Hopes of reconciliation between Morocco and Algeria returned with gusto to the forefront of political and media attention. And then… on 21 August, the Algerian Arabic-language daily *al-Khabar* reported that, according to inhabitants of the frontier zone, Moroccan security forces had cut off the retreat of the armed group suspected of having perpetrated the massacre at Bechar. On 22 August, *al-Hayat* in London carried the headline: '14 children massacred in Algeria. Morocco assists in surrounding an armed group.' An AFP dispatch dated 25 August announced in the same vein that: 'the arrest in Morocco of an Algerian Islamist group suspected of the killing of 29 people at Bechar on 15 August confirms that the normalisation of relations with Algeria is a priority for Rabat.'

The next day, however, the Moroccan government's spokesman, Khalid Alioua, denied 'any infiltration of Algerian armed elements' across the border and affirmed that no Algerians were being held by Morocco. 'The Algero–Moroccan frontier is secure and intact and no infiltration across it is possible.' Algiers was not pleased. The daily *Le Matin* announced, in an article entitled *'Le Maghreb n'est pas pour demain'* (roughly, 'Maghribi Unity: *Not* Coming Soon') that:

> The honeymoon appears to be over and the reopening of the border indefinitely postponed. Algeria affirms that there is categorical proof of Moroccan complicity [with the terrorists]. Let down by the laconic

28

statement released by the spokesperson for the Moroccan government, Bouteflika has revealed that Morocco 'trains and finances' Islamist terrorists and sends drugs into our country. Our western neighbour is even accused of plotting against Algeria.[21]

On 3 September, addressing electoral rallies at Annaba and at Hassi Messaoud, Bouteflika returned to the offensive: 'Why should we want to go to a country that does not respect us? Why should we go to these countries [Tunisia and Morocco] to spend hard currency buying second-hand clothes from the Far East? [...] Algeria is not the country it was in the 1980s. We will no longer be milked by our neighbours or by any state that holds its sovereignty in thrall to outside powers.'

Relations between the neighbours went into freefall. A segment of the Moroccan press decided to hit back at Algerian accusations: 'Moroccans are entitled to tell a man who first opened his eyes at Oujda,[22] who grew up there and who thrived as a militant of the Maghrib, that it would be better for him not to waste his time in the deviations of the past, and instead that he should return with us to the present, so that together we may turn towards the future.'[23] On Monday 20 September, the Algerian daily *al-Khabar* reported that 80 kilograms of TNT, originating in Morocco, had been seized by Algerian border guards. On 22 September, in a press conference given in New York, on the fringes of the UN General Assembly, Bouteflika announced that: 'We are experiencing a major moral crisis in Algeria. It is not the fault of Moroccans or Tunisians. There is a general moral crisis which has stimulated an enormous black market between the three countries of the Maghrib. It gives me no pleasure to say it, it pains me to do so, but Morocco *is* an international supplier of drugs. The young generation in Algeria has been completely, I do mean completely, cut down by this traffic in drugs.' Before a stupefied audience, the President pressed his attack, this time with accusations of other kinds of trafficking: 'As regards the tragedy that my country has experienced , there has been on the Moroccan side, let us say, a blind eye turned to certain things, notably arms smuggling. I do not think that we can talk of fraternity and at the same time kick each other's shins.'[24]

A week later, two jeeps carrying a dozen Algerian soldiers made a point by penetrating two and a half kilometres inside the Moroccan frontier at al-Hajra al-Kahla, in the south, firing into the air and damaging a border post. The incursion, announced several days later by the French newspaper *Libération*,[25] considerably aggravated the tension. The Moroccan weekly *Maroc-Hebdo* hardened its line: 'President Bouteflika is a mythomaniac. How terrible when someone who claims to be one's brother turns out to be a joker! We genuinely believed the displays put on by the embittered man of Algiers, but they were excessive. [...] But the Algerian President is a hostage to the

Generals. He may really have some affection for Morocco. But he is watched, receives instructions, is led. A serf. In short, we have to do with an impotent man. He entered into discussions with His Majesty Hassan II in terms which left no room for ambiguity. He lied.'[26]

So is everything definitively off between Morocco and Algeria? Not exactly... On 22 October 1999, the Algerian President nonetheless declared from Formentera, an island in the Balearics, that 'the stability of Algeria is of a piece with the stability of Morocco and that of the Alawite throne', and expressed his desire to implement the 'construction of a sovereign Maghrib'.[27] The episodes marking the summer of 1999 illustrate the extreme levels of tension that can be reached between the two countries, in which domestic political calculations play a significant role (the crisis in relations with Morocco occurred at precisely the moment of Bouteflika's first difficulties with the army), alongside the persistent weight of reactions and suspicions born of recent history. Rapprochement, so difficult between governments, is nonetheless occurring within Algerian and Moroccan societies themselves. The 'Berber question' is a perfect example of the dynamics shared by, and circulating between, Algerians and Moroccans, and of the commonality of terms in which such dynamics find expression.

Summer 2001: Simultaneity – the Berber Question

The Berber question, recognised as a cultural factor in Morocco through the Berberism of Mohjoubi Aherdane's Mouvement Populaire, and severely repressed in Algeria at the time of the 'Berber Spring' in 1980, has re-emerged in both countries. In Morocco, the Agadir Charter, concerning Berber cultural and linguistic rights, was signed on 5 August 1991 by a number of Amazigh cultural associations. This was the first collective text produced by what we shall call the Amazigh cultural movement, and it called for a revision of official Moroccan history. In 1993, the Moroccan historian Mostafa Hassani Idrissi, fearing the disappearance of the teaching of ancient history in schools, wrote:

> The history of antiquity, let us state quite clearly, in no way obstructs the development of a homogeneous image of the nation. On the contrary, it permits us to emphasise the community of origin of Amazigh and Arab.[28] It permits every Moroccan to consider the history of the Arabs, even from the earliest times, as his own, and in the same way it simultaneously brings every Moroccan to regard the Imazighen as his ancestors and their history, notably their resistance to Romanisation, as his own.[29]

On 1 March 2001, a 'Berber manifesto' was adopted; it caused a sensation for having questioned the traditional, Arab-Islamic basis of Moroccan official history.[30] In the summer of 2001, Abdellah Bonfour wrote in the magazine *L'Essentiel*: 'The political recognition, even voluntary, of the Berber language will not suffice. A whole practice of archaeology, of historical deconstruction, is necessary, as a prelude to an education which must be undertaken. In other words, a critical rereading of our history is urgent.'[31]

This debate on history and Berber culture in Morocco was occurring at the very moment when, in Algeria, mass mobilisation was developing around the same themes. After ten years of terrible civil war and the death of over 100,000 people, Algeria was again in the international media spotlight on 14 June 2001. On that day, almost one million demonstrators attempted to march through the streets of Algiers to demand a transition to democracy, the end of police violence in Kabylia and the respect of linguistic pluralism (in particular, recognition of Tamazight). The march came in the wake of the turbulent 'events' which had shaken Kabylia and other regions, particularly in the east of the country, since April – social protests, rioting, violent expressions of the anger of young people and citizens more generally demanding the improvement of their living conditions. The spectacular demonstration of 14 June, its size and its violent repression by the regime, was a very significant sign of a new situation emerging in Algeria. It marked the end of the exclusive hold on Algeria of the bloody *tête-à-tête* between armed Islamic groups and the state, and announced the active presence of a hitherto silent civil society which had frequently been seen to be 'held hostage'. It demonstrated the political weakness of the Islamists, whether 'moderate' or radical, now clearly identified as having come to agreement with the system in the accords settled with certain ruling circles of the regime, which envisaged an intransigent defence of 'Arabo–Islamic values', and the preservation of the 'high' Arabic language as the essential foundation of national unity.

The 'Kabyle crisis' signalled and amplified the central state's loss of legitimacy, its distance, authoritarianism, and arbitrary rule. The riots in Khenchela, a major town in the east of the country, set in the heart of the Aurès mountains and cradle of the revolution in the 1950s, saw the appearance of slogans declaring 'The Chaouis Against *Le Pouvoir*'.[32] This ethnicisation of the crisis, however, recalls the spectre of a possible Balkanisation of Algeria. The leaders of the revolt in May–June 2001 accused the regime of exploiting precisely this fear, and of playing the old card of Arab–Muslim nationalism, in order to maintain themselves in power. The protestors pointed out the deployment, against the June 14 march, of groups of young men recruited from the popular quarters of the capital, who were sent against the demonstrators with 'anti-Kabyle' and 'pro-Arab–Muslim' slogans. The characterisation of the revolt by the regime as a 'Kabyle' affair, a menace to territorial integrity and national cohesion, was denounced as cynical manipulation by the protestors.

This revolt (whose repercussions continued throughout 2001 and into 2002) points, finally, to a reduction in the regime's margins of manoeuvre. The end of the opacity of *le pouvoir* has weakened the decision makers at the top of the executive, who had been accustomed to working in perfect obscurity. Henceforward, as the young demonstrators in the spring and summer of 2001 made clear, the demand for democracy requires a low profile from the army in the conduct of political affairs, and the recognition of political and cultural plurality. These same aspirations can be seen in Morocco. The King of Morocco, in his Speech from the Throne of 31 July 2001, announced the creation of a Berber Cultural Institute.

The Past and Visions of the Future

Recent history, particularly colonial history, has profoundly divided the 'Maghribi nation' into hostile identities frequently derived from the France of the Third and Fourth republics: a monarchist Morocco imagined by Lyautey, a Jacobin Algerian Republic, single and indivisible. To define oneself is always to oppose oneself to others, and from the 1960s to the 1990s Moroccans and Algerians were frequently hard put to transcend their mutual oppositional dynamic. It is only the application of democratic politics, as yet barely able to speak but undeniably alive, that might potentially reunite the Maghrib, and ever more closely reunify it.

An inventory of differences and a searching-out of possible resemblances can lead to all kinds of visions of the future of relations between Morocco and Algeria. There might be an ever stronger affirmation of obvious singularities, hence a maintenance of a difficult, and sometimes hostile, relationship, or on the contrary it might become possible to move beyond the old, conflicting positions. It is this latter hypothesis which seems most probable in the years to come. At a time when both countries are preparing themselves for the opening of their (economic) borders to Europe within the framework of agreements with the EU, the Maghrib owes it to itself to present its northern neighbours with a united political and economic front. There is no shortage of other factors pleading for an effective union: the impulsion of an impatient, active, massive younger generation, the need to consolidate economies capable of offering opportunity at home to populations drawn away into (often hopeless and clandestine) emigration, the competition of European production, an Islamism still ready to relaunch itself on the back of social despair... In building its unity, the future Maghrib might reconstruct, little by little, the bases of its old inheritance of trans-Mediterranean civilisation; it might thus preserve the possibility of a real dialogue between all those 'Westerners', Christian, Jewish, or Muslim, who live on both sides of the Mediterranean.

NOTES

This article is an amended translation of the introductory essay which first appeared in Benjamin Stora, *Algérie, Maroc. Histoires Parallèles, Destins Croisés,* published by Éditions Zelig (France), Éditions Barzakh (Algeria) and Éditions Tarek (Morocco) in October 2002.

1. On the relationships of temporality in the Maghrib, see the classic texts of Jacques Berque, *Le Maghreb entre deux guerres* (Paris: Seuil 1962). English translation by Jean Stewart; *French North Africa. The Maghrib between two World Wars* (London: Faber and Faber 1967); and Ch-A. Julien, *Histoire de l'Afrique du Nord* 2 vols. (Paris: Payot 1951).
2. On this aspect of the current crisis, see B. Stora, *Algérie, formation d'une nation* (Biarritz: Atlantica 1998) and also *La Guerre invisible, Algérie, années 90* (Paris: FNSP 2001).
3. On this highly complex problem, see the major work by Rémy Leveau, *Le fellah marocain défenseur du trône* (Paris: FNSP 1985).
4. The French assault on Algiers began with the landing of troops at Sidi Fredj (or Sidi Ferruch), north-west of the city, in June 1830.
5. 'Maroc-Algérie, l'entente, la coopération et le bon voisinage, fondements de l'UMA', *Le Matin du Maghreb et du Sahara* 19 May 1999.
6. On 20 August 1953, the Moroccan sultan, Sidi Muhammad ben Yusuf (soon to be King Muhammad V) was deposed by the French protectorate authorities, an action which provoked the violent opposition of the Moroccan population and triggered a crisis which culminated in Moroccan independence in 1956. On the same date in 1955, the second anniversary of the Sultan's deposition, thousands of peasants in the north Constantinois (north-eastern Algeria) rose in revolt on the orders of the FLN. This uprising marked a major turning point in the FLN's insurrection and might be considered as the effective beginning of the Algerian war.
7. Quoted in the Moroccan newspaper *Al-Maghrib* 17 May 1999.
8. Ahmed Taleb Ibrahimi, *De la Décolonisation à la révolution culturelle* (Algiers: SNED 1973) p.225.
9. Ferhat Abbas, *La Nuit coloniale* (Paris: Julliard 1962), the first volume of his memoirs.
10. See his *De la Colonie vers la Province. Le Jeune Algérien* (Paris: Garnier 1981) 2nd edn., 1st edn. 1930 (Editor's note).
11. On Allal al-Fasi, see the reports in the Istiqlal's newspaper, *L'Opinion,* 14, 15 and 16 May 1999, the 25th anniversary of his death.
12. The modernist movement for the reform (*islah*) of Islam, which posited a return to the supposedly original purity of the faith, located in the generation of the immediate followers of the Prophet (*al-salaf al-salih,* the 'pious forefathers'), combined with the rationality of modern thought, so as to revive Islamic culture in the modern world. The movement originated in the Middle East with the Egyptian Muhammad Abduh (1849–1905) as its most influential thinker (Editor's note).
13. Ben Badis (1889–1940) founded the Association of Algerian Muslim *'ulama* in 1931, on the basis of a group of modernist, reform-minded Islamic intellectuals influenced by the *salafiyya* which had gathered around Ben Badis since the mid-1920s (Editor's note).
14. On this question, see Mahfoud Kaddache, *Histoire du Nationalisme Algérien. Question Nationale et Politique Algérienne, 1919–1951* (Algiers: ENAL 1993 [2nd edn.]) 2 vols.
15. Now a generally used ethnonym among berberophones of all regions in North Africa to

designate themselves. The plural of *amazigh* is *imazighen*, and the various dialects of the language are commonly labelled together as *Tamazight*. Tamazight is also the commonly used name for one of the dialects found in Morocco (Editor's note).

16. El Khatir Aboulkacem (doctoral student, EHESS, Paris), untitled paper, forthcoming.

17. The POLISARIO Front (*Front Populaire pour la Libération de la Séguia al-Hamra et du Rio de Oro*).

18. Khadija Mohsen-Finan, *Sahara occidental, les enjeux d'un conflit régional* (Paris: CNRS histoire 1997).

19. See Fatiha Layadi and Narjis Rerhaye, *Maroc, chronique d'une démocratie en devenir* (Casablanca: Eddif 1998).

20. The tendency to movement and exchange irrespective of state policy is nowhere, perhaps, more strikingly illustrated than in the *trabendo* (black marketeering) which flourishes apace along the officially closed Algero–Moroccan border, a frontier regularly described in the Algerian press as 'a sieve' (Editor's note).

21. *Le Matin*, 5 Sept. 1999.

22. The Moroccan town on the Algerian border where Bouteflika was born, 2 March 1937. During the Algerian war of independence, Oujda was the major headquarters in the west of the ALN, and the birthplace of the core elite that would form around Colonel Houari Boumediènne, a group of which Bouteflika was a prominent member (Editor's note).

23. *al-Ahdath al-maghribiyya*, 7 Sept. 1999. The more 'official' daily, *Le Matin du Maghreb et du Sahara* did not enter the fray.

24. *MAP Actualité* 23 Sept. 1999.

25. 'L'Escalade de Bouteflika', *Libération* 11 Oct. 1999.

26. 'Rancunes, mensonges et inimitié', *Maroc Hebdo International* 388 (8–14 Oct. 1999).

27. 'Bouteflika change de ton', *L'Opinion* (the mouthpiece of the Moroccan Istiqlal party) 24 Oct. 1999.

28. On this aspect of the Maghribi nationalist reading of ancient history, see James McDougall, 'Myth and Counter-Myth: "the Berber" as National Signifier in Algerian Historiographies', *Radical History Review* 86 (forthcoming) pp.66–88.

29. Mostefa Hassani Idrissi, 'Les Malheurs de Clio au Maroc', *al-Bayan*, 5 May 1993.

30. See the important work of Mustapha El Qadiry, *L'État national et les Berbères. Le Cas du Maroc. Mythe colonial et négation nationale*, doctoral thesis, Université de Montpellier III, 1995.

31. Abdellah Bonfour, 'l'Enjeu de l'histoire dans le débat sur l'amazighité au Maroc', *L'Essentiel* 3 (Aug. 2000).

32. *Shawiyya (chaoui)* is the Berber dialect spoken in parts of eastern Algeria (the Aurès and Nemencha mountains (Editor's note).

Ideologies of the Nation in Tunisian Cinema

KMAR KCHIR-BENDANA

What is *Tunisian* cinema? Or, what do we understand by 'Tunisian' cinema? Would it be simply the totality of films produced since the country's independence by directors of Tunisian nationality, in Tunisian studios with Tunisian crews and budgets? Or all films shot in Tunisia? These criteria, which are 'national' at least in the sense of juridical and financial 'nationality', are generally appropriate in respect of the 60 or so films which can be considered as constituting a corpus of contemporary (that is, post-independence) Tunisian cinematography. The considerations which I shall develop here revolve around a central question, that of understanding what is signified by 'Tunisian', or *'tunisianité'*, and are intended as an attempt to read, through the diverse marquetry of cultural production represented by these films, the various meanings which they give to the 'nationality' they apparently share.

What can we understand by *'tunisianité'*? And how is such a national identity expressed through such varied artistic works? Or rather, how does *the ideological expression of 'the national'* manifest itself, on different levels, according to different viewpoints and approaches? In other words, what we are seeking to isolate, in sociological terms, is the relation between the material bases of social organisation and the most highly elaborated forms of intellectual, artistic and cultural production; taking the Tunisian cinema as a case study, I observe in this article the field constituted by 40 years' production of films in order to test a *grille de lecture*, experiment with certain definitions, and advance a certain number of hypotheses.

Since I have raised the notion of 'ideology', I should first of all explain which of all its definitions I mean – although several would suit the present purpose. Among them – ideology as the science of ideas (as facts of consciousness, their nature and laws), or, by extension, the study of a system of ideas, that is, of a philosophy of the world and of life or, again, as a classical Marxist reading would have it, the totality of ideas and beliefs particular to a given global historical period, society or class – I opt for the

35

point of view presented by Althusser, that ideology is the imaginary relation of individuals to their real conditions of existence.[1] The term thus designates the totality, not only of representations, but also of practices and behaviour both conscious and unconscious. 'National identity' here does not, then, mean the supposedly 'objective' criteria held to characterise a nation – territorial space, language, and juridical considerations were only just appropriate for the initial steps towards an insufficient definition with which we began. To 'belong to a nation' is to adhere, voluntarily or not, consciously or not, to a representation – not to a political regime, nor to a doctrine or a culture, but to the framework within which all of these are expressed, the ideological form of modern social community.[2] An idea, or ideology, of the nation is not reducible to nationalism, and vice versa; national*ism* might rather be thought of as one possible form of expression of the broader system of a national ideology, a form most often today identified as pathological, as a hypertrophy of national sentiment. For our purposes here, I consider 'nationalism' as one *level* of ideological expression which might be encountered in the reading of our corpus of films – in official discourse, in propaganda, in underlying assumptions – but which might equally be encountered, diffused or explicit, in the writing of some of our films' critics. There are, for example, certain affirmations made here and there in the press or in literature on the subject which deserve attention. Tunisian cinema has a 'national tonality' less acute than that of its Algerian neighbour[3] (where 'national' means what I call 'nationalist'). Tunisian cinema in the 1970s arrived at a certain 'Tunisian ethic';[4] the same decade is said to have witnessed the creation of a 'national cinematographic aesthetic'.[5] Such question-begging uses of the terms 'Tunisian' and 'national' oblige us to interrogate the films themselves in order to investigate what is meant by their being 'Tunisian' or 'national', and what is the ideology of the national in this 'Tunisian' cinema.

One attitude, common to a certain number of films, and whose decoding is extremely simple, is first and most obviously remarkable. Pure political engagement marks those films which take as their subject the political history of nationalism, exalting with a certain gusto a glorious national history, relating the struggle for the country's political liberation from colonialism. One thinks in particular of the films of Omar Khlifi, a director whose début, *al-Fajr* ('The Dawn') of 1966, is considered the first Tunisian film. He would go on to make three further films: *Le rebelle*, ('Rebel', 1968); *Les fellaghas*, ('Bandits', 1970); and *Hurlements*, ('The Roaring', 1972). Khlifi produced a cinema which relates and illustrates in its images exactly what is produced and reproduced by school history books, radio and television programmes, and all the official public histories. These films define themselves as national because they are nationalist. Their content and tone is determined by what 'the nation' says, tells itself, and teaches about itself. The strυ colonialism is idealised, presented as a uniformly heroic enterp way as to serve directly, through cinema, the project of (nationalist epic in line with a state-sponsored cultural productioυ ῀ by unanimism. The creation of the production company SATPEC (*Socieι.* *Anonyme Tunisienne de Production et d'Exploitation Cinématographique*) in 1959, and then the building of a film laboratory at Gammarth, completed in 1967, were essentially political decisions, intended to give the new national cinema an infrastructure which would allow it to develop.

The recent history which the first films set out to dramatise, of course, was not nearly so simple and Manichean as it appears in Khlifi's work. Other directors, recognising the forgotten aspects of official history, revisited it, attempting to repair earlier omissions and tackling subjects which are not generally mentioned in treatments of the country's recent past. Abdellatif Ben Ammar's *Sejnene* (1973 – the title is taken from the name of a small agricultural and mining town in northern Tunisia) dealt with the workers' movement, rereading the history of national liberation through the story of the UGTT (*Union Générale des Travailleurs Tunisiens*, the Tunisian General Workers' Union, founded in 1946). Through the story of a print-worker and his son seen during the events of 1952–54, a crucial period of contemporary Tunisian history, the director sought to restore to the labour movement as a whole its place in the anticolonial struggle. *Et Demain*, ('And Tomorrow', 1972) by Brahim Babaï confronted two crucial problems of the immediate post-independence period – unemployment and the exodus from the countryside. The condition of immigrants in France was the burning subject of the moment when Naceur Ktari made *Les Ambassadeurs* in 1975. The film, set in the *Goutte d'Or* district of Paris (an area heavily populated by North African immigrants), plays on the grandiloquent and misleading title of 'ambassadors' given by the authorities at home to the migrants, whose living and working conditions give the lie to rosy official rhetoric.

Women, although never absent from the more 'officially' nationalist films, (Khlifi's *Hurlements*, for example), became heroines in their own right in this second category, which seemed intent on giving women the place of honour in a 'revised and corrected' national history whose task was the rehabilitation of all those who had previously been forgotten. This was thus a cinematography whose political engagement had a revisionist agenda, but its desire to testify about Tunisian society and history was nonetheless articulated in the same affirmative register as more 'traditional' nationalism. This is true even of a film like *Sejnene*, which, despite its highly original viewpoint, did not depart from the fixed chronological scheme of those key dates accepted by everyone, more or less, as developmental steps of the national movement and through which the history of the struggle for liberation is told via that of the political parties. When, in *Soleil des Hyènes* ('Hyenas Sun', 1976), Ridha Behi mounted a critique in which the ravages of the tourist industry were perceived as acts of rape, (the film showed the brutally penetrative impact of the expansion of tourism in a fishing village, where the new economy smashes social relations, the labour market, the landscape, and property rights...) it was, again, a question of affirming the 'defence of the nation'. Brahim Babaï was working from a similarly nationalist perspective in composing his political statement, *La Nuit de la Décennie* (1990) which dealt with the causes of the 1978 clashes between the regime and the workers' union.

All these films have a second common denominator. They all focus on characters who generally lack consistency and exist only as symbolic flag-wavers. Even when, in the best works, the characters have a certain depth, they nonetheless remain prisoners of prototypes: *the* traitor, *the* patriot; *the* bourgeois, *the* worker, *the* woman – a necessarily positive character – *the* colonist, *the* intellectual, *the* bureaucrat. The ideology of the nation is thus expressed through a gallery of highly characteristic 'Tunisians'! Despite their entirely different genres – since they are, variously, Western-style epics, neo-realist statements or quasi-documentary reportages, these films exhibit the same tendency to address *tunisianité* through a typology of more or less archetypal characters.

Other film makers, nonetheless, understood the impossibility of determining exactly what 'the national' signifies, appreciating that no representation of social or political history can ever exhaust the question of *tunisianité* by giving it a total and definitive form. Their films express in a more nuanced fashion the ambiguities and difficulties of being Tunisian. The 1969 film *Khlifa Lagraa* ('Khelifa the Bald') is emblematic of this approach. Director Hamouda Ben Halima describes with great individuality and a highly poetic economy of style the malaise of a man exceptionally authorised (or condemned) to enter the closed and private world of women by a skin disorder which leaves him bald. A few years later, *Au Pays de Tararini*, (1972) a collective film made up of short cinematic sketches, evoked the old city of Tunis. In its best moments achieving a level of refinement and intimacy comparable with those of Ben Halima's *Khlifa Lagraa*, the film sought to anchor itself in a mythical past, and represents the first appearance of what might be called the nostalgic side of Tunisian cinema. The past is reasserted, here, in warm retrospection, but can the return to certain values and sources of the urbane *Tunisois*, thus reclaimed through a certain stylised imagery, constitute the hallmark of *tunisianité*? An explicit interest in the work of Tunisian novelists characterises this tendency, which finds its legitimate subjects (Khelifa le Teigneux, Tararini, Barg Ellil) in the writings of Ali Douaji[6] and Bechir Khraïef.[7]

Curiously, a film as radical and Brechtian as the Nouveau Théâtre's *La Noce* ('The Wedding') can also be considered, at least as regards its dialogue, as representative of this nostalgic current. However different the films undoubtedly are in form, *La Noce* (1978) can be read alongside Ali Labidi's *Barg Ellil* (1990) which relates in a conventional, televisual style a story of life in Tunis in the fifteenth century, at the time of the Spanish invasion, as well as *Halfaouine, L'enfant des terrasses* (1990) in which Ferid Boughedir amuses himself with his childhood memories, *Soltane el Madina*, (1992) Moncef Dhouib's reflection on the degeneration of the old town's districts, or more recently *Les Silences du Palais* (1994), a film by Moufida Tlatli in which the action takes place around the end of the beylicate in the 1950s. In all these films one can observe a particular attention paid to language in the scripting of the dialogues, which most frequently employ a *tunisois* dialect, vehicle of a certain, specific notion of *tunisianité* which is reductive and not, of course, shared by all.

For other directors, Tunisian identity is to be found in the countryside. Taïeb Louhichi's *L'Ombre de la Terre* ('The Shadow of the Land'), (1982) a chronicle of the life of a nomadic community at the edge of the desert, is the most significant example of a group of films which have sought to glorify the rural world; Ali Abdewahab, in *Om Abbès* (1969), and Omar Khlifi in *Hurlements* (1972), also attached themselves to the effort of rehabilitating – with a great deal of theatricality and rather less accuracy – a bedouin world that had been abandoned and ignored.

A further attempt to problematise dominant notions of 'national identity' emerged in work addressing the delicate question of biculturalism and plural identity, a tendency which emerged relatively early in Tunisian cinema with films like *Mokhtar* (1968) by Sadok Ben Aïcha, which related in episodic fragments the suicide of a young, francophone Tunisian novelist, and *Une si Simple Histoire* (1970) by Abdellatif Ben Ammar, who demanded of his audience a reflection on the *déchirement* of a Tunisian intellectual married to a Frenchwoman. The same director's *Aziza* (1980) similarly explored the difficulties of adapting from traditional ways of life to modern living, through the emigration of an artisan from the heart of the old *medina*, symbol of a disappearing socio-cultural urban network, to a newly built suburb. The changes in socio-economic conditions and values observed through this spatial shift appear limitless, as one of the characters, Aïcha, leaves with a Gulf emir, dazzled by the mirage of an easy life which marriage to him seems to offer.

A concern with boundaries, borders and imposed limitations also animates Mahmoud Ben Mahmoud's *Traversées* (1982), whose action takes place outside Tunisia, and relates the painful failure of the attempted 'crossings' of the title through the story of a Tunisian intellectual's inability to cross a

European frontier. More recently, *Chichkhane*, ('Diamond Dust', 1991) by Mahmoud Ben Mahmoud and Fadhel Jaïbi, and *Les Zazous de la Vague*, (1992) by Mohamed Ali Okbi, both explore (the latter in parodic mood) the complexity of a 'Tunisian identity' subject to the countervailing forces which pull their characters in different directions: these two films address, respectively, cultural mix, and the refusal to accept one's condition in life. The cohabitation of – at least – two identities, 'eastern' and 'western', is treated here in quite different ways, sometimes in a grave and even tragic tone (as in *Diamond Dust*), alternatively in a comical vein *(Les Zazous)*.

In such films, which demonstrate a particular sensitivity arrived at through the development of cinematography in Tunisia more generally, it becomes possible to identify particular expressions of locality and singularity. The appearance of film makers working in this vein, such as Néjia Ben Mabrouk and Nouri Bouzid, consecrated an interest in film capable of scrutinising its characters, one which would endow them with a psychological density transcending simple typologies. Around the characters of their films, these directors construct a meticulously precise and realistic vision of space, décor and dialect, creating a specific ambiance and constituting a depth and sincerity for their protagonists, heroes who can finally be apprehended in the full complexity of their contradictions. Earlier works, it is true, had already given a foretaste of this achievement: well before Néjia Ben Mabrouk's *La Trace* (1982) or the 1986 production *L'Homme de Cendres* by Nouri Bouzid (a true homage to the old city of Sfax), Ahmed Khéchine, in his 1969 film *Sous la Pluie de l'Automne,* succeeded in depicting the conflicts of a poor family in Kairouan with a remarkably sure eye and tone – albeit without ever liberating himself from suppositions about 'the national' as a pre-existing given simply requiring illustration, rather than a problem in need of creative exploration. The culmination of this approach can be seen in Nouri Bouzid's sketch, *C'est Schéhérazade qu'on assassine* ('Murdering Sheherazade') in the collective film *La Guerre du Golfe et Après...*(1992), which addresses the 1991 war in the Gulf, an event translated into a spectacular worldwide phenomenon by its televisual hyper-mediatisation, through the lens of the everyday life of a Tunisian family. The director, concentrating his gaze on small, tightly circumscribed facts, succeeded in exposing a larger reality, one which gained the film a considerable audience. It is, in fact, local, particularistic films, assuming their specificity and presenting it in a way which is globally accessible, which have more recently achieved the greatest success at Tunisian box offices, and which have also most attracted foreign audiences: witness the popular success of *Halfaouine, L'Homme de cendres* and *Les Silences du Palais.*

Yet other directors have opted to ignore, or to refuse, the flagging of national colours; in such films, where some notion of *tunisianité* is not immediately evident, we might ask ourselves what significance such an absence might have. In establishing an *ad hoc* inventory of these films it is quickly apparent that they appeared very early on in Tunisian cinema – films which played on allegory or which effaced certain stock themes of 'Tunisian-ness'. In *Yusra*, (1972) Rachid Ferchiou set the action of his fantastic tale in an indeterminate Mediterranean space, as if to accentuate its ethereal aesthetic. Claude d'Anna and Férid Boughedir's *La Mort Trouble* (1969) explored the master–slave problematic, but in an esoteric style, to investigate the colonial situation from an oblique angle. The Nouveau Théâtre's *Arab* (1988) equally employed the detour of metaphor – in this case, the siege of a derelict cathedral – to explore the threats posed to Tunisia by conflicts in other Arab states, whereas *Les Baliseurs du Désert*, a (1984) film by Naceur Khémir, took refuge in allegory, beyond the limitations of any specific time, to pursue its search for the meaning of lost cultural values.

There is, too, a further wave of films – *Mon Village* (1979) by Mohamed Hammami, in which the village of the title is that of a group of Palestinian *fida'iyin*; *Leïla ma Raison* (1989, the plot is that of a famous, seventh century Arabian legend, mediated through a novel by André Miquel of which the screenplay is an adaptation) by Taïeb Louhichi; *La Ballade de Mamelouk* (1982) by Hafedh Bouassida; *Les Anges,* (1984), *Champagne Amer,* (1986), and *Les Hirondelles ne meurent pas à Jérusalem* (1994), by Ridha Béhi; and finally Naceur Khémir's *Le Collier Perdu de la Colombe* (1988). The makers of these films, perhaps for reasons of marketing and distribution, have deliberately chosen as their setting spaces which evoke Tunisia only indirectly, if at all. Their screenplays, too, employ foreign languages or dialects, or else are couched in literary Arabic, or in an artificial, 'rootless' Arabic, supposedly comprehensible anywhere and thus capable of carrying *tunisianité* – whatever their *tunisianité* would then be – into a market-place otherwise inaccessible to an overly specific local ('national') production. Work in this vein, sacrificing local particularity, has yet to prove its commercial and artistic effectiveness, and the allegorical detours through which it finds expression demonstrate in themselves the difficulties of 'speaking the national' through film – and, thereby, also themselves speak of the complexity which 'Tunisian', if these are 'Tunisian' films, entails.

The brief, panoramic overview which I have attempted to sketch illustrates the variety of Tunisian film-makers' responses to the question of 'the national', whether the question itself is central to their preoccupations or uncomfortably lingers on the periphery of their vision. The inescapability, in any event, of 'national' classification, of 'being national', in whatever sense, and somehow expressing an ideology of the nation, is perhaps a reflection of the overwhelming dominance of what Balibar calls the 'nation-form'[8] in global political and ideological organisation. Contemporary Tunisian cinema is obliged to organise and present itself as a 'national cinema' in a market where it has to face other national cinemas – Algerian, Egyptian, French – and all others (Indian, British, Italian cinema) do likewise, in the face of American cinema, which alone, perhaps, in the global marketplace is capable of transcending (or sufficiently extending?) its own frontiers and specific traits, and of imposing itself as 'transnational'.

NOTES

An earlier version of this article was presented to the Tunisian Association for the Promotion of Film Criticism (ATPCC) in Tunis in 1994. Feature-length films produced in Tunisia since 1956 now (September 2002) number around 100. The production examined here consists of those 60 or so films made in the first 40 years of Tunisian independence.

1. 'L'idéologie et appareils idéologiques d'Etats', *La Pensée* (June 1970). Reprinted in English, 'Ideology and Ideological State Apparatuses' in Louis Althusser, *Essays on Ideology* (London: Verso 1984).
2. See the remarks of Pierre Nora, 'Présentation' in *Les lieux de mémoire*, vol.I, *La nation* (Paris: Gallimard 1986) especially p.x.
3. Guy Hunebelle, in Férid Boughedir, *Introduction aux Cinémas du Maghreb*, special issue of *Ciném'Action*, (Paris, 1980) p.6.
4. Victor Bachy, *Le cinéma de Tunisie, 1956–77*, (Tunis: STD 1978) p.147.
5. Férid Boughedir (note 3) p.67.
6. (1909–49) A Tunisian novelist and short story writer, he was a member of the famous literary and artistic group Taht Essour ('Below the Ramparts') and also wrote radio plays, song lyrics.
7. (1917–83) A writer, born in the Tunisian south, of novels and novellas which were serialised in the Tunis press, notably in the review *al-Fikr.*
8. Etienne Balibar, 'The Nation Form: History and Ideology', in E. Balibar and Immanuel Wallerstein, *Race, Nation, Class: Ambiguous Identities* (London: Verso 1991).

Stories on the Road from Fez to Marrakesh: Oral History on the Margins of National Identity

MOSHE GERSHOVICH

If you travel from Fez to Marrakesh along the winding, mountainous inland road that crosses the Middle Atlas, you are bound to pass through the bustling town of Khenifra.[1] A few kilometres south of there, you may notice an impressive, obelisk-shaped monument atop a hill on the left-hand side of the road. A steep dirt road takes you to the monument and after climbing a few yards you reach its base, which carries a small plaque in Arabic that in translation reads as follows:

> In memory of the great battle of El Hri that took place on the 2nd of Dhu al-Hija 1332 (13 November 1912) between the national resistance, formed of the proud champions of the Middle Atlas tribes led by Moha ou Hammou Zaiani and the French army led by Colonel Laverdure. The battle ended with a great defeat of the French army in spite of its large numbers and its equipment. The French left on the battlefield more than 33 dead officers headed by Colonel Laverdure, more than 700 soldiers, and 176 wounded. In that battle in which the coloniser, as witnessed by its officers, experienced its greatest defeat in North Africa, 182 martyrs gave their lives among the warriors. Their names were not recognised until now. Here are their names according to tribes and communities.[2]

The plaque is dated 1991 and signed by two Moroccan ministers, Moulay Ahmad Alawi and Muhammad El-Ansar. It represents an effort by the Moroccan state to commemorate an important event in the nation's recent history. I am unfamiliar with the exact circumstances that brought about this initiative, but judging from some inaccuracies, most notably the mistake concerning the date of the battle, one may assume that the erection of the monument may have been carried out in a somewhat hasty fashion to meet a ceremonial deadline.[3] Beyond these shortcomings, what caught my attention and led me to include this contemporary sign of a reconstructed past at the

43

outset of this article, is the identification of the 'proud champions of the Middle Atlas tribes' as members of the 'national resistance'.[4]

One may only wonder how Moha ou Hammou and his Zaiani warriors would have reacted to their posthumous induction into the Moroccan pantheon of national heroes. Born in the late 1850s and appointed *qa'id* (tribal governor) of the Zaian in 1886 by sultan Mawlay Hassan I, Moha ou Hammou had distinguished himself as a maverick, an often rebellious and altogether unreliable player in the tangled power game between the government (*Makhzan*) and the tribes of the Middle Atlas.[5] His encounter with the French in 1914 should be understood against the background of his volatile relationship with the pre-colonial Moroccan sultanate. Moreover, while he himself had remained a 'dissident' (the conventional colonial label for Moroccans who resisted French 'peaceful penetration') until his death in 1921, he apparently encouraged close members of his family, including two of his sons, to switch their allegiance and serve as 'partisans' of the French army.[6] Indeed, his own death came in a battle with a Zaiani contingent loyal to the French and led by his own son.[7]

Morabet Moha Ouala was born around 1913 in the *douar* (hamlet) of Ait Lahcen ou Said, part of the Ait Moussa Zaian tribe, in the region of Khenifra.[8] His date and place of birth were registered 23 years later by a French enlistment officer who recorded Moha's induction into the ranks of the French army. Since the registration of newly born children had been virtually non-existent in the Moroccan countryside during the 1910s, we may safely assume that the determination of Moha's date of birth had been made merely upon the officer's judgement of his age. Moha's childhood was rather uneventful. He never went to school, since 'only rich people were allowed to attend it'. All he remembers of that time was 'the back of the mule and the sheep I was guarding'. His enlistment occurred in 1936 at Sidi Bouzakri, a township in the region of Meknes. 'I was there for the weekly market', he recalled. 'Someone named Abou Hammou was calling for people to enlist, and I went with three of my friends.' He underwent basic training in Meknes as a rifleman, a member of the 1st *Régiment des Tirailleurs Marocains* (RTM). Later on he was transferred to the 3rd RTM, and with that regiment he left for France in 1938.

Since Moha's unit was stationed in Alsace, it was spared the harshest fighting of the Spring 1940 campaign. Still, he was wounded in the hand and had to be evacuated to Morocco. After his recovery, he rejoined his unit, now part of the scaled-down armistice army under German supervision. As a member of that force he took part in the brief round of hostilities against the American troops who landed on Morocco's Atlantic shores in November 1942. He was wounded again, more severely this time, and spent three years in a military hospital, thus missing the remainder of the war. The doctors could not remove the bullet that had struck a bone near his neck. Mobaret retired from the French army in 1947 and moved to Khenifra where he acquired a plot of land and worked in agriculture. He has lived in Khenifra ever since, existing on the meagre French pension and invalidity payment sent to him every three months through the Moroccan postal system. Despite his frustration over the lack of substantial material support, he expresses no regret about his decision to serve in French uniform. 'If given the chance', he declares, 'I would have done it a second time.'

Morabet Moha Ouali's story is not unique. If I were to alter a few details, places, and dates, it could fit dozens of personal stories I have collected over the course of two years of field research in Morocco. It is, indeed, the frequency and predictability of these stories that enable the reconstruction of a collective profile of the group to which Mobaret Moha belongs: Moroccan veterans of the French army.

My interest in this group derives from the role that its members often found themselves playing as representatives of the colonial order among their indigenous communities. For most of these men, their enlistment in the ranks of the French army represented the first significant separation from their homes. While wearing the uniforms of that army they travelled to and resided in some of Morocco's main cities. Many among them would eventually find themselves aboard ships taking them overseas to Europe, the Middle East, or Vietnam, to name some of the theatres of war in which Moroccan soldiers were to shed their blood.[9] For those fortunate enough to survive the ordeal and return home relatively unharmed, this experience overseas singled them out in communities that had rarely been exposed to such far-flung external contacts before their forced 'pacification'.

This article gives a collective profile of Moroccan veterans of the French army as an example of a subaltern group located in the margins of colonial and post-colonial discourses. Specifically, I am interested in the effect that military service has had on the shaping of these men's lives as well as on their dual role as agents of change within their home communities and as representatives of those communities to their colonial masters and comrades-in-arms. I explore here aspects of these individuals' non-elite, 'interstitial' historical agency, and its difficult socialisation in the post-colonial era relative to the 'home' nation state, the former colonial power, and – perhaps most importantly – the local community.

In this context I would like to propose a hypothesis, to be fully developed in future work, linking the career patterns of veterans of the Middle Atlas and the integration of that region within post-colonial Moroccan society. My thesis in this regard argues that the French strategy, which aimed at preserving a distinct Berber identity as a safeguard against the spread of anti-colonial indigenous nationalism from the Arabophone urban centres to the mountainous countryside,[10] was significantly compromised by recruitment practices that inadvertently achieved the very result the French had sought to prevent. The principal vehicle for the adoption of Moroccan nationalist ideas among Berber soldiers was language. According to Morabet, prior to his enlistment in the French army he had never been 'in contact with Arabic-speaking Moroccans'. This statement would probably characterise many other Berber-speakers from the Middle Atlas. The French practice of placing Berber speakers in units in which Moroccan colloquial Arabic was used alongside French as the language in which commands were transmitted to the rank and file was one born out of necessity rather than choice: there were never sufficient numbers of French officers and Moroccan NCOs fluent in *Tamazight* (the dialect prevailing in the Middle Atlas) to staff all 'mixed' Moroccan units (that is, those manned by both Moroccan and French personnel). It also reflected the historical progression of the French army's employment of Moroccan soldiers.

The recruitment of Moroccans as soldiers in French military formations began in November 1908, three and a half years before the formal imposition of the dual protectorate regime over the Sherifian empire and a year and a half after the initial landing of a French expeditionary corps in Casablanca. Six auxiliary units were created, each 150–200 strong, composed of local recruits from among the Arabic-speaking population of the *Chaouia* region, with a handful of French commanders. The format of this type of contingent as well as its name – *goum* (from Arabic *qawm*), were based on previous French practice in Algeria. Originally designated to be 'a temporary back-up tribal force raised for specific operations',[11] the *goums* soon proved to be highly useful, flexible and cost-effective, so much so that their number doubled within six years and kept climbing until it reached 50 by the early 1930s. These units operated side-by-side with regular French troops and were fully integrated with French operations aimed at 'pacifying' the Moroccan countryside.[12]

While experimenting with assigning combat roles to its own locally recruited auxiliary troops, during the transition to the Protectorate, the French military command in Morocco was confronted with the need to redefine the future status of soldiers who had served in the pre-colonial Moroccan army. The matter came to a dramatic conclusion shortly after the signing of the Protectorate treaty by Sultan Mawlay 'Abd al-Hafiz, and the subsequent uprising of the sultan's troops stationed in Fez against their French instructors and the foreign inhabitants of the city (mid-April 1912).[13] After suppressing the revolt and executing hundreds of Moroccans, the French disbanded the army (save for the ceremonial 'Black Guard' of the Sultan) and re-admitted those soldiers not implicated in the revolt who wished to continue their service to newly created infantry and cavalry battalions entitled 'Moroccan Auxiliary Troops' within the ranks of the French army.

Treated with open suspicion by their French counterparts, Moroccan soldiers were among the first troops dispatched to France at the outbreak of hostilities in Europe in August 1914, in an obvious measure of precaution against a possible revolt.[14] They participated in the defence of Paris that summer and in trench warfare along the Western Front as well as other theatres of battle (notably the Balkans) for the duration of the Great War. Their bravery, and the heavy casualties they sustained (9,000 killed or missing in action, 17,000 wounded or victims of illness) were widely acknowledged and won them considerable metropolitan respect. The ultimate collective reward for the Moroccan troops came in February 1923, when they became fully integrated within the regular ranks of the French army, thus losing their 'auxiliary' status.[15] Henceforth, the rights and benefits of Moroccan soldiers were to be equated with those of other colonial soldiers serving the tricolour – these, however, remained far inferior to those of metropolitan recruits.

In the shrinking ranks of the post-war French army, the 32,000-strong contingent of Moroccan soldiers acquired a prominent position. They served in the French occupation corps in the Rhineland,[16] and took part in the suppression of revolts in Syria and the Rif as well as in the 'pacification' of southern Morocco. They were garrisoned in France and trained for another general European conflict. In an army composed mostly of short-term conscripts, the volunteer status of Moroccan soldiers,[17] and their tendency to sign long-term contracts up to a maximum of 15 years, warranted them an aura of professionalism and the epithet of 'splendid mercenaries' otherwise reserved only for the Foreign Legion. Their French superiors hailed their courage and resilience, submission to rigorous discipline (often attributed to their presumed 'fatalism') and reliability.[18]

One trait rarely ascribed to Moroccan soldiers, on the other hand, was initiative, or any similar quality associated with intelligence. Moroccan soldiers were supposedly 'born warriors', but hardly to be trusted with complicated, skills-related tasks. A 1939 study of Moroccan soldiers, for example, noted the willingness of some Moroccan recruits 'to learn more or less complicated mechanics', but acknowledged also that 'Moroccan specialists – radio transmitters, vehicle drivers, etc. – are rare since their training is long and more costly than that of young Frenchmen.'[19] The extent to which this perception of Moroccan soldiers and their limitations was rooted in objective, measurable realities, remains unclear, and one must in any case suspect the usability of supposedly objective, measurable indicators, which may have been adequate to assess the qualification of young metropolitan

Frenchmen or urban colonial recruits, but which must have put young men from the countryside at a considerable disadvantage. We should also consider the prevailing perception of 'wild savage countrymen' that probably clouded such assessments of their qualifications and potential.[20]

A good example for disproving such biases would be Taousi Haj Lakbir. I met Taousi in January 1998 at the War Veterans office (*bureau des anciens combattants*) of Beni Mellal, the Middle Atlas' largest town on the Fez–Marrakesh road, where he was residing at the time.[21] I was then at the outset of my research, still exploring interviewing methods and assessing ways to locate individuals whose life stories may best contribute to my goal of reconstructing a collective profile of Moroccan war veterans. With my research assistant IO[22] at my side, I was in the midst of conducting several interviews when a short old man stepped into the room. At first I paid no special attention to the little figure. But, as Taousi began telling his life story, dotted with small details that reflected his crisp memory, I realised how unique and impressive he was.

Taousi was born in 1910 near Kalat Essaraana, a town further south along the Fez–Marrakesh road. He came from a poor family who lived in the countryside and had no direct contact with the French authorities prior to his enlistment. He never attended school and was completely illiterate on joining the ranks of the French army at the age of 20. 'I used my fingerprint to sign a four-year contract,' he recalls. His initial monthly salary was 22.5 anciens francs (i.e., just under one franc per day), far below the payment of French soldiers serving with him. He became a rifleman (*tirailleur*), beginning his service in the 2nd RTM and later moving to the 3rd. After finishing his training, he left with his unit for France, but he did not adjust well to the cold, snowy weather and became ill. Taousi returned to Morocco and took advantage of the limited educational opportunities open to Moroccan soldiers to acquire a solid proficiency in French, learning to read and write in that language. With his improved skills came an accelerated pace of promotion. By 1938, the year in which he returned to France, Taousi had reached the rank of sergeant-major, the highest non-commissioned rank open to Moroccans at the time.

Placed in combat positions from the outbreak of war in 1939, Taousi's regiment was transferred to Belgium in May 1940 along with the bulk of the French army, expecting to meet the German thrust there. However, as Taousi recalls, 'The Germans had encircled Belgium and when we crossed the border they closed our way back.' This simple statement about what was to develop into a colossal *débâcle* illustrates the depth of Taousi's perception of the situation in which he found himself. Such comprehension is highly uncharacteristic of Moroccan war veterans, most of whom remain to this day oblivious to all but the most rudimentary facts related to their military careers.[23] Taousi has apparently devoted considerable time and effort to studying the history of the Second World War, and has acquired a keen awareness of his own role in it.

Taousi recalls with great precision the events of 20 May 1940, the day in which his unit's heroic but futile resistance came to an end. 'I went with a French officer to seek food and a way out,' he recounts. The officer 'climbed a tree and waved a white flag. I asked him: "Why are you doing that?" He responded: "We've been prisoners for ten days already." The officer then dropped his rifle and raised his hands.'

Following their captivity, Taousi and his comrades were marched through Belgium to Germany. Their treatment was harsh. 'Each evening they gathered us like sheep. Each time a soldier rose up, they would shoot. We ate nothing but grass.' Once in Germany the prisoners were taken by train to Berlin where 'The German authorities called civilians to come spit on us.' From there they were shipped to another prisoners' camp located inside the German-occupied zone of north-eastern France.

Thus began Taousi's saga to regain his freedom. He escaped in October 1940 along with another Moroccan sergeant named Hammou ben Mimoun. They hid in a forest for six days and finally managed to cross to the southern zone of France, controlled by the Vichy Government. During their escape, he recalls, they met 'a French woman who told us how to pass a bridge guarded by a German soldier. At noon the bell rang, civilian workers left their work, and we could disguise ourselves among them.' He spent several months in France, during which time he communicated with the local French military headquarters and arranged for his return to Morocco.

Taousi rejoined the ranks of the French army and was promoted to the rank of adjutant. Following the Allied landing in Morocco and the subsequent liberation of North Africa, Taousi joined the Free French Expeditionary Corps and participated in fighting in Italy, France, Germany, and Austria. He retired briefly at the end of the war, but in 1948 was recalled for service and sent to defend French interests in Indochina. He remained on active service until 1954, completing nearly a quarter century of his life in French uniform. Beside the 13 medals and decorations he had been awarded during his career, his reward amounted at the time of our meeting in 1998 to a quarterly pension of 2,027 Moroccan dirhams (then roughly equivalent to $225 or £150).

Taousi is exceptional in his crisp memory and attentiveness to precise details, his sharp mind, and his ability to master the French language to the extent of conducting official correspondence with the French authorities dealing with veterans' affairs in Casablanca. One may wonder what kind of achievement this man could have accomplished had he been given the opportunity to maximise his intellectual potential and leadership skills. In reality, he has been condemned to the pitiful poverty that characterises the overwhelming majority of his fellow veterans.

Insofar as his actual career is compared with those of other veterans I have met and interviewed, Taousi's story is less remarkable. Like many of the 90,000 Moroccan *tirailleurs* who took part in the 1940 Battle of France,[24] and who were fortunate enough to escape death on the battlefield, he became one of about 1.8 million French prisoners of war.[25] A good number of these POWs attempted to escape and a few of them actually succeeded in reaching the territory held by the Vichy government, and from there made their way back to Morocco. Other Moroccan prisoners won early release from POW camps and repatriation to their native land. Once there, they found themselves officially discharged from service, in accordance with the restrictive stipulations of the armistice regime dictated by the Germans and Italians to defeated France. However, a number of these veterans were re-employed in the clandestine network of Moroccan auxiliaries who were trained by French officers in preparation for a future French re-entry into the war on the Allied side. This massive covert operation, one of the few bright spots in France's military record during World War II, took advantage of the existing framework of the *goums* – and of the dismissive attitude of Axis armistice inspectors towards colonial recruits.[26]

Hence, some *tirailleurs*, veterans of the 1940 campaign, were reassigned to *goums* and spent the rest of the war fighting in their ranks. Such a transition was not difficult, since the social background, economic status, and tribal origins of men serving as *tirailleurs* or as *goumiers* seem to have been the same. Indeed, when comparing stories of veterans who were recruited to the French army during the 1930s and early 1940s, one is struck by the apparent arbitrariness of the selection of their designated units.

Witness, for example, the story of Mr Baz Benasser[27] who was born in 1910 and enlisted in the French army in 1935. His original goal was to join a *goum*, so he travelled south from his native region of Midelt (on the south-eastern slopes of the Middle Atlas mountains) to Moulay Ali Sharif in the region of Errachidiyah. For some reason he failed to find the *goum* there, so he reversed his course, returned to Midelt and enlisted as a *tirailleur*. Mr Benasser participated in the 1940 campaign and spent more than two years in a German POW camp. After his release and repatriation, he was asked by a French recruitment officer to rejoin the army. He agreed, but asked to be sent to a *goum* instead of his old *tirailleur* unit. In his mind, 'the *goums* were free. They bought their own food and they were well paid in comparison with the *tirailleurs*. The *tirailleurs* were well equipped, but serving with them was more difficult. You had to carry 15 kg on your back and you walked long distances.'

The liberation of North Africa by Allied troops in November 1942 enabled the French military there to switch its allegiance away from Marshal Pétain's collaborationist Vichy government and to resume active participation in the war against Nazi Germany. For the Moroccan *tirailleurs*, the return to war provided an opportunity to redeem themselves and erase the humiliation of 1940. For their fellow *goumiers* it was an opportunity to demonstrate on a world stage their skills in mountain warfare. While the efforts and sacrifices made by the *tirailleurs* during the last two and a half years of the war certainly matched the record of their World War One predecessors, the performance of the *goums*, now organised in battalion-size *Tabors* and grouped in four regimental-size *groupements*, overshadowed them to win attention, admiration, and apprehension from foe and friend alike. However, along the course of their campaigns from Tunisia to Corsica, Italy, France, Germany, and finally Austria, they also acquired a reputation for their savage appearance, acts of indiscipline, and sheer atrocity (including the rape of Italian women).[28]

A common denominator of virtually all accounts written about the Moroccan *goums* (and the *tirailleurs* for that matter) is the absence of any specific reference to individual Moroccans who served in them.[29] This is hardly surprising, given the fact that none of these veterans ever wrote, let alone published, his memoirs. Hence, the image of World War II veterans, like that of their predecessors of the Great War and the interwar years, has been largely shaped by French views, both in official documentation and commemorative pieces. As might be expected in this context, oral history research among these veterans tends to reveal new angles and challenge some conventional wisdom.

A case in point concerns the reasons that led young Moroccans to enlist as soldiers before and during the Second World War. Contrary to the popular notion at the time, that these men had volunteered out of a quest for adventure and their innate 'warlike tendencies', the reason cited by the overwhelming majority of veterans interviewed is material in nature. The hardship of life in rural Morocco during the transition from virtual freedom to French 'pacification' had been coupled with the impact of the global depression that reached Morocco during the mid-1930s and remained until the end of the war. Recounting his enlistment as a *goumier* in 1943, Timour Ali Oubassou[30] speaks for many other veterans when he says: 'I wanted to have money and to escape misery and oppression. At the time I knew that the world had been at war and that we would be sent abroad where the war was more difficult. However, I didn't have any other choice.'

With the end of the war in sight, French authorities in charge of 'native control' in Morocco began to view with some concern the possible ramifications of the return of liberated Moroccan soldiers to their rural communities. These men, it was felt, could serve as agents of French influence, but also as instigators of anti-French sentiment. They had witnessed first-hand the impact of the Nazi occupation on France, and could easily disprove the prevailing notion of French might that appears to have remained intact throughout the Moroccan countryside during the war.[31] Various measures were drawn up to contain the number of demobilised soldiers returning to their tribal communities without sufficient means of livelihood. Hundreds of veterans were absorbed into the ranks of the Protectorate's public sector, most notably within the police apparatus. Many of them gained access to free or heavily subsidised housing in recently built low-income neighbourhoods such as Hay Mohammadi in Casablanca.[32] However, the dilemma of what to do with demobilised Moroccan veterans took a turn in 1947–49 when France's growing entanglement in Indochina required their re-mobilisation and dispatch to the Far East.[33]

There was a price to be paid for this solution. Fighting in France's war against Nazism could be legitimised, given the Sultan's proclamation, issued at the beginning of the war (September 1939) urging his people to side with France. Participating in a war aimed at the suppression of the national liberation of another colonised people proved to be a far less consensual proposition. North African soldiers who were captured by Vietnamese forces were subjected to indoctrination and invited to renounce their allegiance to France and join the ranks of the rebels. A significant number of them did. They were led by a former *Tirailleur* and prominent member of the Moroccan Communist Party, M'hamed Ben Aomar Lahrech, aka 'Maalouf' or 'Anh Ma.'[34] Some Moroccan prisoners and deserters married in Vietnam and brought their wives back to Morocco. A special section of a cemetery in Casablanca is reserved for these Vietnamese women.[35]

Amid the hardships of confused and inconclusive jungle warfare, culminating in the humiliating defeat at Dien Bien Phu, morale and discipline among the Moroccan contingent in Indochina began to unravel, as is attested by numerous severe acts of desertion and insubordination directed at French officers. The most violent instance of the breakdown of morale was recorded in the 4th battalion of the 2nd RTM during the night of 9–10 July 1952. A few days after an ambush in which his company had lost most of its men, and following a dispute with one of his superior officers, Sergeant Boudjmaa ben Maati, a twice-decorated veteran of World War II, opened fire in the officer's mess, killing six French officers and wounding several others before being shot dead himself. A similar incident had occurred in the same battalion a few months earlier: on 22 March 1953, Private M'hamed ben Mohamed opened fire in the NCOs' dining room, killed two men, wounded two others, and was then shot himself.[36]

Despite the growing tension between France and Morocco, culminating with the exile of Sultan (shortly thereafter King) Muhammad V in August 1953, most Moroccan soldiers remained in the service of France and continued to exercise their duties. Some soldiers (and even a few officers[37]) deserted and joined the ranks of the Liberation Army that staged a brief guerrilla campaign against French targets during the last year of the Protectorate.[38] Only a handful of the scores of veterans I interviewed claimed to have joined the ranks of the resistance movement, although many more declared (retrospective) sympathy for its cause and resentment at the repressive actions undertaken against it by the French. The dilemma is well illustrated in the case of the late Fatoul ou Khalk, as told by his son El Houssine.[39] 'My father', he says, 'joined the French army to earn money, not to fight his Moroccan brothers. There were people [like him] who didn't leave the French army during the period of resistance in 1955, but they also refused to fight against Moroccans. They stayed in the army but didn't fight against the rebels.'[40]

One issue which many veterans who served through the early 1950s seem reluctant to discuss freely concerns the manner in which they reintegrated into society after ending their careers in the French army. Some veterans' transition was facilitated as they moved from their French units directly to the newly created Royal Armed Forces (*Forces Armées Royales,* FAR), or remained in one of the state police apparatuses. Others, mainly handicapped veterans, encountered problems finding suitable livelihoods. As for the manner in which they were received by other Moroccans, most veterans interviewed dismissed any notion of ill-will being expressed towards them; some even recalled a warm, enthusiastic reception. Still, some veterans admit having encountered rejection and abuse on the part of their compatriots. 'I did not integrate easily,' states Tafdoute Elrabi ou Hammou,[41] 'because people were against France and rejected anyone who had served France. People considered those who had worked for France to be traitors, and they were afraid of such people.' Then he adds: 'My wife used to think that way too.'

Faced with negative perceptions, latent or explicit, retired Moroccan veterans have tended to keep to themselves, congregating in small coffee houses typically attached to the *bureau des anciens combattants* of their locality. The overwhelming majority of those veterans I interviewed live in deplorable conditions. Aged, sick, frail, they pass the remaining years of their lives in poverty and purposelessness, desperately reliant on the assistance of their offspring to survive. The pitiful tri-monthly pension they receive from France (via the embassy in Rabat and through the Moroccan postal system),[42] usually amounting to less than $1,000, falls well below what would allow them a minimal level of subsistence in today's Morocco. It is hardly surprising, therefore, that the single common opinion on which virtually all veterans I met seem to agree is that France has mistreated them and ought to compensate them better for the sacrifices they made on its behalf. Indeed, many veterans regarded the mere act of recounting their stories to an impartial but sympathetic stranger like myself as a reclamation of their usurped rights.[43]

The commemoration of the fiftieth anniversary of the end of World War II raised a brief interest in Morocco in the veterans and their story. In 1994, the late king Hassan II inaugurated an exhibition in Rabat, organised by the French embassy and devoted to the 'Liberation of France by Moroccans'. His presence at the event lifted a *de facto* taboo in public discourse on this chapter of Moroccan history and sparked popular and academic interest. Two research groups of Moroccan historians (centred at the universities of Rabat and Kenitra) were formed to study the nation's modern military history, including the involvement of its soldiers in World War II. Useful research has also been conducted by a few independent Moroccan scholars, although most of their work has yet to be published.[44] Given the advanced age of the veterans and their high rate of mortality, the reconstruction of their stories and their collective biographical profile needs to be concluded soon, before they all fade away.

NOTES

This article is part of an oral history research project conducted in Morocco between 1997 and 2000, entitled 'Serving the Tricolor: Moroccan Soldiers in French Uniforms'. I would like to express my gratitude to the Council for the International Exchange of Scholars, the Fulbright International Educational Exchange Programme, and the Moroccan–American Commission for Educational and Cultural Exchange for their funding and assistance that allowed me to carry out my research. I would also like to thank James McDougall for his careful editing and perceptive suggestions that helped put the text in its current form.

1. Serving as the regional centre of the Zaian confederation, the population of Khenifra rose from 18,503 in 1960 to 35,802 in 1971 and 75,454 in 1982. Twenty years later it has most likely surpassed the 100,000 mark thus rising beyond the level of a medium-sized town. On the development of Khenifra and other urban centres of the Middle Atlas, see Mohammed Kerbout, 'Quelques aspects de l'urbanisation des régions marginales et leur signification: le cas du Moyen-Atlas et du bassin de la Moulouya', in *La Ville moyenne au Maghreb: Enjeu de la décentralisation et du développement local* (Eighth Sefrou Colloquium, 1991) pp.45–58.

2. In translating the text I was aided by my research assistant, Hamid Nouamani, a native of the nearby village of Ouaoumana. All responsibility for inaccuracies that may have occurred in translations, however, lies with me alone.

3. The battle took place on 13 November 1914, not 1912. The Muslim calendar (*hijri*) date was 24 Dhu al-Hijja, not the 2nd. For a detailed eye-witness account by one of the battle's French survivors, see Jean Pichon, *Le Maroc au début de la guerre mondiale: el-Herri: Vendredi, 13 novembre 1914* (Paris: Charles-Lavauzelle 1936).

4. The anniversaries of the El-Hri battle and other incidents of successful resistance to French and Spanish rule in Morocco are occasionally celebrated in the current Moroccan press. Note for example the 13 Nov. 1996 issue of *Le Matin du Sahara et du Maghreb* (a semi-official

daily affiliated to the Palace) which devoted four pages (7–10) to the 82nd anniversary of El-Hri. Similar space was devoted to the 63rd anniversary of the Bou Gafer (Jabel Saghro) campaign of 1933 in the 12 Feb. 1996 issue of the same newspaper pp.5–8).

5. Scattered information about his life and early career was gathered in an unpublished study composed in 1924 by a French field intelligence officer, Lt Chanzi, chief of the Alemsid bureau. The study mentions a coalition which Moha ou Hammou forged in 1888 with the Ait Sokhman tribe to resist an attempt by the Sultan to penetrate their lands. In the midst of the conflict the Zaiani leader defected to the *makhzan* camp, but when Mawlay Hassan organised a punitive expedition to attack the Ait Sokhman, Moha ou Hammou refused his support, causing the expedition's failure. A copy of this study, entitled *Organisation du commandement marocain*, is available in the Protectorate's archives, now housed at the French Diplomatic Archive (*Archives Diplomatiques*) at Nantes (series Maroc/Meknes, file 89). An interesting detail in Moha ou Hammou's pre-colonial career concerns his family ties with the ruling 'Alawi dynasty. In 1907 he married his daughter to the future sultan, 'Abd al-'Hafiz, who was then on the verge of challenging his brother, reigning sultan 'Abd al-'Aziz. On this episode see C.R. Pennell, *Morocco since 1830: A History* (London: Hurst and New York: NYU Press 2000) pp.137–41. A recent contribution to the study of Moha ou Hammou's life is an Arabic translation of a biography, originally published in Marrakesh in 1929 by another French intelligence officer, François Berger. The translator and editor is Mohamed Bouasta and it was published in Fez (Imprimerie Info-Print) in 1999. I am thankful to my colleague Michael Peyron for his insight on the original French 'classic'.

6. See Daniel Rivet, *Lyautey et l'institution du protectorat français au Maroc, 1912–1925* (Paris: L'Harmattan 1988) vol.II, pp.82–3, 99.

7. On the circumstances surrounding his death see Berger, *Moha ou Hammou al-Zaiani*, pp.95–103. Note the similarities between this story and Ibn Khaldun's account of the death of the legendary Berber Jewish queen, the Kahina, during the early phase of the Arab/Muslim invasion of the Maghrib.

8. My interview with Mr Morabet was conducted in September 2000 at his residence in Khenifra. I was accompanied by Hamid Nouamani (note 2) who also transcribed and translated the interview.

9. For a concise but fairly inclusive account of the role played by Moroccan units within the ranks of the French Army consult Anthony Clayton, *France, Soldiers and Africa* (London: Brassey's Defence Publishers 1988) pp.262–81,291–305 and *passim*.

10. On this policy see Chapter II in Charles-Robert Ageron, *Politiques Coloniales au Maghreb* (Paris: Presses Universitaires de France 1972) pp.109–48.

11. Thus defined by a 7 Dec. 1909 memorandum by the *Section d'Afrique* of the metropolitan General Staff, series 1H (*Algérie*), file 1013, French military archives (*Service Historique de l'Armée de Terre*, Château de Vincennes, Paris).

12. On the history of the *goums* see my article, 'French Control over the Moroccan Countryside: The Transformation of the Goums, 1934–42', *The Maghreb Review* 22/1–2 (1997) pp.123–36.

13. For a contemporary French account of these events, see Jacques Hubert, *Les Journées sanglantes de Fez. 17–18–19 avril 1912* (Paris: Librairie Chapelot 1913).

14. Resident-General Lyautey actually 'volunteered' these troops without being asked to do so by his superiors in Paris. 'Take my five [*tirailleurs*] battalions and my five[*spahi*] squadrons,' he advised War Minister Alexandre Millerand. 'They are marvellous. You will ask more of them from me.' Quoted by Maurice Durosoy, 'Soldats Marocains', in *Renseignements Coloniaux*, supplement to the *Bulletin du Comité de l'Afrique Française* (July 1932) pp.286–90. One may question the sincerity of this statement that proved nonetheless remarkably accurate.

15. The original bill on this matter was passed in the *Chambre des députés* on 25 Nov. 1915, but it was blocked in the *Sénat* and removed from the agenda shortly thereafter in order to avoid embarrassment to the Sultan, since Morocco had maintained an official neutrality in the war.

16. On that episode and its racial undertones see my article, 'The Sharifian Star over the Rhine: Moroccan Soldiers in French Uniforms in Germany, 1919–25', *Morocco: Journal of the*

Society of Moroccan Studies 2 (1997) pp.55–64.

17. In Algeria and Senegal the French introduced conscription in 1912 and 1919 respectively. A similar motion was considered for Morocco as well, but it was postponed indefinitely in the early 1920s due to the tenuous state of 'pacification'. During the 1930s, years of the global Great Depression, the number of Moroccans seeking to enlist as soldiers generally exceeded the vacancies.

18. For further discussion of French perceptions of Moroccan soldiers, see my book, *French Military Rule in Morocco: Colonialism and its Consequences* (London and Portland OR: Frank Cass, 2000) ch.6, pp.167–205.

19. Berruyer (Captain), 'La situation morale du soldat marocain en France'. Unpublished research paper (*mémoire en stage*) submitted in 1939 to the *Centre des Hautes Etudes d'Administration Musulmane* (C.H.E.A.M. now renamed *Centre des hautes études sur l'Asie et l'Afrique moderne*) in Paris; classified there in vol.3, no.46 *bis*.

20. Rural Moroccan soldiers were not unique in being labelled 'wild mountain countrymen', 'natural warriors', etc. (and intellectually inferior to their 'civilised' masters). Such characterisations were also used in respect of Highland Scots, Indian Sikhs, and Nepalese Gurkhas in the British army, or Algerian Kabyle (*zouave* from Kabyle *azwaw*) recruits in the French.

21. While preparing the initial draft of this essay in the summer of 2001, I received news that Taousi Haj Lakbir has been spending his retirement between Beni Mellal and a home he had acquired in Coigniers, France. This represents an interesting trend, the extent of which is hard to determine, but it came to my attention through occasional and anecdotal reference as I was carrying out my research. Taking advantage of their ability to enter France without the visa required of other Moroccans, some veterans have developed the habit of moving back and forth between the two countries and trading in goods purchased in Europe. Apparently, this trend has come to the attention of French agencies handling veterans' affairs in southern France, whose interim response to the 'problem' has been to relocate their offices from the Gironde (in the south-west) to Caen on the Normandy coast. I am thankful to M. Philippe Pagés, director of the *Service des Anciens Combattants et de l'Appareillage des Handicapés* (an extension of the French embassy located in Casablanca that handles Moroccan veterans' affairs) for enlightening me on this matter.

22. A resident of neighbouring Ksiba, IO, who prefers to remain anonymous, served as my research assistant in the Beni Mellal area and helped me translate the interview with Mr Taousi. I wish to thank him for the work he did for me at the time, as well as my friend Bill Lawrence who acquainted me with IO.

23. Moroccan war veterans are not unique, of course, in having such 'limited understanding' of the battlefield. Indeed, it is quite common, and reasonable, for rank-and-file frontline soldiers to retain rank-and-file frontline perceptions. Their 'confusion' is probably a more veridical representation of the reality of the experience of battle than the 'actual' facts as seen on maps at HQ – and by later historians. An additional factor is that the veterans I interviewed were attempting to recall events in their lives that had taken place five or six decades earlier. In such circumstances it is hardly surprising that one's memory may merge different episodes into a synthesis. Such synthetic memory work is also quite common in story-telling; witness the account of another veteran, Boubeddi Ben Ayyad, whom I interviewed in September 1999 in his hometown of Khemisset. Recounting the same battle in May 1940 in Belgium, Ben Ayyad stated that 'we [French and Moroccan forces] were helped by the British planes while the Germans were backed by the Italian planes. The Russians were fighting the Germans from the other side.' In fact, Italy entered the war only two weeks after the end of the Belgian campaign while the USSR had remained neutral until its invasion by Germany a year later. In a sense it could be argued that Mr Ben Ayyad was summarising the whole war in a single, dramatic image, thus magnifying the event in a way that approximated his own experience of it while synthesising the historical information into digestible form for his listeners.

24. This figure is cited in the second part of a detailed study of the history of the Moroccan *tirailleurs* by Lt Col. Lugand, 'Historique des Tirailleurs Marocains', *Revue Historique de l'Armée* (Sept. 1952) p.32. This figure is repeated in a recent commemorative volume issued

jointly by French and Moroccan military historical societies to honour the contribution of Moroccans to France's war between 1939–45. In their introduction to *Frères d'Armes: Mémoire marocaine d'une histoire partagée* (Le Plessis Robinson, France: Imprimerie Blanchard 1999), the five authors of the volume specify the number of Moroccan fatalities in the 1940 campaign as 2100 and the number of Moroccan prisoners as 18,000.

25. See Andrew Sherman, *The Fall of France, 1940* (London: Longman 2000) p.19.

26. On the conduct of that operation see my article on the *Goums* (note 12).

27. He was interviewed in Khenifra in Aug. 2000.

28. The history of the *goums* during the latter part of World War II has been the subject of numerous commemorative books by French and American authors who had commanded them or fought by their side. The most recent contribution to this genre is Edward L. Bimberg, *The Moroccan Goums: Tribal Warriors in a Modern War* (Westport CT: Greenwood Press, 1999). For an earlier account from a French perspective see also Jacques Augarde, *La longue route des tabors* (Paris: Éditions France Empire 1983). For an earlier fictional account see Joseph Peyré, *La Légende du goumier Saïd* (Paris: Flammarion 1950).

29. A good example of the absence of any reference to Moroccans is a commemorative piece by Jean Durkeheim, *Tirailleur Couscous* (Paris: France Empire 1965). The author served as an NCO in various RTM units.

30. Interviewed in Beni Mellal in Jan. 1998.

31. Issues related to the post-war integration of liberated Moroccan soldiers were discussed in several unpublished papers available at *C.H.E.A.M.*. Note specifically two studies submitted in 1945 by Captain De Marouil, *Le retour des goums au pays* vol.30/759, and by Major Turnier, *Le retour des goums au Maroc* vol.30/765].

32. Thus, 153 of the 508 veterans included in my database were listed as residents of Casablanca. Of them, 38 had resided in Hay Mohammadi. The availability of special housing for veterans was not limited to Casablanca. While interviewing in Midelt in Aug. 2000, I happened to converse with Mr El Houssine ou Khalk, the son of a deceased veteran who had served in the *goum* and retired in 1955. The father chose to move to Midelt in order to give his children educational opportunities he had never had. The family used to live in a neighbourhood reserved exclusively for veterans.

33. At its height, the Moroccan contingent in Indochina included three armoured (*spahi* – originally cavalry) regiments, 14 *tirailleur* battalions and nine *tabors* of *goums*. The make-up and size of this contingent changed frequently.

34. See Abdallah Saaf, *Histoire d'Anh Ma* (Paris: L'Harmattan, 1996).

35. See also Nelcya Delanoë 'Les Marocains "ralliés" au Viet-Minh. Une histoire virtuelle, 1947–72–2000' a paper presented in Nov. 2000 to a colloquium in honour of Charles-Robert Ageron, and published in the conference proceedings *La Guerre d'Algérie au miroir des décolonisations françaises* (Paris: Société Française d'histoire d'Outre-mer, 2000).

36. Information regarding these incidents and several others is available in series 10H *Indochine*, file 371, French military archive (Service Historique de l'Armée de Terre), Château de Vincennes.

37. Since this article (and my research project in general) focuses on rank-and-file soldiers, I have refrained from discussing the colonial history of the Moroccan officer corps. In 1919 the French inaugurated the Royal Military Academy in Meknes where dozens of Moroccan officers were educated. On the colonial history of that institution, the career patterns of its graduates, and their transition to the ranks of the post-colonial Royal Armed Forces, see my article, 'A Moroccan St-Cyr', *Middle Eastern Studies* 28/2 (April 1992) pp.231–57.

38. See Zaki M'Barek, 'La désertion des soldats marocains de l'armée française à l'Armée de Libération du Maghreb (A.L.M.): Rôle militaire, impact psycho-politique (1955–1956)', *Maroc-Europe* 7 (1994) pp.235–71. An interesting fictional character, representing the soldiers who switched to the side of the resistance at this time, is Faqih in Leila Abouzeid's novella, *Year of the Elephant* (originally published in Arabic in 1984; transl. Barbara Parmenter (Austin, TX: University of Texas Press 1989). A veteran of Indochina who had lost a leg at Dien Bien Phu, he is helped by the heroine to escape from Casablanca to the Spanish occupation zone in northern Morocco.

39. See note 32.
40. The extent of the French authorities' actual use of Moroccan soldiers to fight their compatriots in the Liberation Army remains unclear. Since most armed resistance took place in the countryside, it seems likely that *goum* units saw more counter-insurgency action than did their *tirailleur* counterparts. This hypothesis is supported by a series of reports (available in file 1344 of *série 3H: Maroc* at the military archives in Vincennes) issued by the Rabat military sub-division during the final weeks of 1955, concerning the erosion of morale and discipline among *goums* whose unit cohesiveness had been eroded due to desertions. Concurrent reports from the Meknes region (found in file *Maroc/DI/79* at the diplomatic archives in Nantes) discuss the spread of nationalist agitation among local *goums*.
41. Interviewed in Ouaoumanna in Feb. 1999.
42. An amendment to the law regulating veterans' benefits, passed by the French legislature more than four decades ago, set the amount paid to Moroccan veterans at about half of that received by an Algerian veteran of similar seniority and rank. A French veteran is entitled ten times the Moroccan's amount. The sum fixed at that time has been augmented only twice to account for inflation. Unlike their French counterparts, direct relatives of deceased Moroccan veterans (widows, orphans) are not entitled to any portion of this pension. The *Service des Anciens Combattants et de l'Appareillage des Handicapés* (see note 21) does provide some medical facilities and treatment free of charge. However, using those facilities requires veterans to appear in person, thus making it accessible mainly to veterans who reside in Casablanca. In addition, the Service operates two medical trucks and staff that circulate through various cities on a monthly rotation in conjunction with local *Bureaux des Anciens Combattants*. Despite all the goodwill and resources invested in this operation, anecdotal evidence suggests that it is of very limited benefit and falls short of addressing the growing needs of the population it strives to serve.
43. A typical situation at the beginning of interviews would be for veterans to mistake me for a Frenchman, and to refuse to talk to me. Once assured that I was American, however, they would change their demeanour completely and express great eagerness to recount their hardships and frustrations at their treatment by France.
44. A good example of this type of new scholarship is Driss Maghraoui's article, 'The Moroccan Colonial Soldiers: Between Selective Memory and Collective Memory', in Ali Abdullatif Ahmida (ed.), *Beyond Colonialism and Nationalism in the Maghrib* (New York: Palgrave 2000) pp.49–70. That article is part of Maghraoui's unpublished Ph.D. dissertation (University of California at Santa Cruz, 2001), entitled 'Soldiers without Citizenship: Collective Memory and the Culture of French Colonialism.'

Echoes of National Liberation:
Turkey Viewed from
the Maghrib in the 1920s

ODILE MOREAU

The distant aim towards which this article hopes to contribute is that of elucidating the emergence of ideas of the nation, and the structures of the 'nation' state, in North Africa, a process of which the beginnings, I argue, ought to be situated in the early 1920s. This decade has long been considered as encompassing the 'hollow years' *(les années creuses)* of the history of Maghribi nationalism, a lull preceding the stormy nationalist agitation of the 1930s, and there has thus been a tendency for the study of this period to be somewhat neglected. This has largely remained the case despite the evident effervescence which the 1920s saw throughout North Africa.[1] Nationalist politics took shape from the early years of the decade in Tunisia, with the founding of the Destour *(Hizb al-hurr al-Dustur al-Tunisi,* the Independent Tunisian Constitutional Party, often referred to as the 'Old' Destour), on 4 June 1920. Contestation took a very different form in Morocco, with the emergence of the armed resistance movement in the Rif led by Muhammad Ibn 'Abd al-Krim al-Khattabi in 1921, and his 'Republic of the Rif' which expressed both wholly modern desires for statehood – at least on the part of its architect – and an older established style of authority.[2] In Algeria, there was an unprecedented flowering of the Arabic language press, the coalescing of the Islamic reformist movement ('Abd al-Hamid ben Badis' first journal *al-Muntaqid* appeared in 1925), and massive labour migration to France, where the *Étoile Nord-Africaine*, first expression of revolutionary-populist nationalism, was formed in 1926.

The emergence of images and ideas of the nation in the Maghrib, however, for too long considered in isolation from the rest of the world,[3] ought also to be situated in a wider context – that of the epochal events occurring during the 1920s elsewhere in the Mediterranean, and most particularly in Turkey, where Mustafa Kemal's movement first prosecuted a successful war of independence against the Western powers, the only Muslim society to do so, and then proceeded to abolish those multisecular symbols of Islam, the Ottoman sultanate and the caliphate. The more immediate goal of this article is to investigate some of the ways in which North Africans saw, and responded to, the Turkish nationalist movement, and the radical institutional transformations undertaken by the young Turkish republic. I hope in this way to contribute to an understanding of the links – which had by no means been entirely severed in the early twentieth century – between the Maghrib and, initially, the Ottoman empire, and later Turkey, as well as to an appreciation of some of the overlooked complexities of the formation of nationalism in North Africa itself.

The War of Independence

The 1920s in Turkey witnessed the end of a world, or at least, the end of a world in itself, in the Braudelian sense of that phrase, with the collapse of the Ottoman empire. Despite its weakened presence on the international stage, the Ottoman state had continued, after the Berlin Congress of 1878 (at which the empire lost some two-fifths of its territory), to play a role in world affairs. Its engagement in the First World War alongside Austria–Hungary and Germany both testified to this and, as it turned out, brought about the end of the empire, with the central powers' defeat bringing about the end of Ottoman dominion in its remaining Arab provinces and eventually in Anatolia as well.[4] The armistice of Mudros (30 October 1918) announced the partition of the defunct empire and simultaneously opened the question of succession to its rule. The ensuing events, between the Mudros agreement and that of Mudanya almost exactly four years later (11 October 1922), aroused the interest of an international public, including that of 'French' North Africa.

The Turkish national movement led by Mustafa Kemal was most immediately a response to the allied occupation of Anatolia and the *Diktat* of Mudros, which were quickly followed by apparent steps towards the establishment of a Greater Armenia in the east and of a Greek state of Pontus in the west.[5] The call to 'save the nation' was expressed through various nationalist congresses. The Protocol of Amasya (21 June 1919), a revolutionary manifesto, asserted the integrity and independence of the endangered fatherland and the incapacity of the existing government to exercise its functions. Thereafter, local congresses met in Anatolia, at Erzurum, Balikesir, Alasehir… during the months of July and August, 1919. The Istanbul government was declared incompetent, independence was demanded and the establishment of any foreign mandate refused outright. These meetings culminated in the National Congress at Sivas in central Anatolia (4–11 September), which confirmed the resolutions taken at

Erzurum and amplified them into a call for national mobilisation, the National Pact *(Misak-i millî)*, which defined the national territory to be liberated and was adopted on 17 February 1920, by the Ottoman parliament in Istanbul. By voting the Pact, the assembly thus adopted the positions taken at Erzurum and Sivas, the Kemalist election victory in November 1919 having produced a nationalist majority in the parliament. This last assembly of the old state went on to vote itself out of existence on 18 March, 1920, and the very next day, Mustafa Kemal addressed a circular to the civil and military authorities in which he announced the forthcoming meeting, in Ankara, of a new assembly which would assume extraordinary powers. The new National Assembly met for the first time on 23 April. This insurgent parliament immediately set about the procurement of hard currency from Soviet Russia, an alliance which caused alarm among the Entente powers and served to heighten their concern about the nationalist movement, whose early victories over the Greek army, and over French detachments in Cilicia, accentuated the perception of its posing a serious threat.

With open conflict now engaged between a rump Ottoman government under allied control and the insurgent nationalists based in Ankara, the Treaty of Sèvres, an agreement for the empire's dismemberment, was nonetheless signed on 10 August 1920, but the nationalist victories won by the movement now under Mustafa Kemal's overall leadership, climaxing with the armistice of Mudanya between victorious Turkish nationalist, and defeated Greek and British, forces, opened the way for the new negotiations with the allies which resulted in the Treaty of Lausanne (24 July 1923). Its terms were virtually concordant with the demands expressed in the National Pact. The Turkish victory produced a shock wave in the west and in the Arab and Muslim worlds, at a time when almost half of the world's Muslims lived under British rule.[6]

Certainly, the links which had subsisted between the Ottoman world and the Maghrib had become ever more tenuous. To French control in Algeria and Tunisia was added, with the Treaty of Ouchy of 15 October 1912, the annexation of Tripolitania and Cyrenaica by Italy (Italian domination of Libya was thus recognised by the Ottoman government, although the caliph retained a nominal, spiritual authority over these territories' Muslim populations), while Morocco had of course never been under Ottoman authority. But nothing that occurred in the eastern Mediterranean left the Maghrib indifferent, and the reverse was also true. Certain symbolic, spiritual ties persisted to connect North Africans (at least Algerians and, perhaps more particularly, Tunisians) to the Ottoman seat of the caliphate. And the example of victorious Turkish nationalism could hardly be ignored by North African societies under French domination. Indeed, the seismic events centred in Anatolia radiated throughout the Mediterranean basin.

Maghribi views of Turkey's nationalist movement, and of its emblematic hero, Mustafa Kemal in particular, shifted significantly over time. With the victories of the war of independence, between 1920 and 1923, he was considered, throughout the Arab world, as a hero of Islam, an archetypal warrior chief *(ghazi)*, and indeed as a candidate for the caliphate. After the abolition of the caliphate, he was attacked and vilified.[7] The discourse of the independence movement assumed, in its early stages, a specifically Islamic character.[8] It was addressed to 'Muslim compatriots', and aimed to wrest 'Islamic lands' and 'Islamic peoples' from foreign domination. Mustafa Kemal's supporters, in Turkey and elsewhere,[9] envisaged the reconstitution and liberation of the caliphate, rather than its suppression. In his speech at Ankara in January 1920, the Turkish nationalist leader laid out the projected reforms necessary 'so that Turkey may take her place among the civilised nations, extending her hand to all her Muslim brothers so as to ensure the success of the Islamic world, of whose revival there can be no doubt.'[10]

The *fetva* (religious ruling of opinion) issued on 11 April 1920 by the *şeykh ul-islam* (Istanbul's senior religious official), pronouncing the double – civic and spiritual – 'excommunication' of the nationalist 'rebels', contested this religious dimension of the struggle. From then on a state of civil war existed between the nationalists and the so-called 'army of the caliphate'. In response, the *mufti*s (officials competent to issue rulings on questions of law) of Anatolia riposted with counter *fetva*s which declared the nationalist insurgency to be a legitimate *jihad.*

Such contests over the Islamic legitimacy of rule and struggle could hardly be without echoes among other Muslim populations, (to whom they were also, in any event, addressed) living under foreign occupation beyond Anatolia. In the Maghrib, they found a particularly ready audience. A certain sympathy for the centre of the former empire could exist here, untroubled by the particular forms of Arab nationalist expression which had emerged in the Mashriq (particularly in Syria) in opposition to Turkish rule during the last years of the Ottoman state. The example of Turkey at war in defence of Islam and liberty was received as an encouragement in local struggles against other occupiers. In 1920, demonstrations in Tunis in favour of the territorial integrity and independence of Turkey aroused concern among the French authorities. Placards were posted on the walls of the Great Mosque, calling for protests against the occupation of the Ottoman capital, seat of the caliphate, and summoning the population of Tunis to demonstrate outside the palace of the Bey at one o'clock in the afternoon.[11] A delegation issuing from this meeting was received at the French Residency. When Kemalist victories were reported, Turkish flags were flown from houses, prayers were said in mosques and processions, bearing flower-bedecked portraits of Mustafa Kemal, marched through the streets. It was reported that it was a very long time since such displays of joy had been seen in Tunis.[12]

In Algeria, news of Turkey circulated in cafés and popular opinion rejoiced at Turkish victories. After the nationalist victory over Greek troops at the Sakarya river (September 1921), Messali Hadj, later the leader of populist Algerian nationalism, was arrested for shouting *vivats* to Mustafa Kemal Pasha.[13] Similarly, in Morocco, the success of Turkish arms aroused popular enthusiasm throughout the country, including in the Spanish zone. The French consul at Tangier reported his 'impression of a great satisfaction' felt by the Moroccans at news of the nationalists' progress.[14] More evidently visible solidarity was sought from the Maghribi population through the collection of funds – but the support thus garnered for the Turkish cause was, again, of local, symbolic significance rather than a participatory effort in aid of the war itself. The *shaykh* of the Derqawiyya order in Morocco organised a collection intended to finance a celebration, to be held among the members of the order, of 'the defeat of the infidels'. It turned out to be a huge picnic in a garden near Tangier, attracting some 500 participants.[15] Similar fundraising events were held in Algeria.

The reaction of Maghribi opinion to events in Turkey was not monolithic, however, nor was it necessarily felt that it must be prejudicial to France. The Muslims of Morocco apparently considered Mustafa Kemal's victories as 'the revenge of free Turkey against its Greek and British oppressors'; and they were said to express open satisfaction with the 'moral support' offered by France to the government in Ankara.[16] In the blossoming inter-war competition of empires, the French attempted to draw advantages from events in Anatolia. The Moroccan press reported on an exchange of telegrams between the Sultan of Morocco and Poincaré, the French President. It was reported that French policy regarding the war in Anatolia had produced a favourable impression on the population, who 'saw the reassertion of those ties that bind France and Islam'.[17] At the end of the war, France had indeed been numbered among the powers expecting to share in the dismemberment of the empire, and anticipated territorial gains which would increase French influence in the region. However, by the time of the new armistice, signed in October 1922, relations with the emerging Turkey had greatly changed. A first Franco-Turkish armistice was agreed in Cilicia as early as 30 May 1920. A French envoy, Franklin-Bouillon, was sent for a secret meeting with Mustafa Kemal himself in the summer of 1921. By directly negotiating with the delegates at Ankara, the French government offered the nationalist insurgents an implicit recognition. Franklin-Bouillon left Anatolia on 1 August without having reached agreement with the Ankara government, but new negotiations took place between 24 September and 20 October, culminating in a Franco–Turkish accord signed in Ankara on 20 October. France was thus presented in the metropolitan press as the prime mover for peace in the Middle East, a new stance which did not leave indifferent the temporal and spiritual authorities of the colonised Maghrib. The discourse of 'French Islamic policy' invoked at this time was no doubt intended to recall the privileged relations which had previously bound France to the Sublime State since the sixteenth century, through the diplomatic efforts maintained under François I, Louis XIV, Napoléon III … In the aftermath of the Ankara Accord, France was presented as having established herself, or rather, as having *re*-established herself, as a reliable friend of Turkey. The French press sought to present the agreement with Ankara as a reconciliation of the French Republic with the whole Muslim world, *via* the normalisation of her relations with the people of Turkey.

Of course, all of this was intended to bolster French prestige, and French domination in North Africa, not to encourage Maghribi links with the east. More substantial efforts at harnessing Maghribi solidarity undertaken by the Red Crescent in aid of 'the Muslim populations of Asia Minor, victims of the war' were actively discouraged by the French colonial authorities. It was thought, in fact, that there could be nothing but difficulties arising from the opportunity which might be given to the populations of North Africa of establishing new links with the formerly Ottoman Mashriq. The prospect of such new relations between Turkey and the Muslims of the Maghrib was regarded by North Africa's rulers with alarm.[18] In fact, however, if the new government in Ankara did dispatch a secret mission to Tunisia in the spring of 1923, led by one Ahmed el Karaï, its subversive potential was probably quite limited.[19] The mission apparently intended to link up with the Destour, but the policy of the new Turkey was in no way given to involvement in external anti-colonial struggles – except in speech making. Indeed, Turkish representatives, approached by young Tunisian nationalists, would declare themselves strictly disinterested in the affairs of France's Muslim colonies.[20] The 1923 mission was more likely concerned with gathering support and Islamic legitimacy for its own cause at home.

The Sultanate and Caliphate

The institutional transformation of the young Turkish state developed through three key moments: first came the abolition of the sultanate (the Ottoman dynasty's institution of temporal power) by the Grand National Assembly, in November 1922, shortly after the armistice of Mudanya. In consequence of this destitution of the monarchy, the Turkish Republic was proclaimed on 29 October 1923, with Mustafa Kemal as President and Ankara as the new state's capital. Finally, on 3 March 1924, the Assembly voted to completely remove any remaining Ottoman authority by legislating the spiritual institution of the caliphate out of existence.

The initial impression produced in the religio-intellectual circles of the Maghrib by the deposition of the Sultan was unfavourable. The lettered élites of Fez were disturbed by so unexpected an event, considered a kind of 'religious revolution'. Reported sentiments were of disconcerting surprise, a certain 'malaise', and disquiet.[21] The opinion of younger, modernist groups of intellectuals like Allal al-Fasi, on the contrary, was all in favour of Mustafa Kemal, whose separation of spiritual from temporal authority was viewed with approval as an essential element of progress in civilisation.[22]

In direct contrast to this response, the announcement of the reduction of the caliphate to a purely spiritual power caused profound dismay and stupefaction within the *makhzen*. The evident example thus set in Turkey was, the Moroccan court clearly feared, liable to spread – including among the subjects of the alawite Commander of the Faithful.[23]

At the other end of the Maghrib, the Bey of Tunis, struck by the irregular election of the new caliph, and remarking that the title of 'Highness' now borne by Abdülmecid II was analogous to his own, apparently entertained the idea of having himself proclaimed caliph of Tunisia's Muslims. With prayers in some mosques of Tunis being said in the name of the new caliph while others continued to be pronounced in the name of the deposed sultan Vahideddin, the Bey considered summoning the *shaykh al-islam* to resolve the question.[24] The French authorities discouraged the notion. Worried about possible repercussions on relations with the Ankara government, they further observed that such a new investiture of the Bey could only contribute to his own authority *vis-à-vis* the protecting power, while simultaneously signalling, to Muslim audiences and the other European powers, an intrusion into the religious domain on the part of the French government which could only damage French Islamic policy. The *shaykh al-islam* was apprised of the government's position, and an audience with the Bey was sought by the Resident General to dissuade his ambition.

The suppression of the caliphate itself, when it came, provoked an outburst of emotion in Tunisia. A meeting in the courts of the Great Mosque in Tunis assembled a number of students and leading personalities of the city in what was seen as a demonstration of the solidarity of Muslims with their nominal head and their attachment to the caliphal dynasty.[25] In the wave of competing claims to the title which followed the divestiture of the last Ottoman caliph, Algerians and Tunisians were generally supportive of Abdülmecid's case for reinstatement.[26] Moroccans, who of course considered their own sultan as the only *amîr al-mu'minîn* (Commander of the Faithful) who mattered, were nonetheless hostile to the pretensions of the ageing King of the Hijaz, the Hashemite *sharif* Husayn ibn 'Ali, to supplant the sultan of Constantinople. Maghribi religious authorities were not, however, free to engage fully in these turbulent discussions beyond the borders of the Maghrib itself: when the Islamic congresses of Ankara and Jeddah (1921) were announced, Resident General Lyautey did not consider it appropriate for a Moroccan delegation to attend, and although the authorities in Algiers and Tunis anticipated the dispatch of representative *'ulama* from the communities under their control, and no instructions were given them from Paris on the position they should endeavour to impose relative to the question of the caliphate, it was eventually decided that the presence of Algerian *'ulama* at the congresses would be 'inopportune'.[27] Despite this, however, it appears that certain North African delegates did attend these gatherings, having made their way to the Mashriq by clandestine means.

What, in fact, did the French hope would be the repercussions in North Africa of the Kemalist policies unfolding in Ankara? In sum, it was anticipated that many Muslims, particularly in Tunis, who had nothing but sympathy for Constantinople and who had retained a symbolic tie of solidarity with the seat of Islamic power in the east, would be disaffected by the apparently anti-religious swing of this 'country where, in their minds, they situate the heart of their faith'. The hoped for antipathy against revolutionary Turkey was expected to result in a net gain for French imperial policy in Africa.[28]

What role did North Africa play in the mobilisation of the Islamic world around the issue of the caliphate? A Committee for the Caliphate was created in Tunis by a group of young, modernist bourgeois associated with the Destour. Its president was Tawfiq al-Madani, an enthusiast for Mustafa Kemal known to the protectorate authorities as a turcophile, and who had welcomed the nationalists' separation of political from caliphal authority. The protectorate's police mused that:

> according to him [i.e. Madani], the Destour cannot show itself hostile to the government of Mustafa Kemal which has abolished the sultanate and caliphate; but, given the reaction of the Tunisian population to the Kemalists' violations of what they consider an inviolable religious dogma, the Committee of the Destour has allowed the creation alongside it of a group for the re-establishment of the caliphate, which it intends thereafter to merge into itself. This Committee for the Caliphate is in contact with similar bodies in Egypt, and has become at the same time a centre for pan-Islamic activity.[29]

In fact, it appears that the Tunisians also attempted to employ French diplomatic pressure to negotiate a new role for the re-established caliph, while at the same time orchestrating their usual, anti-French campaigns. Madani intervened with the French authorities to request a modification of the Treaty of Lausanne, which would stipulate that the caliph should renounce his rights to any political, legislative or administrative action over the countries which had been separated from Turkey at the partition of the empire. The committee simultaneously engaged in a kind of non-governmental diplomacy of its own, although its action was minimised by the protectorate government. Madani himself corresponded in person with Abdülmecid, and the Committee dispatched a telegram to the Turkish chargé d'affaires in Paris, in protest at the caliph's deposition.[30] Only months before this, the Destour – and notably Madani – had been responsible for the telegrams of congratulation dispatched by Tunisians to the Kemalist government on the occasion of the signature of the Lausanne treaty in July 1923.[31]

While undeniably supporting Mustafa Kemal and the symbolism of liberation he represented, the Destour diverged from Turkey's radical policy on the question of the caliphate and pursued its own agenda on the matter. Events in Turkey, indeed, were not simply of great significance in themselves, but acquired entirely new importance as they were worked into independent agendas and instrumentalised in other contexts, in the Maghrib as elsewhere, by colonial powers, emerging nationalist movements and public opinion in the colonised Muslim world at large.

But before long it would no longer be possible to draw on Turkey for such inspiration. In September 1923, Jilali Ben Ramdan, a member of the Tunisian Bey's Grand Council, visited the caliph, and was joined by 'Abd al-Aziz al-Tha'alibi, founder and leader of the Destour, who had gone to Turkey to represent 'the Tunisian people' at the Islamic Congress which was to take place after the entry of Mustafa Kemal's troops into Istanbul in October. The abolition of the caliphate would force a change of strategies, as it finally eliminated the possibility of finding in Turkey a platform from which, and an audience by whom, such 'representatives of the Tunisian people' could make themselves heard. It appears, in fact, that this moment (October 1923) marks the last occasion on which such representations could take place in the old heart of the empire. The caliphate was the last embodiment of a link to Islamic sovereignty which North Africans could still hold on to, beyond the political frame imposed by France and her empire, and it was perhaps in this that the old Ottoman monarchy had retained its importance. It was this tie, however tenuously symbolic, to a spiritual sovereignty that the young, modernist nationalists in Tunisia, for example, sought to maintain in their notion of a re-established caliphate divested of temporal authority. The Kemalist government, through the radical reforms adopted in the domestic sphere and its position of neutrality in foreign policy, resolutely turned its back on these other, external, demands from its 'Muslim brothers' and set itself to the construction of a new nation state oriented towards Europe.

The religious dimension of Turkey's own war of independence, and its previous openness towards the Islamic world, were thoroughly erased. The disappointments of the Libyan *shaykh* al-Sanusi, who had been mobilised at the side of Mustafa Kemal, may be taken to summarise this change of tack on the part of the young Republic. The *shaykh*, a leading figure in the Italo–Turkish war of 1911–12 and then during the First World War, had been employed, along with his spiritual authority, to bring together the Arab and Kurdish tribes of the east and south-east of Anatolia. The mirage of his eventual accession to the caliphate, in the event of his successfully carrying out this charge, had even been conjured up before him. He would be greatly disillusioned to discover that, in fact, he was to have no place at all in the new Turkey, and left the country to end his days in exile in the Hijaz.[32]

Conclusions

Views of Mustafa Kemal, in North Africa as elsewhere, were strongly affective. The figure of the nationalist-insurgent General, the President of the Turkish Republic, is above all understood – in contrast to the images dominant in Turkey itself – in terms neither of specifically *national* liberation nor of republican politics but in the register of Islam. Recognised as *ghazi* during the war of independence, he would be condemned for the abolition of the caliphate, although after his death in 1938 there re-emerged something of a posthumous celebration of him, again as 'Hero of Islam'.

The controversial nature of his policy perhaps only added to his personal aura, and among Maghribi populations he commanded great popularity as an iconic figure, a conquering hero in times of crisis. This can be seen clearly in the popular imagery of which he was the subject in the Arab world. Images – on tea-caddies, for example – were produced particularly in Egypt; when these were banned as subversive in the Maghrib,[33] locally produced illustrations took their place. Postcards bearing Mustafa Kemal's portrait and celebrating the successes of the nationalist armies were introduced to Algeria from Tunisia, and circulated in cafés and through newsagents.

The French authorities, as ever extremely suspicious, attempted to limit and neutralise as much as possible any contact between the populations of the colonial Maghrib and the eastern Mediterranean – forbidding fund raising for aid efforts, hindering travel and preventing participation in the assemblies held to discuss the issue of the caliphate. North Africans were clearly not indifferent to the drama being played out in Turkey, and the relative isolation of 'French North Africa' from the Mashriq was by no means total. In the

Maghrib, Turkey was a country at once distant and familiar. Events there during the 1920s were at the centre of the preoccupations of Maghribi elites, who engaged, in religious, intellectual and political terms, in debates and action provoked by the stimuli of news from the east. Intellectuals in exile, like Tha'alibi, attempted to represent the Maghrib in debates taking place in the Mashriq relative to the destinies of the Islamic world.

It may be, however, that the opportunities opened up by the nationalist victory for this kind of effort were eventually suppressed by the subsequent destitution of the caliphate, and the turning of Kemalist Turkey away from the Arab world and its 'Muslim brothers', towards its own programme of radical reform, designed to produce a new Turkish nation state decisively cut off from its Ottoman past. At the same time, events in Turkey had local, symbolic significance in North Africa quite independent of actual, personal connections between the two extremities of the Mediterranean. The institution of caliphate was North Africans' last point of identification with a sovereignty outside, and independent of, the French empire. Its importance, particularly for modernist elites who wholeheartedly approved the abolition of the sultanate, was perhaps derived from this aspect. The re-establishment of the caliphate as a purely spiritual centre of authority in liberated, modern Turkey might have been a way to safeguard this connection, however tenuous, that held the Maghrib to an Islamic figurehead beyond the boundaries and control of French influence. And if imperial France had hoped to benefit both from her own involvement in Anatolia, and from the Maghribi reaction to Kemalist policies, Maghribis themselves (at least in Tunisia) were not averse to attempting to enlist French diplomatic support in the service of their own aims, while continuing to see in Anatolia an example of successful liberation, a motivating factor in the development of their own nationalist movements. This model was, if not exactly an example to follow, at least one from which inspiration might be drawn, and one which, in its tumultuousness, provoked new, effervescent activity.

NOTES

1. Cf. 'Entre histoire culturelle et histoire politique: la Tunisie des années vingt', *Watha'iq* 24–25, 1998–99, published by the Institut Supérieur d'Histoire du Mouvement National, University of Tunis.
2. See C.R. Pennel, *Morocco since 1830. A History* (London: Hurst 2000) pp.192–3 and the same author's *A Country with a Government and a Flag: The Rif War in Morocco, 1921–1926* (Wisbech, Cambridgeshire: MENAS Press 1986).
3. See, in this regard, Julia Clancy-Smith, 'Introduction' in Clancy-Smith (ed.), *North Africa, Islam and the Mediterranean World* (London: Frank Cass 2001), originally published as a special issue of the *Journal of North African Studies* 6/1 (Spring 2001). The isolation of Maghribi history from that of the rest of the Mediterranean, a tendency dominant until very recently, is itself a complex fact of historical scholarship which deserves some attention

(Editor's note).

4. The formerly Ottoman regencies of Algiers and Tunis were lost, of course, in 1830 and 1881; Egypt had been effectively autonomous since 1811 and was occupied by Britain in 1882, and the Libyan provinces were lost to Italian colonialism beginning in 1911. The remaining Syrian and Iraqi provinces were occupied by British troops at the end of the war, with the Arabian peninsula having risen in the Arab revolt from 1916.

5. Greek troops were landed at Izmir on 15 May 1919.

6. See O. Kologlu, *Türk çadaslasmasi, 1919–1938, Islama etki, islamdan tepki* [*Turkish Modernisation: Influence on Islam, Reaction of Islam*] (Istanbul: Boyut kitaplari 1995) p.13.

7. Cf. O. Kologlu, *Gazi'nin çaginda Islam dünyasi* [*The Islamic World at the Time of the Gazi*], (Istanbul: Boyut kitaplari 1994) p.9.

8. Cf. O. Moreau, 'La dimension religieuse de la guerre d'indépendance' in M. Bazin, S. Kançal, R. Perez, J. Thobie (eds.), *La Turquie entre trois mondes* (Paris: L'Harmattan 1998) pp. 381–95.

9. Notably in India, where a congress on the caliphate met on 17 Feb. 1920 and published a manifesto favourable to Turkey. The Muslim population of India in general was an important source of support for the Kemalist movement.

10. Service Historique de la Marine (French Naval Archive), Château de Vincennes, Paris (hereafter SHM), 1 BB7, 25, No.1580, rapport établi par les autorités militaires françaises, 13 Jan. 1921.

11. *Le Temps* 22 Mar. 1920.

12. *Belag* 11 Oct. 1920, quoted in O. Kologlu, *Gazi'nin çaginda, Islam dünyasi* (note 7) p.232.

13. B. Stora, in I. Gökalp and F. Georgeon (eds.), *Kemalizm ve Islam Dünyasi* [*Kemalism and the Islamic World*], (Istanbul: Arba 1990) pp.177–8.

14. Agence et Consulat Général de France à Tanger, Afrique, No.429: L'Agent diplomatique de France, Tanger, to Ministre des Affaires étrangères, 16 Sept. 1922. Microfilm archives, Institut Supérieur de l'Histoire du Mouvement National, Tunis; microfilmed documents of the Archives du Ministère des Affaires étrangères (French Foreign Ministry Archives, Quai d'Orsay, Paris), (hereafter A.E.), bob.528, C.2, folio 231.

15. Ibid.; and Agence et Consulat de France à Tanger, Afrique, No.447: Le Chargé d'Affaires de France à Tanger to Ministre des Affaires étrangères, 12 Oct. 1922. A.E., Quai d'Orsay, bob.528, C.2, folio 275.

16. Résidence générale de la République Française au Maroc, Rabat: Direction des Affaires Politiques et Commerciales, Afrique, No.1683: Le Maréchal de France, Lyautey, to Ministre de Affaires étrangères, 15 Nov. 1922. A.E. , Quai d'Orsay, bob.528, C.2, folio 34.

17. *Le Matin, Le Temps,* 3 Oct. 1922 ; cf. also Délégué de la Résidence Générale, Rabat to Maréchal Lyautey, Paris (coded), No.4.349S.G.P.; personal communication to Maréchal Lyautey from His Majesty the Sultan. A.E., Quai d'Orsay, bob.528, C.2.

18. Ministère des Colonies, Service des Affaires Musulmanes: le Ministre des Colonies to Ministre des Affaires étrangères, Paris, 8 Nov. 1922. A.E., Quai d'Orsay, bob.528, C.3, folio 2.

19. Ministère des Affaires étrangères, Direction des Affaires politiques et commerciales: Commandement de Constantinople du gouvernement de la Grande Assemblée Nationale Turque, bureau privé No.718, to Direction de la police de Constantinople. S.d., Quai d'Orsay, bob.533, C.19, folio 166.

20. Ambassade de France en Suisse, Berne, to Ministère des Affaires étrangères, No.520, 22 Dec. 1921. A.E., Quai d'Orsay, bob.623, C.319, folio 1 (Editor's note).

21. Army of Occupation in Western Morocco, region of Fez : Service des Renseignements, No.315/R.C., confidential: General Maurial, commandant la région de Fez to Monsieur le Commissaire, Résident Général de la République Française au Maroc (Direction du Service des Renseignements): Fès, 18 Nov. 1922. A.E., Quai d'Orsay, bob.528, C.3, folio 55; 'Note sur la répercussion des événements d'Orient dans l'opinion publique Fassi' by Paul Marty, Fez, 18 Nov. 1922, attached to Ibid. A.E., Quai d'Orsay, bob.528, C.3, folio 57; Résidence Générale de la République Française au Maroc: Direction des Affaires politiques et commerciales, Afrique, No.1683: Le Maréchal de France Lyautey to Ministre des Affaires

étrangères, Rabat, 15 Nov. 1922. A.E., Quai d'Orsay, bob.528, C.2, folio 36.

22. Id., folio 59. cf. Résidence Générale de la République de France au Maroc, Afrique, No.1016: Le Ministre Plénipotentiaire, Délégué à la Résidence Générale de la République Française au Maroc to Ministre des Affaires étrangères, Rabat, 28 Oct. 1924. A.E., Quai d'Orsay, bob.529, C.5, folios 195–97.

23. Protectorat de la République Française au Maroc, Gouvernement Chérifien, Direction des Affaires chérifiennes: note by Monsieur Marc, Conseiller chérifien, to Monsieur le Maréchal de France, Résident Général, Rabat, 10 Nov. 1922. A.E., Quai d'Orsay, bob.528, C.3, folio 13.

24. Résidence Générale de France à Tunis, Direction des Affaires politiques et commerciales, No.435, Afrique: Le Résident Général to Ministre des Affaires étrangères. A.E., Quai d'Orsay, bob.528, C.3, p. 74, Affaires étrangères, (decoded telegram), Tunis, 25 Nov. 1922, also bob.529, C.4, folio 173.

25. Ministère des Affaires étrangères, Direction des Affaires politiques et commerciales, Asie: Ministre des Affaires étrangères to Monsieur le Haut-Commissaire à Constantinople, à Beyrouth: Paris, 20 July 1921. A.E., Quai d'Orsay, bob.528, C.2, folio 75.

26. Ibid.

27. Ibid., and Ministère de l'Intérieur, Service des Affaires algériennes, 1er bureau: Ministre de l'intérieur to Ministre des Affaires étrangères, Paris, 29 July 1921. A.E., Quai d'Orsay, bob.528., C.2, folio 84.

28. Ministère des Affaires étrangères, Quai d'Orsay, note for the Directeur Politique sur la politique en Orient, 8 Nov. 1922. A.E., Quai d'Orsay, bob.528, C.3, folios 5–8.

29. Résidence Générale de France à Tunis, Direction des Affaires politiques et commerciales, Afrique, no. 303: Le Résident de la République Française à Tunis to Ministre des Affaires étrangères: Tunis, 17 Feb. 1923. A.E., Quai d'Orsay, bob.528, C.3, folio 206.

30. Résidence Générale de France à Tunis, Direction des Affaires politiques et commerciales, no.435, Afrique: Le Résident Général to Ministre des Affaires étrangères, (undated). A.E., Quai d'Orsay, bob.529, C.4, folio 173.

31. Telegram *'au nom du peuple tunisien'* from the Destour to Chargé d'affaires, Turkish Legation in Paris. A.E., Quai d'Orsay, bob.529, C.4, folio 47.

32. Cf. O. Moreau, 'La Dimension religieuse de la guerre d'indépendance' (note 8).

33. Ministère des Affaires étrangères, Sous-Direction d'Afrique: Note to Sous-directeur des relations commerciales, Paris, 20 Aug. 1924. A.E., Quai d'Orsay, bob.529, C.5, folio 111.

Libya's Refugees, their Places of Exile, and the Shaping of their National Idea

ANNA BALDINETTI

This article is intended as a preliminary discussion of research in progress which focuses on the history of Libyan exiles during the colonial period. Rather than a presentation of finished arguments it is an exploration of certain key issues and problems concerning the history of incipient Libyan nationalism and the spaces of exile in which it developed.[1]

A considerable literature on colonial Libya has been published in Italian in recent years. However, most of these studies are devoted to the international, military and diplomatic aspects of the Italian colonial experience, and they have been undertaken mainly by scholars of contemporary Italian history.[2] Libyan historians, on the other hand, have been essentially engaged in the writing of works addressed to large audiences from an anti-colonial perspective, in the translation of Italian studies and in the collection of sources and chronology. The Libyan Studies Centre in Tripoli[3] has done remarkable work in collecting oral sources for the history of anti-colonial resistance. The history of the *jihad* is embodied in a few studies which consider armed opposition, but there does not yet exist any global evaluation of the movement as a whole.[4] There is also a lack of studies addressing the impact of Italian colonialism and its consequences in terms of the social transformation of pre-colonial Libyan society, the one exception being Ali Abdullatif Ahmida's *The Making of Modern Libya*, recently published in America.[5]

The research presented here focuses on the impact of the experience of Italian colonialism on indigenous Libyan society, and on reactions to the colonisation of Libya in neighbouring Arab countries, especially Egypt. My central hypothesis is that Libyan refugees' activities abroad, from 1911 to 1951, can be regarded as the first nucleus of Libyan nationalism. It was through experiences undergone during the period of exile that new structures of loyalty and solidarity emerged, ones which replaced the traditional roles played by ethnic membership, tribal loyalties, kinship, brotherhood bonds, and affiliation to the pre-colonial Ottoman *wilaya*. Thus it was largely the refugees who gave birth to the associations that led ultimately to the formation of political parties.

As Lisa Anderson notes, until the 1920s, the dominant idioms of political identity in Libya were those of Islam and the Ottoman empire; the idea of nationalism, of a nation based on Arabism, did not yet exist.[6] While some scholars date the origins of Libyan nationalism back to 1911, with the Italo–Turkish war and the beginning of resistance to occupation, or even earlier,[7] this seems to me to be unfounded. At this early date, the idea of *watan*, understood to signify the union of the three pre-colonial Ottoman provinces in one 'Libyan nation', was not current. Overall, the history of the origins of Libyan nationalism has not generally received much attention from scholars. The history of Libyan refugees in the colonial period, and their relation to the development of nationalism, has been particularly neglected; no major contribution has yet been made in this area, besides a few studies in Arabic on the communities of exiles in Tunisia and Syria.[8]

The methodological framework informing my approach follows what Israel Gershoni describes as the 'new narrative' of Arab nationalism: 'the protagonists of the new narrative are not bodies of ideas or their proponents, a handful of representative writers or intellectuals; they are, rather, national movements subsuming elite and non-elite groups, official and unofficial parties and organisations, as well as economic forces, systems, and institutions.'[9] I consider this approach appropriate to the Libyan case owing to the peculiarities of the creation of the Libyan nation state, an 'artificial' result of the colonial experience. Nationalism here, as in many other parts of the world, can be understood mainly as the result of 'invented tradition' articulated by emergent social groups and cultural–political activities that crossed pre-colonial, and colonial, borders. As yet, only a very small literature has discussed issues related to these aspects of Libyan nationalism, and no study provides a general interpretation of it.[10]

The Places of Libyans' Exile

The exile of Libyans between 1911 and independence in 1951 involved many countries: Tunisia, Algeria, Syria, Chad, Turkey, Palestine, Niger. Whilst it is difficult to give precise figures, the number of people performing *hijra* out of colonial Libya is probably to be measured in the hundreds of thousands.[11]

Establishing the exact number of exiles, however, is extremely difficult, for a number of reasons. First, no census data exist for the nomadic tribes. Secondly, refugees frequently emigrated from one country to another following subsequent expulsions, in order to reunite members of their family or tribe, or to seek work. For example, during the 1930s, the French authorities in Egypt tried to recruit Libyans living there to work in Tunisian phosphate mines. Also, currently available data is not uniformly reliable.[12]

The Italian diplomatic documentation gives figures only for returning refugees, and it may be suspected that the authorities had some interest in overestimating the numbers of returnees in order to demonstrate the success of Italian policy. On the Libyan side, the number of refugees given by the Libyan Studies Centre is based mainly on the collection of oral sources and may itself be exaggerated.

Tunisia

The successive waves of refugees' departures can be correlated with the different periods of colonial rule. The first departure occurred with the initial stages of the Italian occupation of Tripolitania, and the first country of destination was Tunisia. French diplomatic documents report that about 35,000 Libyans emigrated to Tunisia during the first year of occupation.

This first wave of migration to Tunisia concerned mainly tribes from the Agilat, Zuara (such as the Mahamid tribes), Josh (such as the Siaan tribes) and Nalut *cazas*;[13] it was principally a movement of nomadic populations, of the poorest social groups. Frequently it was the elderly, women and children who emigrated, leaving their menfolk to organise resistance in Tripolitania. This was the case, for example, of the Tripolitanian refugees who settled in the area of Gabès on the Tunisian south-east coast. Again, however, there are difficulties in positively establishing the identities of those Tripolitanian tribes which emigrated to Tunisia as a direct result of Italian occupation, as many of those present in the territory of the French protectorate (and in its records) after 1911 had already emigrated before the invasion. In fact, after the defeat (in 1858) of the local resistance, led by Ghuma[14] to the second Ottoman occupation of Tripolitania, many Tripolitanian tribes moved to Tunisia. The French authorities, in order to identify those Tripolitanians who had settled in Tunisia before the Italian invasion, asked them to prove their payments of the *majba*, a capitation tax (or poll tax), introduced by Mohammed Bey in 1856, for which all adult male Tunisians were liable. Conversely, some of those migrants who had settled in Tunisia before 1911 registered themselves on the protectorate's lists as Italian citizens – in order not to have to pay the *majba*.

Moreover, it would appear that some Tunisians, following certain encouragements from the Young Tunisians, claimed to be Tripolitanians in order to benefit from Italian protection.[15] This was not, of course, a reflection of any support on the part of the Young Tunisians for Italian colonial policy; demonstrations against the Italian invasion of Tripolitania and initiatives of solidarity with Tripolitanians were organised by the Young Tunisians.[16] Their propaganda in favour of Italian citizenship was a function of their activity against the French authorities (in particular, a counterweight to French 'naturalisation' measures aimed at encouraging Tunisians to take French citizenship).

The Italian authorities were concerned at the movement of population into exile and hence, already during the first months of 1913, they sent a mission to Tunis with an assignment to persuade the refugees to return to Libya. Among those targeted figured some notables and chiefs like Sulayman al-Baruni and Musa Bey Grada who, in the Ottoman administration, had held the offices of *mutasarrif* of Jebel Gharbi and *ra's al-baladiyya* of Jefren, and *shaykh* Sof, the great grandson of Ghuma, the hero of the Tripolitanian resistance to the second Ottoman occupation.

With the promise of influential offices in the colonial administration for Libyan notables, and particularly for al-Baruni, to whom, it seems, a promise of Berber autonomy was made,[17] the Italian authorities aimed to guarantee the return of the refugees. Many tribes returned voluntarily to Tripolitania but others came back in response to the threat of expulsion for life from their native country. Both facts suggest that, already in the first years after 1911, Libyans did not believe that the Italian occupation would be of short duration. The 'rallying' of notables and chiefs to the colonial regime was due to Italian assurances that they could keep their wealth and retain the privileges of their social status; some also tried to garner new advantages from their return to their homeland; for example, one *shaykh* 'Abd al-Latif asked to be appointed *mudir* of Sorman, in place of a rival *shaykh*, in recognition of his voluntary return.[18]

As for ordinary people, the major factor influencing their return from Tunisia was neither the promises nor the threats, but the conditions which the French authorities imposed on their presence in the Regency. The refugees had three choices: they could sell all their goods and leave for Constantinople, stay in Tunisia as French subjects, liable to taxation and conscription, or go back to their country. Some did not return, but opted instead for further migration; *shaykh* Sof with some hundreds of people emigrated to Syria. It should also be noted that despite the hard conditions they imposed on Tripolitanian migrants, the French authorities did not necessarily desire their return to Libya; many were employed as workers in the Tunisian mining industry.

Egypt

It is similarly difficult to establish the number of refugees in Egypt. Many enrolled themselves in the lists of 'Libyan subjects' kept by the Italian Consulate, but in most cases such recognition concerned only the heads of families. Besides, there were also Cyrenaican–Tripolitanian tribes in Egypt who had moved there before the Italian invasion. Many of those who migrated to Egypt settled in the town of al-Fayyum and in the surrounding area. This first generation of refugees lived generally in good conditions and more or less all of them were engaged as agricultural labourers. Al-Fayyum was chosen as many people originally from Cyrenaica already lived in that area, having bought land there during the reign of Khedive Ismail (1863–79).[19] The area was also highly strategic: it was the starting point of the caravans that supplied goods and arms to the Libyan rebels.

The refugees became integrated in their places of exile at different levels. In Egypt, for example, the Libyans who settled in Cairo and Alexandria worked in business, while those in the region of al-Fayyum worked in agriculture. In the 1940s, all the refugees from al-Fayyum returned from exile, whereas those living in Cairo and Alexandria did not thereafter leave Egypt.[20]

Syria

If, for obvious reasons, the flow of refugees principally concerned immediately neighbouring countries, different reasons directed Libyans towards Syria. The refugees who moved to Syria between 1911 and 1916 were mainly from the coastal towns, in particular from Tripoli, Bengazi and Misurata. Emigration by sea to the Syrian provinces was, for them, doubtless the quickest and more comfortable route, although not the cheapest. Many of these exiles belonged to the bureaucratic or intellectual classes. Their social capital, as well as the personal property that some of them possessed, helped them to become integrated in Syrian society. The Ottoman authorities facilitated Libyan immigration from their last, lost North African provinces and many former Ottoman officials chose Syria as their place of exile. It is very probable that they counted on the possibility of finding in the Syrian administration the same offices they had held in Libya. The authorities also facilitated their settlement in other ways, including the disbursement of money for the building of new houses.[21] This first wave of emigration to Syria also involved the families of journalists and, in general, families of those intellectuals who had denounced and opposed Italy's expansionist policy before the military invasion. As was the case with emigration westwards by land, the bulk of the refugees initially arriving on the Syrian coast consisted of women, children and the elderly, as the adult men followed later.

A considerable movement of return to Tripolitania took place in 1919, in response to the enactment of new constitutional legislation (*al-Qanun al-Asasi*). This gave Tripolitanians full citizenship, a delegation to the Italian Government, the election of their own Parliament and guaranteed the respect of local customs and traditions. Sources report that about 100,000 Libyans came back to Tripolitania, mainly from Tunisia, but also from Egypt and Palestine.[22]

In the 1920s, with the onset of fascist colonial policy, a second large wave of emigration took place. At the same time, the pattern of activities among the refugees changed. Instead of collecting arms, money and supplies in support of the current primary resistance in Tripolitania, Cyrenaica and Fezzan, they began to form political associations, and from these new platforms started to press for the independence of Libya.

The Changing Structure of Libyan Exile: the Refugee Associations and the First Signs of Political Activity

The most important Libyan refugee association was founded in Damascus in 1925. Named *al-Jaliyya al-tarabulusiyya bi-Suria* (The Tripolitanian Colony in Syria), it denounced in the Syrian press the atrocities committed by fascist troops in Libya. Until 1928, the association was clandestine, as Syrian law (now under French mandate) forbade civil servants from engaging in political activity. In 1928, the Tripolitanian Bashir al-Sa'dawi, who before the Italian occupation had held at Khoms, his native town, different positions in the Ottoman administration,[23] was chosen as leader of the association and its name was changed to *al-Lajna al-tanfidhiyya li'l-jaliyya al-tarabulusiyya al-barqawiyya* (The Executive Committee of Tripolitanian and Cyrenaican exiles). The new title proclaimed the association's desire to represent all Libyans. Also in 1928, this same group issued a first Nationalist Charter, calling for the establishment of a national Libyan Government, with a Muslim leader to be chosen by the people, the introduction of Arabic as the sole official language, and the reorganisation of *habus* (*waqf*).[24] The main activity of the association at this time was the running of a large information campaign throughout the Muslim world.

However, due to its geographical position and its own, internal political development, Egypt was the preferred centre of Libyan refugees' activities. In 1924, The Welfare Association of the Libyan Bond, or Libyan–Egyptian Committee (*Jam'iyya Khayriyya li-Khatt Libiyya*) was established in Cairo. It gathered together the Libyan Senussis, and enjoyed strong support from famous Egyptian nationalists, such as Hamad al-Basil Pasha[25] and Saleh Pasha Lamlul. The Committee, in order to gain official recognition from the Egyptian Government, ostensibly supplied aid to the Libyan refugees in Egypt, but behind this official activity lay a political association whose aim was to support the resistance in Cyrenaica.

In the same year, 1924, the Co-operation Association of North African Exiles (*Jam'iyyat ta'awun jaliyyat Ifriqiyya al-shamaliyya*) was established, and beside Libyans, it gathered together Moroccans, Tunisians and Algerians. The primary goals of the Association were the extension and promotion of mutual acquaintance among Tripolitanians, Algerians, Moroccans and Tunisians and the defence of their rights. The leadership of the association was mainly Libyan and one of its most important supporters was the leading Egyptian nationalist, 'Abd al-Rahman 'Azzam.[26] A special section was formed under the aegis of the Association, called the Committee for the Cultural Development of North Africa, which had the brief of collecting, and where necessary translating, everything that was published about North Africa in both the Arab and the Western press. The Committee's organ was a revue called *al-Zuhra*.[27] A few months after its foundation, the Committee opened a branch in Alexandria. The Alexandria branch soon became autonomous: it laid down its own rules and was named The Maghribi Association of Charity in Alexandria (*Jam'iyyat al-khayriyya al-maghribiyya bi'l-Iskandariyya*).

Cairo was also the centre of the Committee of National Action in Tripolitania and Cyrenaica which united those Libyan notables who emigrated after the conquest of Libya was completed by an Italy now under fascist rule. The Committee engaged in strong propaganda against Italy in the Mediterranean and Muslim countries. Like the Syrian association, it called for the establishment of a national government with the head of state elected by the people, respect for Muslim religion and law, a general amnesty, and the implementation of a peace treaty with Italy.

There were also other refugee associations established in Egypt, such as The Aid Committee for Libya, which co-operated with all the Senussis exiled in Egypt and was headed by *shaykh* Senussi Hasan Driss Sharif; the Alexandria Tripolitanian Bloc; The Association of Tripolitanians living in Egypt, whose head was Massawd Mahruq; and The Egyptian Committee for the Defence of Libyan Interests, which tried to develop a huge movement against the Italian occupation through the publication of pamphlets addressed to Muslims all over the world.

In January 1925, on the analogy of *Jam'iyyat al-Rabita al-Sharqiyya* (Society of the Eastern Bond),[28] a new association, named *al-Rabita al-Tarabulusiyya* (The Tripolitanian Bond), was formed. Egyptian nationalists also played a very important part in this association: the house of 'Abd al-Rahman 'Azzam served as a clandestine meeting place for the association and *shaykh* 'Abd al-Aziz Jawish[29] was one of its founding members.[30] It remains to be shown, however, what were the real intentions behind Egyptian leaders' involvement in this activity – was their goal an independent Libya as a sovereign national state, or as a part of Egypt?

As we have seen, the Libyans were supported by Wafd party leaders of the calibre of 'Abd al-Rahman 'Azzam and Hamad al-Basil. It remains an open question, however, as to whether the Egyptian nationalists supported Libyan demands for independence because they recognised a shared idea of a 'Libyan' nation, or whether their support was an act of solidarity articulating an agenda of 'Arab unity', a unity which would be led by Egypt. The latter supposition is quite well-founded. For example, already in 1924 Hamad al-

Basil suggested to the Italian authorities that Tripolitania be united with Cyrenaica into an independent principality, whose Government should be assigned to a Prince of the Egyptian ruling family to be chosen by the Kings of Italy and Egypt. All the Senussi tribes would come under the government of the Kingdom of Egypt. The Italian Government would forgo all rights to interfere in the united Libyan principality's internal affairs, but would retain the right to represent it abroad.[31]

Development of the Associations' Activities

In the 1930s, a second large movement of the return of refugees to Libya took place, after the proclamation issued by Governor Badoglio (28 February 1929), announcing an amnesty for political offences and the restitution of confiscated property. In most cases, however, the refugees' return seems to have been principally motivated by the difficult economic conditions they experienced abroad during this period of global crisis.

The British and Egyptian authorities did not hamper the return of refugees from Egypt; some Egyptian politicians acted as mediators to ensure the respect of all conditions upon which their return was seen to depend. It seems that about 10,000 Libyans left Egypt between 1929 and 1938. On the other hand, the return of refugees from French-controlled territories was more difficult, as the Libyans who worked in the Tunisian mines were bound by contract to their French employers. Nevertheless, refugees did also come back from Tunisia: between 1929 and 1933 more than 7,000 left the country.[32]

Despite these movements of return, it was in the heightened political atmosphere of the 1930s that the associations of exiles abroad intensified their political activity and started more actively campaigning for independence. A major turning point was the execution of Omar al Mukhtar (16 September 1931) and the 'pacification' of Cyrenaica; the refugees tried to internationalise the Libyan question as much as possible and the associations of refugees, acting as transnational bodies, attempted to coordinate their activities. Al-Lajna al-tanfidhiyya established in 1929 a Tunisian Branch, which was an integral part of the Syrian-based parent association. In December 1931, a delegation from this association took part in the Islamic Congress in Jerusalem, and produced a report formulating their demands. In the same year, the association published the book *The Black and Red Atrocities or Civilisation by Iron and Fire*.[33] The refugees were aware that anti-colonial propaganda was the only weapon available to them with which they could stimulate public opinion to take an interest in Libya. The book collected testimonies of Italian brutality in Libya. According to some Arabic sources, 20,000 copies circulated in Arab-Islamic countries, but Italian diplomatic documents report that its distribution had no such reach.[34]

On 5 April 1932, the first members' meeting of the *Lajna al-tanfidhiyya* was called. The association changed its name to *Jam'iyyat al-dife' al-tarabulusi al-barqawi* (The Defence Association of Tripolitania and Cyrenaica) and decided to increase its contacts abroad beyond those established in the Muslim world. In September 1936, the Association issued its complete programme: the establishment of a national Libyan Government with a Muslim leader to be chosen by the people, the establishment of an assembly to draw up a new Constitution, the introduction of Arabic as the official language, and the reorganisation of *habus* properties.

The outbreak of war in 1939 was regarded by the refugees as an opportunity to regain control of their country. A conference was held in Alexandria, in October 1939, at which Tripolitanians and Cyrenaicans tried to overcome their differences, and where it was decided that responsibility for leadership of the movement should be entrusted to Sayyid Idris al-Senussi. However, after Italy entered the war the Tripolitanian and Cyrenaican refugees could not agree on a policy of co-operation with Britain, and their common attempt to use the war to further the fight for independence came to a standstill.[35]

Political Action Moves to Libya

After the end of the Second World War, and the end of Italian colonial rule, a number of political parties were founded in Libya. Independence was their common goal, but they did not agree on the means for its attainment. Three main tendencies can be discerned among these movements: those who accepted Muhammad Idris al-Sanussi as King of a united Libya, those who were ready to accept a foreign mandate over the country for a period preparatory to complete independence, and those who dreamt of setting up a democratic, constitutional republic. Those who now returned from exile, especially from Egypt, played an active role in the formation of these political parties.

Already in 1940, 'Abd al-Rahman 'Azzam had formed in Cairo The Tripolitanian Committee, composed of those Tripolitanians who objected to the proposal of Idris al-Senussi as 'Emir-in-Chief' for a united Libya. In 1944, the leading members of this committee returned to Tripolitania.[36] Two other groups whose members returned to Libya after the war, The Egyptian–Tripolitanian Union Party and the Omar al-Mukhtar Club, were both strongly influenced by Egyptian pan-Arabist ideology.

The Omar al-Mukhtar Club (*Nadi Omar al-Mukhtar*),[37] named after the hero of the Cyrenaican resistance, was formed among exiles in Cairo in 1942. A year later the Club began a revival in Benghazi thanks to a number of refugees who had come back from Egypt; it encouraged sporting and cultural activities among Cyrenaican youth and promoted the publication of a sports review, named *al-Barqa al-Riyadiyya*. Benghazi became the headquarters of the organisation and branches were established in Derna, Barce and other towns. In 1944, the Club manifested its first signs of political activity, focusing its criticism on the British Administration. The Club was constantly influenced by Egypt in different ways: by the refugees who returned from Egypt, by Egyptian employees in the administration, by Egyptian nationalistic ideas which circulated through the Egyptian press. A further development occurred in 1946 with the transformation of the sports review *Barqa al-Riyadiyya* into *al-Watan*, now the weekly political organ of the Club. This change confirmed the fact that the Omar al-Mukhtar Club was now primarily a political organisation. In the same year, the Club formed a section called *Kashshaf*, a troop of Boy Scouts. It was affiliated with the International Federation of Boy Scouts.[38] In 1950, the Club, following the Law of Associations which stipulated that the name of any person, whether living or dead, could not be used as the title for any political organisation, changed its name to The National Association (*al-Jam'iyya al-Wataniyya*). The Omar al-Mukhtar Club, and later the National Association, was one of the first associations to fight, within the country, for the independence and unity of all Libya.

The Egyptian–Tripolitanian Union Party was formed in Tripoli in November 1946 by a small group of dissidents from the Free National Bloc. Its aim was the union of Libya with Egypt under the Egyptian Crown, with a common defence and a common foreign policy. Libya would have preserved some independence as a sort of autonomous province under a Vice-Regent (Idris al-Sanussi), and would retain its own administration and legislature. According to some archival sources it seems that 'Abd al-Rahman 'Azzam had a strong influence upon the Union, as he worked hard for a Libyan connection with Egypt. His own primary motive was thought to be to become Egyptian Governor-General of Libya.[39]

Bashir al-Sa'dawi, leader of the exiles' movement in Syria, who in the meantime had been appointed adviser to 'Abd al-Aziz Ibn Sa'ud in his own newly created Kingdom of Saudi Arabia, returned to the scene in Cairo, where in March 1947 he established the Libyan Liberation Committee (*Hay'at tahrir Libiya*). Its aim was to bring together the different nationalist tendencies both from Cyrenaica and Tripolitania. The programme of the Liberation Committee included the following: action for the independence of Libya, co-operation with the Arab League, and maintenance of Libyan unity during the struggle for freedom. The Liberation Committee was also strongly supported by al-'Azzam, then Secretary-General of the new Arab League. He made an appeal to the people of Libya asking them to recognise the Committee, to be united, and to co-operate in order to obtain the freedom of the country, without paying attention to the differences of opinion among the political parties.[40]

Libyans' experiences of exile, however, were not to end with the independence of a united Libya when it did come in 1951. Some of those who returned from exile and fought for the freedom of their country were forced into exile again in 1952, after the election of Idris. Among those to be found in this new wave of refugees was Bashir al-Sa'dawi.

Conclusion

As I mentioned at the outset, the aim here has been merely to draw out general issues and identify key patterns in an area where much exploration remains to be done. The main aim of my work is to explore the history, ideology and organisation of the Libyan refugee associations, principally those which were active in Egypt. The first objective is to understand the differences as well as similarities between these organisations and the nature of their contacts with nationalist movements in other countries. In the light of an adequate account of these movements of persons, ideas and activities, it will be possible more carefully to scrutinise, and more precisely to situate, the history of the shaping of the idea of a Libyan nation.

The role played by the exiles' associations in the shaping of a Libyan national idea must also, however, be analysed in conjunction with a number of other, related, questions. One such is the intellectual production of Libyan refugees. Did the Libyan intellectuals in exile play an active role in formulating Libyan nationalism and in creating a collective image of 'the Libyan nation'? The most famous poets of the time emigrated to Egypt: Husayn Muhammad al-Ahlafi, Amin al-Hafi, Miftah Umar al-Haqq, Sa'id Shalbi, to name only a few. Their texts include some common features but is it possible to call their works an *oeuvre*, a 'literature of Libyan emigration'? Did the so-called 'Egyptian National Literature' of the 1930s influence their compositions?[41]

Further questions also remain concerning the role of Egyptian intellectuals. In spite of a ban imposed by the Italians from the 1920s onwards, the number of Libyan students attending classes at al-Azhar increased. What was the role played by al-Azhar and the brotherhoods in the refugees' organisations? In the early stages of the Italian occupation, some brotherhoods (*Shadhiliyya, Madaniyya*) actually supported Italian colonial expansion as a strategy of countering the Sanussi tendency towards supremacy.

Research in this area must also take account of Italian propaganda in Egyptian nationalist circles. As a counterweight to the activity of Libyan refugees, the Italian authorities published a number of pamphlets in Arabic, and established an Italian 'information centre' in Cairo. In addition, the colonial authorities made contact with the Young Egypt Movement and also with such notable Arab and Muslim nationalists as Shakib Arslan. Some of these (including Arslan himself) were led to reverse their previous positions and made favourable statements regarding the Italian presence in Libya. Were these changes of opinion brought about simply by gifts granted by the Italians?

In conclusion, as we have seen, key issues related to the development of Libyan nationalism remain in need of more thorough investigation. In particular, and although, as André Martel has pointed out[42], the historical course taken by Libya has to be distinguished in a number of ways from those of its neighbours, Libyan nationalism and Libyan history more generally must be included in, as well as compared with, the broader history of the contemporary experiences of the Maghrib, and its Mediterranean context, as part of a larger, interconnected whole.[43]

NOTES

1. This research project was initially presented at the seminar *Reshaping the Individual and Power Relations in the Context of Colonial Experiences*, Tampere, Sept. 1997, part of the European Science Foundation's research programme *Individual and Society in the Mediterranean Muslim World*. The proceedings contain the first general outline of the project. Anna Baldinetti, 'The Libyan Refugees, Egyptian Nationalism and the Shaping of the Idea of a Libyan Nation' in Kirsi Virtanen (ed.), *Individual, Ideologies and Society. Tracing the Mosaic of Mediterranean History* (Tampere: TAPRI Research Report No. 89 2001).

2. For a discussion of the literature, see Nicola Labanca, 'Gli studi italiani sul colonialismo italiano in Libia', *Journal of Libyan Studies* 2/1 (2001) pp.69–79.

3. The Libyan Studies Centre/Markaz jihad al-libiyyina li-l-dirasat al-ta'rikhiyya was established in 1977, with its main centre in Tripoli and branches in certain other towns. See Hans Schlüter, 'The Libyan Studies Centre', *Libyan Studies* 11 (1980) pp.101–2. The Centre's main activity is the collection of documents on contemporary Libya, and especially on the colonial period. The oral archives section preserves the recordings and trancriptions of some thousands of interviews held with *mujahidin*, veterans of the anticolonial resistance struggle. In Tunisia, the Institut Supérieur de l'Histoire du Mouvement National/al-Ma'had al-'ali li-ta'rikh al-haraka 'l-wataniyya maintains a similar archive of recorded interviews at the Manouba campus of the University of Tunis. On the Libyan state's programme to assemble this history, and its relation to other, local tribal histories, see John Davis, 'The Social Relations of the Production of History' in Elizabeth Tonkin *et al* (eds.), *History and Ethnicity* (London: Routledge 1989) ch.7.

4. For a review of Libyan studies on Italian colonialism see Pierluigi Venuta, 'Libyan Studies on Italian Colonialism: Bibliographical and Historiographical Considerations', *Journal of Libyan Studies* 2/1 (2001) pp.48–60.

5. Ali Abdullatif Ahmida, *The Making of Modern Libya. State Formation, Colonisation, and Resistance, 1830–1932* (Albany: SUNY Press 1994).

6. See Lisa Anderson, 'The Development of Nationalist Sentiment in Libya, 1908–1922' in Rashid Khalidi, Lisa Anderson, Muhammad Muslih, Reeva S. Simon (eds.), *The Origins of Arab Nationalism* (New York: Columbia University Press 1991).

7. For further discussion of this issue see Simone Bernini, *Studi sulle origini del nazionalismo arabo in Libia*, *Journal of Libyan Studies* 2/1 (2001) pp.95–103.

8. Ibrahim Ahmad Abu al-Qasim, *al-Muhajiruna al-Libiyyuna bi al-bilad al-tunisiyya (1911–1957)*, (Tunis: Mu'assasat 'Abd al-Karim bin 'Abd Allah 1992); Tisir Ibn Musa, *Kifah al-Libiyyina al-siyasi fi bilad al-Sham* (Tripoli: Markaz al-Jihad 1983); Ahmad al-Tahir al-Zawi, *Jihad al-Libiyyina fi diyar al-hijra min sanat 1924 ila sanat 1950* (Tripoli: Dar al-Firjani 1976). Data on the refugees are also to be found in Adrian Pelt, *Libyan Independence and the United Nations: A Case of Planned Decolonisation* (New Haven: Yale University Press 1970).

9. Israel Gershoni, 'Rethinking the Formation of Arab Nationalism in the Middle East 1920–45. Old and New Narratives' in James P. Jankowski and Israel Gershoni (eds.), *Rethinking Nationalism in the Arab Middle East* (New York: Columbia University Press 1997) p.13.

10. For an overview and discussion of the literature related to Libyan nationalism and the Libyan nation state see Michel Le Gall, 'Forging the Nation-State: Some Issues in the Historiography of Modern Libya' in Michel Le Gall and Kenneth Perkins (eds.), *The Maghrib in Question. Essays in History and Historiography* (Austin: University of Texas Press 1997).

11. On the significance of *hijra* from colonised land, see Muhammad Masud, 'The Obligation to Migrate. The Doctrine of *hijra* in Islamic Law' in Dale F. Eickelman and James P. Piscatori (eds.), *Muslim Travellers. Pilgrimage, Migration and the Religious Imagination* (London: Routledge 1990). For other examples in the colonial Maghrib, see Julia A. Clancy-Smith, *Rebel and Saint. Muslim Notables, Populist Protest, Colonial Encounters (Algeria and Tunisia, 1800–1904)* (Berkeley and Los Angeles: University of California Press 1994), ch. 5, and Charles-Robert Ageron, 'L'émigration des Musulmans algériens et l'exode de Tlemcen (1830–1911)', *Annales: Economies, Sociétés, Civilisations* 22/3 (1967) pp.1047–66 (Editor's note).

12. The data presented here have been collected from several archives, in particular Archivio Storico Diplomatico del Ministero degli Affari Esteri (Rome), (hereafter cited as ASMAE); Archives d'Outre-Mer (Aix-en-Provence), (hereafter cited as AOM); Archives Nationales de Tunisie (hereafter cited as ANT); Public Record Office (London), (hereafter cited as PRO); Dar al watha'q al-qawmiyya (Cairo) (hereafter cited as DAW). As this is still a work in progress I have taken the liberty of citing only archives and files referred to, without giving specific references to individual documents.

13. For detailed information on these tribes see Enrico De Agostini, *Le popolazioni della Tripolitania* (Tripoli: Governo della Tripolitania 1917).

14. Ghuma bin Khalifa (1795–1858), head of the al-Mahamid tribes, and 'Abd al-Jalil Sayf al-Nasser, head of the Awlad Sulayman tribes, were the leaders of the Arab resistance to the second Ottoman occupation of Tripolitania, which began in 1835. 'Abd al-Jalil was defeated in 1842, while Ghuma resisted until 1858. Ghuma did not only mobilise Arabs and Berbers, nomads and sedentaries but also some Tunisian tribes. On Ghuma see Bradford G. Martin, 'Ghuma bin Khalifa: a Libyan Rebel, 1795–1858' in S. Derengil and S. Kuneralp (eds.), *Studies in Ottoman Diplomatic History* (Istanbul: 1990), Muhammad al-Tawir, *al-Shaykh Ghuma al-Mahmudi 'ala al-'Uthmaniyyin* (Tripoli: Dar al-Firjani 1995) 2nd edn.

15. ANT: A 280–9/9, A 280/3, A 280–9/19, A 280/9–12, A2 80–9/19.

16. See Ali Mahjoubi, *Les Origines du mouvement national en Tunisie 1904–1934* (Tunis: Publications de l'Université de Tunis 1982) pp.129–38; Anna Baldinetti (ed.), *David Santillana L'uomo e il giurista. Scritti inediti 1878/1920* (Rome: Istituto per l'Oriente 1995) pp.43–63.

17. ASMAE: ASMAI Libia 122/1–8. Sulayman al-Baruni (1870–1940), after the Young Turks' revolution of 1908 was an elected deputy at the Ottoman parliament in Istanbul, representing the Jebel liwa'. In 1911 he returned to Tripolitania to promote resistance against the Italians; he played an active role in the resistance and was one of the 'Council of Four' in the Tripolitanian Republic established in 1918. On his political activities see J. E. Peterson, 'Arab Nationalism and the Idealist Politician: the Career of Sulayman al-Baruni' in James Piscatori and George S. Harris (eds.), *Law, Personalities, and Politics of the Middle East. Essays in Honor of Majid Khadduri* (Boulder, CO: Westview Press 1987).

18. ASMAE: ASMAI Libia 125/2, ASMAI Libia 122/1, AMAI Libia 122/1–8.

19. ASMAE: AE 192, AE 196/4, AE 188/14.
20. This emerged in interviews I carried out in Oct.–Nov. 1998 in Cairo, among Libyans settled there, and in al-Fayyum with some members of the al-Basil family. At this stage I am not yet able to assess the influence of, for example, the course of the war in 1940–42 on the return of al-Fayyum's Libyan population.
21. Ibn Musa (note 8) *Kifah al-Libiyyina* pp.13–38.
22. ANT: MN 10/1; ASMAE: ASMAI Libia 150/22, ASMAI Libia 150/30.
23. Bashir al-Sa'dawi (1884–?) was, from his exile, one of the most active opponents of the Italian occupation of Libya. In 1912 he emigrated to Istanbul, later to the Hijaz and then Lebanon, where was appointed *qa'imaqam* (a senior administrative post). In 1920 he returned to Tripoli, before emigrating a second time (in 1923) to Damascus, where he established *The Tripolitanian and Cyrenaican Defence Committee* and devoted himself to the struggle for Libyan independence. See Muhammad Fu'ad Shukri, *Libiyya haditha: watha'iq tahririha wa istiqlaliha* (Cairo: Matba 'et el- I'tima 1957) in particular Vol.II.
24. That is, properties made over by pious endowment for the upkeep of religious institutions (mosques, schools) or the maintenance of religious officials and scholars.
25. Hamad al-Basil Pasha (1871–940), a bedouin notable from the region of al-Fayyum, was one of the first members of the *Wafd*. In 1919 he was exiled to Malta with Sa'd Zaghlul; later (in 1924) he acted as Vice-President of the Chamber of Deputies, and was Vice-President of the *Wafd* until Nov. 1932.
26. 'Abd al-Rahman 'Azzam (1893–197?) is considered not only an Egyptian nationalist, but one of the first Arab nationalists. From 1915 to 1923 he took part in the Libyan resistance, and was later a member of the *Wafd*. In 1936 he was appointed Egypt's Minister plenipotentiary to Iraq and Iran, and from 1945 to 1952 was the first Secretary-General of the Arab League. On 'Azzam's political activity up to 1936 see Ralph M. Coury, *The Making of an Egyptian Arab Nationalist. The Early Years of Azzam Pasha, 1893–1936* (Reading: Ithaca Press 1998).
27. Not to be confused with the long-established political newspaper of the same title, published at the same time in Tunis (Editor's note).
28. The *Jam'iyyat al-Rabita al-Sharqiyya* was founded in 1922 with the aim of promoting ties between Eastern peoples. In 1928 the society started to publish a review, *Majallat al-Rabita al-Sharqiyya*, which more than once reported on Italian atrocities in Libya.
29. 'Abd al-'Aziz Jawish (1876–1929) was an activist of the Nationalist Party.
30. ASMAE: AE 192/1, 192/2, 196/4; AOM: GGA 29H13.
31. ASMAE: ASMAI Libia 150/20–88.
32. ASMAE: ASMAI Affari Politici 80, ASMAI Libia 150/21–89, Affari Politici 1931–45 Libia 1/1.
33. *al-Faza'ia al-sud wa al-humr aw al-tamdin bi-al-hamid wa al-nar* (Damascus: l-Halqa al-Ula, Lajnat tasgil al-Faza'ia 1931).
34. ASMAE: Affari Politici 1931/45 Libia 5/3.
35. On these years, see Majid Khadduri, *Modern Libya. A Study in Political Development* (Baltimore: The Johns Hopkins Press 1963) pp.28–52; Ibn Musa (note 8) pp.139–53; Muhammad Fu'ad Shukri (note 23) vol.I, pp.203–67.
36. PRO: FO371/63177 1947.
37. On this association see Anna Baldinetti, 'Note sul nazionalismo libico: l'attività dell'associazione 'Umar al-Mukhtar', *Journal of Libyan Studies* 2/1 (2001) pp.61–8.
38. It was, similarly, in young people's cultural and sports associations, including the Scout movement, that the nucleus of nationalist mobilisation among the young was formed in colonial Algeria and Tunisia (Editor's note).
39. PRO, FO 371/63187 1947.
40. PRO 371/63212.
41. For a discussion of this issue see Israel Gershoni and James P. Jankowski, *Egypt, Islam and the Arabs. The Search for Egyptian Nationhood, 1900–1930* (Oxford and New York: Oxford University Press 1986) in particular pp.191–227.
42. See André Martel, 'Histoire contemporaine de la Libye. Dimensions et recherches' in

Annuaire de l'Afrique du Nord, 1966, pp.781–92, and the same author's *La Libye 1835–1990 Essai de géopolitique historique* (Paris: PUF 1991).

43. Only in recent years have Western historians begun to include Libya in the Maghrib, whose historiography has long been affected by what Mohamed Abed Jabri has called the 'the colonial heritage', that is, the habit by which 'Maghrib' was used only to refer to the former French colonies of North Africa. See Mohamed Abed Jabri, 'Evolution of the Maghrib Concept: Facts and Perspectives', in Halim Barakat (ed.), *Contemporary North Africa: Issues of Development and Integration* (London and Sydney: Croom Helm 1985) pp.63–86.

Martyrs and Patriots:
Ethnic, National and Transnational
Dimensions of Kabyle Politics

PAUL A. SILVERSTEIN

A Kenza a yelli / D iseflan neghli / F Lzzayer uzekka / A Kenza a yelli / Ur
tru ara
O Kenza my daughter / We have sacrificed our lives/ For the Algeria of
tomorrow /
O Kenza my daughter /Do not cry
'Kenza', written in 1993 by Lounès Matoub for the daughter of
the recently assassinated Kabyle journalist and playwright, Tahar Djaout

One of the many facets of the current civil war in Algeria, a war in which an
estimated 125,000 people have been killed since 1992, has been the renewed
importance of regional dynamics within the Algerian nation-state. From car
bombings in Algiers, to village massacres in the Mitidja plain, to deadly
roadblocks on the country's major arteries, the conflict has been enacted in
spatial as well as ideological terms. Kabylia in particular has been a site not
only of the diffuse violence associated with the battle between the military
and Islamist militias, but more importantly of increasingly violent
confrontations between Kabyle civilians and the central state. This article
focuses on the latter aspect of the conflict and the consequences it entails for
the reinvention of Kabyle political subjectivity.

Placing the current conflict in a longer history of Kabyle struggles for
cultural, linguistic, and political representation, the article explores the
tensions between the ethnic, national, and transnational dimensions of Kabyle
politics. With a particular focus on the representation and enactment of the
Kabyle struggle in the diaspora, I seek to understand these dynamics through
the changing image of the martyr-patriot as successively victimised by forces
of colonialism, Islamism, and the independent Algerian state. I argue that,
while Kabyle politics have become progressively transnationalised, they
nonetheless remain firmly ensconced in local-level concerns over the social
and economic conditions of a future, post-war Algerian nation.

Wartime Nationalism

One of four minoritised Berberophone regions in Algeria,[1] Kabylia has a long history of resistance to central authority. Although its western edges lie only a few miles east of the capital, it was the last region to be successfully 'pacified' by the French in 1856 – some 26 years after the fall of Ottoman Algiers to the French expeditionary force. An area of steep mountains and stark valleys, it was the site of a series of insurrections during the colonial period, most significantly in February 1871 when an estimated 200,000 local fighters rose up in response to the harsh policies instituted by the civilian colonial government.

During the war of national liberation (1954–62), Kabylia was likewise an important centre of resistance, with many of the uprising's military leaders originating in the region, and the first congress of the revolutionary National Liberation Front (FLN) held in the Soummam Valley near Akbou in August 1956. Kabylia witnessed some of the most intense guerilla warfare, with the armed *maquis* recruiting heavily from the countryside and finding widespread emotional and logistical support among the local population. As traditional techniques of warfare proved ineffective against such guerrilla organisation, the French army pursued its infamous 'scorched earth' (*terre brulée*) policy, napalming villages, destroying crops and flocks, and relocating hundreds of thousands of inhabitants from designated 'forbidden zones' (*zones interdites*) to military-run '*regroupement*' camps. As a result, the entire population of the region became a party to the violence of the war.

However, this history of anti-colonial resistance should by no means imply that Kabylia has been a traditional bastion of FLN control. Rather, Kabylia was the site of a veritable 'war within the war', with FLN units battling those of the rival revolutionary organisation, the Algerian National Movement (MNA). Even within the mainstream nationalist movement, Kabyle leaders often represented an oppositional voice, articulating a vision of an independent Algeria as secular and multicultural – an *Algérie algérienne* – that did not conform to the more dominant Arab-Islamist ideology. Revolutionary songs were composed in Berber, calling upon Kabyle villagers to 'Rise up, Berber son!' (*Kker a mmi-s umazigh*).[2] The most extreme of these groups, led by Rachid Ali Yahia, even called for a rejection of any inclusion of Algeria in the larger Arab world, on the basis that Algeria was rightfully Berber in nature.[3] Beginning in 1949, such supporters of a multi-ethnic Algeria were successively excluded from the nationalist movement in a general purge that has become known as the movement's 'Berberist crisis' (*crise berbériste*).[4] Kabyle Francophone intellectuals like Mouloud Mammeri and Mouloud Feraoun were condemned for their anachronistic 'regionalism' in the nationalist newspapers, and prominent Kabyle leaders within the FLN, most notably Abbane Ramdane and, later, Krim Belkacem, were assassinated.[5]

These tensions between visions of an 'Algerian Algeria' (*Algérie algérienne*) and an 'Arab-Muslim Algeria' (*Algérie arabo-musulmane*) resurfaced after independence in 1962. The Algiers Charter, adopted in April 1964 as Algeria's *de facto* constitution, declared Algeria to be an 'Arab-Muslim country' and decried regionalist identities as 'feudal survivals' and 'obstacles to national integration'. Perceiving this direction in the ruling FLN ideology, the Kabyle war hero Hocine Aït Ahmed founded the first rival political party in independent Algeria, the Socialist Forces Front (FFS), in September 1963 and subsequently led a ten-month guerrilla insurrection throughout Kabylia against the Algerian national army and the 'ethnic fascism' of president Ahmed Ben Bella. While the revolt failed to gain widespread support, the FFS remained a strong oppositional (though unarmed) force to the Algerian regime in both Kabylia and in France even after Aït Ahmed's arrest and flight to Europe in 1965.

In the years that followed, the FLN government glossed over these conflicts and employed anodyne images of the war to forge national consensus around itself as the natural inheritor of revolutionary leadership. It portrayed the 1954–62 struggle as a continuation of the anti-colonial resistance of the nineteenth-century, from Abd al-Qadir's resistance war (1834–47) through the Kabyle insurrection of 1871 to the uprising in Sétif and Guelma (8 May 1945). In so doing, the FLN posited a singular Algerian colonial subject across time and space, a subject who, confronted with the violence of colonialism, responded in kind.[6] Armed with the now-famous rally-call, 'One hero, the people', the Algerian state presented the war as a 'spontaneous movement' of a colonised proletariat. Through this experience of struggle, the FLN anticipated the production of a new national consciousness, free from the pitfalls of regionalism, religious rivalry, and class interest. Employing a 'cult of the martyr' (*chahid*, pl. *chouhada*), FLN ideologues foresaw the construction of an Algerian 'new man'[7], purged of the urban cultural decadence and rural economic poverty imposed by colonialism, culturally and spiritually liberated by a 'decolonisation of the mind' (*décolonisation des esprits*) based in a fusion of Arab nationalism and socialism.[8]

Such a narrative represents an exemplary case of the politics of forgetting that Ernest Renan posited in his famous 1882 lecture as the basis of any national unity.[9] Since the early-1980s, Kabyle activists have questioned this univocal narrative and actively recalled the memory of forgotten or assassinated Kabyle leaders. On the one hand, these efforts represent an appropriation of Algeria's revolutionary past into current Kabyle *qua* 'Amazigh' struggles for cultural and linguistic recognition – the creation of a (fictive) genealogy of specifically *Amazigh* (Berber) activism.[10] Berberocentric Kabyle associations, such as the *Association de Culture Berbère* (ACB) in Paris, have sponsored talks and conferences on wartime personages like Abbane, Krim, and Ferhat Abbas. On the other hand, the re-narration of the Algerian War constitutes an effort to re-insert Kabyle particularity into the definition of the Algerian nation. The war figures as a major formative experience in several autobiographies published during the 1990s by prominent Kabyle militants, with the authors in question demonstrating their key participation in the war effort as young children.[11] In privileging this period, the authors assert themselves as *Algerian* patriots and promulgate this patriotism as perfectly compatible with their later Berber activism.

Diasporic Dimensions of Post-War Politics

These attempts to position Kabyle particularity within the Algerian national imaginary have been coupled with an embrace of the transnational context in which such demands are made. With the growing hegemony of the FLN in Algeria, the locus of Kabyle struggle shifted to France. While Ben Bella and later President Houari Boumediènne suppressed Berber cultural expression (including the Kabyle radio programme which had played 8–10 hours per day on France 2 from 1958 to 1962) and pursued a project of Arabisation of the Algerian media and education system,[12] in France a number of Kabyle immigrants and exiles actively voiced their support for Berber language and culture. The activism of these militants succeeded to a large degree in politicising the Kabyle emigrant community against FLN hegemony, thus laying the groundwork for the later foundation of the Berber Cultural Movement (MCB) in the 1980s, as well as a supranational World Amazigh Congress (CMA) in the 1990s.

To a great extent, this diasporic post-war activism was simply a continuation of emigrant nationalist militancy. Algerian emigration to metropolitan France was almost exclusively composed of male Kabyle labourers until 1920, with the Kabyle immigrant community in the Hexagon numbering an estimated 120,000 by the beginning of the 1954 war of decolonisation.[13] It was in France, among these workers, that the first Algerian nationalist party, the *Étoile Nord-Africaine* (ENA) was formed in the 1920s. Likewise, it was there, under the direction of Messali Hadj, that the ENA, banned in 1936, was reborn as the *Parti du Peuple Algérien* (PPA). Also banned, the PPA survived underground before acquiring a legal, electoralist cover organisation, the *Mouvement pour la Triomphe des Libértés Démocratiques* (MTLD), in 1946. The PPA/MTLD would later (in 1953–54) split into the FLN and the MNA. Thirty-five of the sixty-four founding members of the PPA were of Kabyle origin, including Amar Imache, second in command under Messali, who would later break from the PPA and found his own Berberist *Parti de l'Unité Algerienne.*[14]

Drawing on this earlier history, in March 1967, a group of Paris-based scholars (including Mouloud Mammeri), artists (including singer Taos Amrouch), and FFS activists (including Bessaoud Mohand Arab) founded the *Académie Berbère d'Echanges et de Recherches Culturels* (later renamed in 1969 as *Agraw Imazighen*). While originally dedicated to the 'universal' and 'harmonious cooperation between all humanity', the Agraw's goals became increasingly irredentist – 'to introduce the larger public to the history and civilisation of Berbers, including the promotion of the language and culture' as stated in the second article of its 1969 statutes. Adopting the appellation *Imazighen* ('free men'), members of the Academy worked to standardise Berber (Tamazight) and develop a neo-Tifinagh orthographic script. At the same time, the Academy was actively involved in the social life of the Kabyle emigrant community, publicising Algerian and French policy changes of relevance to the community and pushing its ideology of a 'Berber nation' through the medium of *cafés arabes* and the variety of village assemblies (*tajmaât*s) transposed onto the French urban landscape (see Salem Chaker, endnote 2, p.44). In spite of these efforts, however, the Academy maintained its primary presence among Kabyle student groups in the university system.

This intellectual slant of Kabyle expatriate activism was underlined in the 1973 formation of the *Groupe d'Etudes Berbères* at the Université de Paris-VIII-Vincennes. Dedicated to teaching Berber language and culture, the *Groupe* received national and international recognition, garnering the participation of many sympathetic, non-Kabyle scholars including such eminent names as Pierre Bourdieu and Ernest Gellner. In 1978, the *Groupe* formed the *Ateliers Imedyazen*, a publication cooperative in Paris, to diffuse such intellectual debates to a more popular level. Over the course of the next several years, the cooperative published works on linguistics, theatre, poetry and other literature, including translations into Tamazight (of Brecht, among others), grammar manuals, *dossiers de presse* that followed events in Algeria, and political communiqués, including the 1979 FFS party platform. These publications were further paralleled by the growth of a Kabyle recording industry in France, and particularly the invention of the *neo-chanson kabyle* by mostly expatriate recording artists (notably Lounis Aït-Menguellet, Idir, Ferhat M'henni, and Lounès Matoub). Drawing on the earlier sung poetry of Taos Amrouche and the musical commentary on exile (*el-ghorba*) by Slimane Azem, these singer-songwriters adopted traditional poetry into 'revolutionary songs of struggle', and eventually came to play direct political roles in the struggle for Berber linguistic rights. Given this development of emigrant cultural production, as Salem Chaker has remarked, 'it would not be an exaggeration to say that thousands of young Kabyles have learned to read and write in their language from those works published in France'.[15]

Berber Springs

In March–April 1980, Kabylia became once again the centre of resistance to the central state. Following the cancellation, by the governor of the *wilaya* of Tizi-Ouzou, of a lecture on ancient Berber poetry, which was to have been given at the University of Tizi Ouzou on 10 March by Mouloud Mammeri, students occupied the university. When security forces arrived, violent confrontations broke out which would last for two weeks, culminating in widespread student demonstrations, a general strike throughout the region, and the eventual loss of life (36 dead, hundreds wounded) when the newly-installed president Chadli Benjedid called in the military.

These events, collectively known as the 'Berber Spring' (*Printemps Berbère*, or simply *Tafsut*), had several repercussions. In the first place, as a number of observers have noted, it concretised the previously amorphous MCB and initiated Berberism as a political force in post-colonial Algeria.[16] Successive waves of contestation to state authority in October 1988, the autumn of 1994, July 1998, and April 2001 mapped directly onto this early moment of confrontation in terms of both its spatial and ideological dimensions. Secondly, the Berber Spring produced a set of martyrs whose deaths squarely indexed the Kabyle political struggle against the Algerian state. The annual commemorations of Tafsut generally begin with moments of silence for those fallen in 1980, as well as for those Kabyles who have died since at the hands of state or Islamist forces. Thirdly, it reinforced the ties between Kabylia and the diasporic community abroad. The events themselves were well covered in the Kabyle emigrant media in France, particularly as published by Imedyazen. The nascent *Ateliers de Culture Berbère* (now the ACB), formed in 1979 by dissident members of the *Groupe d'Études Berbères*, organised a protest in front of the Algerian embassy in Paris.

Indeed, Tafsut arguably had the effect of politicising the 'second generation' of Kabyles in France, those born away from the quotidian realities of Berber cultural life. Within a year of the events, newly-elected Socialist president François Mitterrand legalised the foundation of immigrant non-profit associations in France, paving the way for what would become known as the 'Beur Movement'.[17] Presenting themselves as post-modern cultural hybrids, these young Franco-Maghribis publicly demonstrated against racism and for their civil rights in a series of demonstrations and artistic productions. While many of their cultural and political activities were oriented towards the improvement of the daily lives of Beur youth living in the deprived and troublesome suburban housing developments (*cités*) of Paris, Lyon, and Marseille, others targeted the Maghrib, seeking to identify a common cause among youth on both sides of the Mediterranean. Beur media (newspapers, radio stations, etc.) in particular became increasingly the main source of news of North African events for immigrants in France. During the riots of October 1988 in Algeria, the Paris-based Radio-Beur provided the only source of immediate, un-censored news on either side of the Mediterranean, devoting its entire airtime to the events, taking live calls from eyewitnesses in Algiers, and broadcasting this information via satellite back to listeners in North Africa.[18]

Moreover, as many of the Beur militants were of Kabyle origin, it is of little surprise that a disproportionate number of their interventions adopted particularly Berber signs to express this identification as cultural mediators. Many of the Beur theatre troupes (e.g., 'Kahina'[19]), musical groups (e.g., 'Djurdjura'[20]), radio stations (Radio Tiwizi[21]), and novelists (e.g., Tassadit Imache) devoted themselves to popularising artistic genres deemed native to Kabylia and drew political inspiration from the annals of Kabyle resistance leaders. Most importantly, this period witnessed a proliferation of Kabyle cultural associations in France: the ACB and the *Association Berbère des Recherches, Information, Documentation et Animation* (ABRIDA) in the Paris region, *Afus deg Wfus* ('Hand in Hand') in Roubaix, *Assiren* in Lyon, and a number of subsidiary branches of the ACB formed throughout the country.[22] Throughout the 1980s and 1990s, these associations sponsored talks on Berber history and culture, taught courses in Tamazight, served as electoral bases for Kabyle political parties, functioned as community centres for local immigrant populations (offering day-care and after-school tutoring services), and staged public celebrations of Kabyle seasonal festivals. These latter festivities, through their accompanying slide shows of Algeria, dance demonstrations, and musical performances, function as primers in Berber culture for the younger generation born in the diaspora.

Not surprisingly, the most important ritual within the yearly cycle is the commemoration of Tafsut, the *sine qua non* activity of diasporic Kabyle cultural associations around the globe. During my anthropological fieldwork among the Kabyle communities of Paris and New York in the mid-1990s, I had the opportunity of participating in six different Tafsut commemorations. While each of the events included the standard remembrance of the martyred students and the narration of the history of Amazigh activism from colonial times to the present, they also served as moments for the articulation of particular political platforms keyed to recent events in Algeria and beyond. The first set of celebrations I witnessed occurred in April 1995 in Paris, in the midst of the generalised Kabyle boycott of the 1994–95 Algerian school year organised by the MCB in protest at the government's Arabisation policies and in hopes of having Tamazight recognised as a 'national and official language' of Algeria. The festivities largely focused on the school strike, with banners decorating the auditoria with slogans like *Tamazight di likul* ('Tamazight in the Schools') and *Tamazight ass-a azekka* ('Tamazight, Today, Tomorrow'), Amazigh flags flying, participants wearing military uniforms signifying a Kabylia at war, and heated debates over the effectiveness of the boycott and the political divisions within the MCB that it had made evident.

One celebration hosted by the Association Tikli of Saint-Denis and MCB-France of Argenteuil held on 14 April 1995 segued into a relatively well-attended protest (60 protestors, 20 Compagnie Républicaine de Sécurité [CRS] riot police) in front of the Algerian embassy the following day. In a parallel celebration by the ACB held the following weekend in the Belleville neighbourhood of Paris, speakers were invited from the various MCB factions (associated with the rival FFS and the Algerian Rally for Culture and Democracy [RCD] political parties) to present their versions of the school boycott strategies and results, and the debate pointed particularly to the differences in these perspectives. In both celebrations, the current civil war was brought directly into the commemorations, with minutes of silence observed for its victims and many of their photographs prominently displayed in the foyers and reception halls.

In contrast, if the 1995 celebrations sought to forge a direct link between Tafsut and the ongoing struggles for linguistic recognition in Algeria, the 1996 Tafsut demonstrations focused more clearly on the French scene. To mark the occasion, the ACB organised a conference on 'Berberity in France', inviting researchers and local activists to debate the role and future of Amazigh identity in the French model of 'integration. In particular, the concern was how to present Amazigh identity as a third option between assimilation and Islamism for young Beurs in the French *cités*. At a parallel conference on 'The Amazigh Question' organised by MCB-France, the debate similarly focused on the place of Amazigh language and culture in the French, as well as the Algerian, nation-state. Alongside testimonies to their cultural trajectories by young Beur men and women, Catalan and Occitan militants were also invited to share their struggles for linguistic and cultural recognition in France. In incorporating these other marginals of the nation-state, the organisers were pointing to the 'universality' of the Amazigh movement and its particular repercussions in the diaspora community in France. These multiple celebrations, in all their divergences, indicate not only the growing transnationalisation of Kabyle politics, but also the tensions between local and global dimensions of the Berber struggle.

The Binary Logic of the Civil War

These tensions have only been exacerbated by the ongoing civil war in Algeria that has hit Kabylia particularly hard in terms of both physical and economic violence.[23] While the economic crisis precipitated by the vertiginous drop in hydrocarbon prices in the mid-1980s has affected all Algerians, it has particularly touched Kabylia, which, having neither agricultural nor mineral resources, has been historically dependent on its ability to export manpower to urban centres and abroad – avenues of migration today largely closed by unemployment and increased border restrictions. While the civil war has not produced as many casualties in Kabylia as in other provinces, it has had visceral effects on the lives of Kabyle men and women. The roads throughout the region have been subject to periodic 'false roadblocks' by Islamist militias that have on occasion resulted in the slaughter of busloads of travellers. Kabyle intellectuals and artists have been the targets of death threats and violence, particularly evidenced by the May 1993 assassination of the author and journalist Tahar Djaout,[24] and the September 1994 kidnapping, and June 1998 assassination, of singer/activist Lounès Matoub. Threatened and actual lethal violence has resulted in the flight of many public figures abroad. Prolonged demonstrations in April 1995, July 1998, and April 2001 have pitted Kabyle civilians against government forces, demonstrations that in many cases have turned violent. All of this has meant an increased presence of police, gendarme, and military forces in the region whose combined effect has been to heighten a general sense of insecurity.

Given this violence, civil war politics in Kabylia has tended to operate as a dual classification system, following a strict binary logic that has alternately opposed Berberists to the state, on the one hand, and to Islamists, on the other. With the founding of the secularist RCD party after the 1989 constitutional reforms, this binary opposition has taken on a recursive character, with political life in Kabylia largely dictated by the FFS/RCD split. The FFS has consistently espoused a position of reconciliation with the outlawed Islamic Salvation Front (FIS) as the only possible means to resolving the civil war. The party was a co-signatory with the FIS of the Sant'Egidio platform which called for a negotiated, multiparty solution and a civil peace; it boycotted the 1995 presidential elections, and has consistently refused to take part in the various military governments that have ruled Algeria since 1992.[25] In contrast, the RCD took part in national elections in 1995 and 1999, and participated in the coalition government under Abdelaziz Bouteflika, who became president in 1999. More significantly, the RCD has advocated a hard-line (*éradicateur*) position that has rejected any dialogue with Islamist forces. In its literature, it has consistently opposed any 'Middle Eastern or Afghan identity' for Algeria supposedly proffered by the 'peons of the Islamist International', and instead has called upon Kabyles to rise up in 'resistance' following the 'spirit of independence' of the 'eternal Jugurtha'.[26] Moreover, it has brought this discourse to action, supporting the government's formation of 'Self-Defence Groups' (*Groupes de Légitime Défense*, GLDs – civilian militia armed by the state and charged with protecting local populations from Islamist incursions; universally referred to as 'patriots') in Kabyle villages. While these 'patriot' groups may produce a sense of agency for certain Kabyles, they have often resulted in an increase rather than decrease of violence, as they have been specifically targeted by Islamist militias and – it is alleged – even employed by corrupt mayors for private affairs of vengeance.[27]

Beyond these divergences in the enactment of civil war politics, the FFS and the RCD are understood by many Kabyles I interviewed to function as rival village clans (*lessfuf*, sing. *ssef*, '*çoffs*' in the older French ethnographic literature), as embodiments of the ritualised antagonism that is written into village social relations and spatial arrangements, and that occasionally results in violent encounters read as wars of 'honour' (*nnif*). More broadly, these *lessfuf* often come to represent, in the structuralist logic of dual classification systems, two opposed moral universes, often designated with left-hand/right-hand terminology.[28] In the case of the *lessfuf* of Kabyle politics, the FFS and RCD are firstly seen to correspond to two opposed political generations, with the FFS drawing its symbolic capital from the war of national liberation, and the RCD attempting to claim a monopoly over those who came of age in the Berber Spring. Furthermore, they are seen as having discrete territorial claims, with the FFS claiming geographical prominence in the province of Bejaïa (the eastern district of Kabylia) and the RCD dominating the *wilaya* of Tizi-Ouzou. Finally, they are seen as corresponding to two distinct classes, with the FFS drawing from the ranks of maraboutic (i.e., localised saintly) lineages, while the RCD, with its avowed secularist ideology, clearly appealing to the larger population of the laity.

Obviously, these distinctions are ideal-typic and only approximate the complex reality of civil war politics, where brothers and sisters find themselves on opposite sides of the Islamist/Berberist split, not to mention the FFS/RCD one. Nonetheless, these popular perceptions, coupled with the irreconcilable political platforms of the two parties, have resulted in the fragmentation of the MCB into factions aligned with each party, making concerted political action difficult. Indeed, although the 1994–95 school boycott did result in the government's creation of a High Amazigh Commission (HCA) to oversee the eventual introduction of Tamazight into the media and school system, it broke down prematurely – without meeting its original objectives of forcing the officialisation and nationalisation of Tamazight – due to internal strife between the MCB factions. Subsequent popular mobilisations against the state have likewise found themselves bifurcated and weakened by the constant doubling of organisational committees, marches, and demands.

In France, the Algerian civil war has clearly politicised immigrant cultural activism along similar lines of binary opposition as has taken place in Algeria. As with the first Algerian War, the civil war has played itself out on French soil in political assassinations (the 1995 assassination of FIS leader Imam Sahraoui), terrorist attacks (the summer 1995 bombings of underground railway stations and markets in Paris and Lyon, attributed to Algerian Armed Islamic Groups [*al-jama'at al-islamiyya al-musallaha/Groupes Islamiques Armés*, GIA]), and the increased militarisation of immigrant neighbourhoods.[29] At the same time, with the failure of the Beur Movement and the rise of a French neo-racism (most visible in the electoral gains of Jean-Marie Le Pen's National Front) that appropriated the Beurs' claims of a 'right to difference' in order to justify policies of exclusion and 'national preference', more and more Franco-Maghribis became alternately attracted to Islamist and Berberist movements. Both offered visions of identity and belonging that, while often posed in strict opposition to one another, shared the common trait of presenting an alternative to official (but, as ever, ambivalent) French policies of assimilation or integration. Both sought to re-suture these children of immigrants, deemed to be in a state of social and cultural disarray, to larger imagined worlds – whether an *umma* or a *Tamazgha* – that extended across the Mediterranean and beyond.

Nowhere were these divisions more evident than in the events surrounding the 1995 Algerian presidential elections. Contrasting directly with the paucity of turnout for the 1991 legislative elections that nearly brought the FIS to power, 620,000 immigrant voters, or over a third of the estimated Algerian nationals in France, turned out to vote, with a remarkable number of the younger generation exercising their double nationality.[30] In discussions at the polling places, young Franco-Algerians explained to me their decision to vote as motivated by two factors: a desire to end the violence in Algeria, and a hope to one day emigrate to a post-war Algeria for work, as there was 'nothing left' for them in France. While 65 per cent of voters in Algeria and France voted for the ruling General Liamine Zéroual, the remaining 35 per cent were split between the Berberist RCD and the 'moderate'-Islamist Hamas.[31]

As immigrant politics became increasingly factionalised between Islamist and Berberist tendencies, so too was French Kabyle politics divided along RCD/FFS lines. In the 1995 elections, both parties engaged in heavy electioneering, with the RCD pushing its candidate Said Sadi, and the FFS joining the FIS and the FLN in publicly calling for a boycott. Moreover, these political divisions came to map onto Berber cultural associations in France, with the ACB serving as the *de facto* French headquarters of the RCD, other groups like Paris-based Tamazgha remaining close to the FFS, and yet others, like MCB-France, remaining purposively non-allied. With both the FFS and RCD simultaneously having official 'immigration' wings, it is clear that the diaspora has become more than ever a central locus of Kabyle politics.

Within this context of diasporic civil war politics, the RCD (via the ACB) has proved most apt at playing the French state's game, consistently expressing an anti-Islamist position that dovetails with France's official policy of state secularism (*laïcité*). In an open letter to the candidates for the 1995 French presidential elections, the RCD wing of the MCB described the Republican school system as the 'principal instrument of integration and social promotion' and claimed that it needed to be protected against Islamist 'manipulation'.[32] Appealing to a democratic image of Berber culture drawn directly from the colonial 'Kabyle Myth',[33] the letter urged the institutional encouragement of *berbérité* as the true cultural 'soul' of North African immigrants and as the key to their future 'integration' in France. This radically anti-Islamist (indeed, anti-Islam*ic*) position was further articulated at the ACB's 1995 celebration of Tafsut mentioned above. Not only were the walls of the conference and reception rooms plastered with laminated newspaper clippings recounting recent political assassinations by the GIA, and a moment of silence was observed at the beginning of the conferences for these 'martyrs' of the recent struggle, but I was several times berated as an American citizen for my country's harbouring of 'Islamic terrorists'. The Algerian civil war, in this sense, had extended not only across the Mediterranean, but across the Atlantic as well.

The Pitfalls of Transnational Consciousness

The transnationalisation of civil war binary logic has increasingly extended beyond the France-Algeria nexus. Kabyle politics is increasingly articulated and debated over a variety of global media, from Berber satellite radio and television networks, to a variety of Berberocentric internet sites, to email list-servers like Amazigh-Net and Algeria-Net. The list-servers in particular have fostered an imagined community of Kabyles living around the world, who use the newsgroups to stay informed of recent developments in Algeria and to help formulate political positions and platforms. The interest in and access to these groups has accelerated in the ten years of their existence, with upwards of seventy email messages being posted per day to the list-servers by 2002. While Amazigh-Net is officially non-partisan, it nonetheless remains clearly biased towards a Berberist (if not *éradicateur*) narrative of the civil war, with messages supporting Islamist positions being largely excluded from the discourse.

Alongside these electronic media, Kabyle politics has been transnationalised via sports.[34] Arguably the *sine qua non* sign of membership in a putative 'Berber nation' has been support for the *Jeunesse Sportive de Kabylie* (JSK) football club. One of the premier clubs in Algerian (and African) soccer – with eleven national club championships, four Algerian Cups, two Africa Club Champions' Cups, one Africa Cup Winners' Cup, and one Africa Super Cup – the JSK has consistently been a thorn in the side of hegemonic, Arab-Islamist Algerian nationalism. Since 1977, JSK matches have been moments for the articulation of pro-Kabyle ideologies in the form of chants in Tamazight and banners written in Tifinagh. Their stadium in Tizi-Ouzou has been the site for Tafsut commemoration ceremonies and concerts by Matoub, Ferhat, and Aït-Menguellet, each of whom has written songs in the team's honour. Likewise, yellow JSK shirts have become the *de facto* uniform of protestors taking part in the 1998 and 2001 demonstrations in Kabylia against the Algerian state.

Moreover, the JSK's moral strength as an icon of Amazigh politics has transcended the borders of Algeria. Kabyle youth in France, under the aegis of various Berber cultural associations, have established local JSK supporters' clubs and parallel soccer teams, such as the ACB's FC Berbère. At the end of a match against a rival club in Drancy in February 1995, a supporter of FC Berbère, a young boy of Kabyle origin, was shot and killed. For the next year, the ACB set up a memorial to him on its premises, placing his picture alongside those of Tahar Djaout and other Kabyle 'martyrs' putatively killed by Islamists during the civil war.

Likewise, in the town of Goulmima, in the southeastern sub-Atlas region of Morocco where I have conducted ethnographic research for the last several years, JSK support has become a local phenomenon of Berber ethnic pride. Since the 1980s, if not earlier, Goulmima has been a regional centre of Amazigh activism and opposition to the monarchy. Part of the historical periphery or *bled es-siba* ('land of dissidence') that has been, according to local townspeople, in continual revolt against central power since time immemorial, Goulmima has on more than one occasion, and most recently in 1994, seen its local leaders arrested by the state police and imprisoned for their support of regionalist platforms or supposed linguistic 'sectarianism'. Such repression has merely reinforced the sense of local political solidarity, with cultural associations multiplying and Tifinagh graffiti plastering much of the public wall space. Much of the graffiti refers to the JSK, which in the case of Goulmima refers not only to the Kabyle soccer club, but also to the local team – the *Jeunesse Sportive du Ksar* – named in honour of the fortified citadel (*ksar*) that occupies the historical centre of the town. In December 2000, the Goulmima JSK won the local Ramadan tournament, a month long competition against neighbouring communes. In the stands of the championship match Amazigh flags flew high, and after the victory the yellow-jerseyed team was serenaded with an all-night celebration featuring Berber folksinging and poetry recitals. In this way, whether in its publicity via the 'Fan de JSK' website, or through participation in one of its filial clubs throughout the Berberophone world, support for the JSK has come to index the transnational dimensions of Kabyle politics.

Finally, the most dramatic case of the growth of a global 'Berber nation' was the creation of a World Amazigh Congress (*Congrès Mondial Amazigh*, CMA) in 1995. Consisting of member associations from throughout North Africa, the Sahel (the sub-Saharan rim – Mauritania, Mali, Burkina-Faso) and the diaspora (including nine European countries, the United States, and Canada), the CMA has met several times, in the Canary Islands, Lyon and Brussels in hopes of establishing 'true Amazigh sovereignty' throughout 'Tamazgha' – the imagined spatial entity encompassing all lands in which Amazigh people reside.[35] However, while clearly transnational in scope, the Congress is organised largely along national lines, with an administrative structure (executive and legislative branches) that mimic those of a nation-state, and representatives elected from each national entity. Indeed, alliances and conflicts within the Congress have largely followed such national lines, with friction occurring particularly between Moroccan and Algerian member associations. Moreover, the Congress's activities have been largely oriented towards a world of nation-states and borrow directly from the language of universalism – whether it be publicising the violation of Twareg human rights in Niger or calling for the official recognition of Tamazight as a 'national language' in Morocco and Algeria.

Furthermore, the internecine divisions within Kabyle politics have plagued the CMA. Originally established by the Paris-based association, Tamazgha, the Congress was in its early days closely aligned with the FFS. Indeed, the RCD viewed the institution as a waste of valuable time and resources that should have been prioritised towards ending the Algerian civil war and gaining Kabyle cultural rights in Kabylia proper. In this sense, it saw the CMA as effectively putting the transnational cart before the national horse, and encouraged its member association (including the ACB, and more generally the *Fédération des Associations Culturelles Amazighes de France* [FACAF]) to take no part in the Congress. However, after the relatively successful first meeting of the Congress in Tafira, especially in terms of the clear widespread international support the Congress seemed to garner, the RCD-affiliated associations sought to join the CMA and gain positions of power – a move that Tamazgha characterised as a 'usurpation' by *'Berbères de service'*, lackeys in the pay of the 'Arabo-Muslim regimes'.[36] This move fractured the CMA into two Congresses – one of officers newly elected at Lyon in 1999 and generally allied with the RCD; the other tracing historical descent from the Tamazgha-based CMA and meeting in Brussels in opposition – both claiming rights to the CMA name and institutional structure.[37] At the time of writing, these rights were being determined by a civil court in Créteil, France. Regardless of the final court decision, what is clear is that the binary logic of civil war, with its competing claims to patriotism and martyrdom, has recursively determined Kabyle (and more largely Amazigh) politics at the local, national, and transnational levels.

Lounès Matoub: A Martyr for Tamazight

Before concluding this article, I want to examine two recent instances of Kabyle martyrdom that indicate the tensions within the spatial and ideological dimensions of Kabyle politics. The first case is that of outspoken singer-activist Lounès Matoub who was assassinated on 25 June 1998 at a false roadblock near Tizi-Ouzou, and whose death sparked several weeks of riots in Kabylia.[38] In large part, the anger generated by his death derived from Matoub's unparalleled following among the younger generation of Kabyle activists, in large part because his life replicated, and stood as a symbol for, their triumphs, defeats, and hopes. Born in 1956, in the midst of the Algerian war of liberation, he was among the last to grow up with the Francophone educational system. Like many of his generation, he migrated to France in search of work, and began his singing career under the patronage of the established Kabyle singer, Idir. His first major concert took place in April 1980, at the exact moment of the Berber Spring. Wearing an army uniform on stage to show his solidarity with a Kabylia 'at war', he endeavoured to give a public concert in Kabylia on each subsequent anniversary of the 1980 events.[39]

While Matoub was never arrested – as many of his comrades were – for his explicit support of Kabyle cultural and linguistic rights, his songs, a mix of oriental *cha'abi* musical orchestration with politicised Berber (Tamazight) lyrics, were often banned from Algerian airwaves. During the October 1988 riots, he was shot five times by a policeman and left for dead at the side of a road. After the outbreak of the civil war in 1992, his name appeared on GIA hit lists with those of other artists and intellectuals. Despite these warnings, Matoub remained in Algeria and, on September 25, 1994, he was abducted, held for two weeks in a GIA mountain stronghold, condemned to death, and released only when his MCB supporters threatened 'total war' on the Islamists, and he swore an oath to discontinue his musical career. On the eve of his assassination, the 'guerrilla singer',[40] increasingly affiliated with the RCD, had just finished the final edits on a new album, *'Open Letter To...'*; in what would become a posthumous release, he pointed the finger at both the government and the Islamists for having betrayed Algeria.

A self-proclaimed rebel,[41] Matoub was the subject of deep controversy, with every aspect of his life submitted to detailed scrutiny. His abduction and assassination were both the subject of highly publicised *affaires* that threatened to tear Kabyle politics asunder. In 1996, the militant singer-songwriter Ferhat M'Henni, then president of the FFS wing of the MCB, accused Matoub of having faked his own kidnapping as part of a 'strategy for the destabilisation of Kabylia for the purposes of the clan in power'.[42] Matoub responded not only by publicly accusing Ferhat of implicitly supporting the GIA, but also by extending the same opprobrium to the unaligned singer Lounis Aït-Menguellat who had refused to comment on Ferhat's accusation. Aït-Menguellat, hailed by Kateb Yacine as Algeria's greatest poet, responded by denouncing Matoub as a 'megalomaniac' whose accusations amounted to a 'death threat' against himself and his family permanently residing, unlike Matoub, in Algeria.[43] Indeed, the 'affair' concerned not only differences in political strategy, but also claims to cultural authenticity and belonging – over the modalities of legitimately representing Kabylia.

Matoub's assassination has been subjected to similar scrutiny. While the death was originally attributed by the Algerian government to the GIA, and indeed several suspects were subsequently arrested, no closure has been brought to the case. Among many rival conspiracy theories that have been proffered since his death, the 'Algerian Free Officers' Movement' (*Mouvement Algérien des Officiers Libres*, MAOL), an expatriate group of dissident Algerian officers modelled on Nasser's movement of the 1950s and claiming to represent a substantial force within the Algerian army, posted a document on its Internet web site claiming that Matoub's death was the result of a conspiracy between the RCD and an Algerian military faction to create a martyr and provoke a generalised Kabyle uprising against Islamists. The document was widely circulated by email and became the subject of much discussion on the Amazigh-oriented list-servers. Like Mohamed Boudiaf's assassination six years' previously, Matoub's death would prove to be a Rorschach test for the younger generation of Kabyle militants.[44]

In spite of these controversies, Matoub remained an uncompromising critic of the government's Arabisation policies and consistently and publicly demanded the officialisation and nationalisation of Tamazight. This position allowed his assassination to be readily linked to the 1991 Arabic-only law that was scheduled to be implemented on 5 July 1998, the 36th anniversary of Algeria's independence and ten days after Matoub's death. The law mandated the exclusive use of Arabic in all aspects of public life (including commercial enterprises, educational facilities, the media, and associations) and called for hefty fines for all violations.[45] Given the close correspondence of these two events, it is little wonder that many Kabyle youth treated Matoub's murder as part of a longer government assault on Berber language and culture. Within hours of his death, huge crowds had gathered in Matoub's natal village and around the Mohamed Nédir Hospital in Tizi-Ouzou where his body had been taken. Yelling anti-government slogans – '*Pouvoir, Assassin*' ('Government, Assassins') – the crowd clearly laid the blame for Matoub's death at the feet of the state. In an ensuing week of riots throughout Kabyle cities and towns (Tizi Ouzou, Bejaïa, Tazmalt, Akbou, Sidi Aïch), young demonstrators attacked hundreds of regional government offices and damaged public property, often clashing with state riot police. In direct defiance of the new law, they covered Arabic signs with slogans such as '*Ass-a, Azekka. Tamazight Tella*' ('Tamazight, Today and Tomorrow'). Responding to Matoub's 'call to arms' at the end of his autobiography,[46] an amorphous group, the Armed Berber Movement, threatened in a crude leaflet not only a 'traditional' vendetta against Matoub's killers, but the wholesale 'elimination' of Algerians attempting to apply the new law. While the FFS and RCD wings of the MCB both publicly condemned such violence, they nonetheless utilised the tragedy to forge a new unity, jointly petitioning the government to abrogate the language policy.

Massinissa Guermah: A New Martyr?

While Matoub's assassination could easily be linked to Kabyle struggles more generally, and in his death he could be made a martyr for a Berberist ideology, the 18 April 2001 murder of 18-year-old Mohammed (Massinissa) Guermah was more problematically encapsulated in extant political categories.[47] Killed by a gendarme while in police custody in the village of Beni Douala, news of Guermah's death quickly transformed into public performances of explicit outrage against the state, drawing thousands of male youth into the streets of Beni Douala, Tizi Ouzou, Akbou, Amizour, Azazga, Bouira, and many other rural *douars* and urban centres throughout the region. Accusing the government (*le pouvoir*) of being 'assassins' and 'refusing pardon' (*ulac smah*) to Guermah's killers, they hurled rocks and home-made Molotov cocktails at police forces and other symbols of state power. The police response with tear gas and live ammunition launched a two-week cycle of protest and violent repression in which an estimated 60 young men were killed and as many as 300 injured in what many referred to as Kabylia's own *intifada*. While the violence eventually subsided into a 'peaceful mobilisation' – including 'black marches' (*marches noires*) of mourning and general strikes – there remained a fundamental sense that the region's political situation had irrevocably changed. As one local editorialist commented, 'Since [the death of Massinissa], nothing has been as it was before in Kabylia. In fact, nothing will be as before'.[48]

To a great extent, the form of the confrontation with police replicated that which had occurred after Matoub's death, from the targeting of state institutions (police stations, ministries, social security offices) to the kinds of slogans yelled and graffiti spray-painted. Indeed, it is highly likely that many of those who participated in the June–July 1998 riots also took part in those of April 2001. The timing of the latter violence with the 21st anniversary of the Berber Spring is clearly not coincidental, as such commemorations have often descended into violent confrontations with state agents. Indeed, one could make a strong claim that the youth on the street constituted a third generation of post-war Kabyle resistance, taking the baton from the Hocine Aït Ahmeds and Saïd Sadis.

Indeed, many were quick to make such links. Bouteflika, for one, in his first public address on the Kabyle riots, a full eleven days after the killing of Guermah, linked the violence to a history of ethnic difference, attributing it to a perdurable 'identity crisis' provoked by certain 'people fomenting divisions and separatism'. Meanwhile, both the FFS and the RCD, in an effort to reclaim the protests, attempted to portray the youths' actions within a history of state repression of Kabylia. In an interview in *Le Parisien* (22 May 2001), Sadi echoed Bouteflika's earlier statement by characterising the mobilisation as the 'consequence of an identity denial (*déni identitaire*)'. Likewise, the FFS, while denouncing Bouteflika's invocation of 'the phantom of separatism' and instead laying the blame for the violence with the 'real decision-makers' (*décideurs réels*), i.e., the military-security generals who are the real power-holders in Algeria, utilised the upheaval to address a memorandum to the government demanding, among other things, the recognition of Tamazight as an official and national language of Algeria. In the end, both parties desperately struggled to remain visible through organised marches and demonstrations throughout Algeria and the diaspora.

Similarly, diasporic Kabyles and other Amazigh communities outside of Kabylia tended to approach the insurrection through the lens of identity politics. Demonstrations in Paris, Marseille, Rabat, and elsewhere with large Berberophone communities were called to denounce the 'repression and persecution of cultural identity in Kabylia' and to express solidarity with those 'Amazigh brothers' who 'are being assassinated for [their qualities of] dignity, liberty, and Amazigh identity'. Wearing traditional Kabyle clothing and marching under banners featuring Tamazight writing and photographs of Matoub, the supporters yelled ethno-nationalist slogans such as 'Free the

Kabyles' and 'We are not Arabs'. Malika Matoub, the outspoken sister of the assassinated singer, expressed such a link to a history of ethnic struggle in perhaps the most dramatic fashion: 'Before they killed us bit by bit (*à petit feu*), but today it's a genocide!'

However, this portrayal of the events as part of a longer, *ethnic* struggle does not account for the novelty of the insurrection as perceived by local observers in Kabylia. For the young men and women who had suffered through nine years of bloody civil war, cultural claims were more often than not superseded by demands for the concrete socio-economic improvements promised by Abdelaziz Bouteflika during his 1999 presidential campaign.[49] Again and again the youth on the street made reference to a generalised state of *hogra*, of marginalisation and inequality, of a lack of justice in their everyday life, of being 'second-class citizens' (*citoyens de seconde zone*). They not only denounced the government's use of violence, but also 'refused pardon' for its corruption in the apportioning of jobs and housing. In other words, the desperation expressed by the young demonstrators was not the particular rage of a Kabyle minority, but that of an entire generation of Algerians who had grown up in an Algeria in which the glories of the war of national liberation were but a distant memory, whose only sense of patriotism was determined by socio-economic marginality and the violence of civil war.

Nonetheless, it may not be feasible to separate the ethnic from the social dimensions of the uprising. If nothing else, the activism of the MCB in the region since the early-1980s has created a widespread awareness of Kabylia's tradition of resistance, of its historical distinctiveness and marginalisation from the central state. Such a cultural awareness, combined with the larger wartime socio-economic conditions that have particularly affected Kabylia, constituted the proverbial 'powder keg' that Guermah's killing ignited. As Mounir Boudjemaa opined, 'There exists a sentiment of oppression and injustice that Berbers have always felt for authorities ... Every abuse is thus interpreted as an anti-Berber attitude'.[50]

However, the demonstrations that followed were not simply a repeat of October 1988 or July 1998, and the youth in the street in many ways arguably constituted a new generation and signalled a new epoch for Kabyle politics. In attacking government offices, taking over the streets, erecting barricades of torn up road signs and traffic lights, and even demanding papers of passing motorists, the youth symbolically asserted themselves as the new *pouvoir* in the region. This overturning of authority was not limited to that of Algiers, but targeted the hierarchies of Kabyle politics as well; in Amizour, among the government buildings ransacked and burned were the offices of the RCD and the FFS. The years of in-fighting between these parties, their respective alliances, or compromises, with the government and the Islamists, and their insistent invocations of national patriotism, had resulted in their growing loss of credibility among the younger generation. For them, the RCD's resignation from Bouteflika's government – on 1 May 2001, several weeks into the disturbances – was much too little too late.

In the place of these national and regional forms of political organisation, the Kabyle uprising embraced two alternate forms of social solidarity, one generally transnational, the other resolutely local. As a youth riot, the confrontations drew on the symbolism and stylistics not only of the October 1988 demonstrations, but of countless other uprisings pitting youth against the police that occurred throughout the 1990s in the *banlieues* of France, as well as in more exotic locations from Los Angeles to Brixton. As with these other events, the variety of globalised media (radio, TV, Internet) provided the circulation of sounds and images to the world and back to the participants themselves. For young Kabyle men and women, such circulation has underwritten an imagination of their transnational solidarity with disenfranchised youth around the globe, be they other North Africans in France or African-Americans in the United States.

Moreover, the rejection of national politics also translated into an embrace of local modes of social organisation. On 17 May 2001, representatives from scores of villages throughout Kabylia met in the small commune of Illoula to found a civil organisation designed to direct the permanent 'peaceful mobilisation' of the region in the post-riot period. Such an organisation amounted to a 'coordination'[51] of traditional village and tribal assemblies, committees of elders (or *tajmaâts*) historically responsible for collective labour, irrigation, feasts, and other group activities that require joint decision-making. The *tajmaâts*, in an unprecedented display of unanimity *vis-à-vis* the state, immediately demanded the postponement of the national high school exam in light of the dislocating effects of the month's events, the expulsion of gendarmes from the region, and the granting of the official status of 'martyr' (*chahid*, and all its concomitant benefits – thus drawing a dramatic parallel between the victims of the Algerian state's recent repression and those of the French state during the revolution) to those killed during the riots. While insisting on the international prosecution of those responsible for the violence, the coordination called for a boycott of the commission established by President Bouteflika to investigate the riots. Whereas the RCD and FFS had hitherto failed to control the rioting youth, the *tajmaâts* succeeded in preserving the peace while coordinating a series of general strikes and the enormous 'black march' on Tizi Ouzou on 21 May 2001. This march, structured around village and tribal groupings from throughout Kabylia, mobilised 500,000 people – five times the population of the city and twenty times more participants than the combined marches organised by the two parties earlier in the month. As such, while members of the coordination of *tajmaâts* claimed to be a 'civil', and not political, group, their actions succeeded in creating a level of locally-oriented popular politics hitherto unknown in the region.

In this respect, Massinissa Guermah may very well have been the first martyr of a new Kabyle political entity transnationally envisioned and locally organised. If the independent Algerian nation-state ideologically created a 'cult of the martyr' for those who gave their lives in the war of national liberation, the new Kabylia has likewise imagined itself into being through the process of creating its own icons through 'black marches' and candlelight vigils. For the April 2001 demonstrators, the blame for the economic and physical violence of the civil war was laid clearly on the shoulders of the *pouvoir* in all of its now morally bankrupt guises – military, Islamist, and even Berberist.

Conclusion

The martyrdoms of Matoub and Guermah point to a set of unresolved tensions between ethnic, national, and transnational dimensions of Kabyle politics exacerbated by the Algerian civil war. On the one hand, Kabyle politics have become more and more transnationally organised, with political parties and cultural movements drawing their strength and coordination increasingly from a diasporic population that includes growing numbers of political refugees and expatriate artists and intellectuals. On the other hand, the civil war has enlarged the rift between the quotidian realities of life in wartime Kabylia and the larger ideological goals of the political parties and cultural movements that claim to represent it. Unemployed Kabyle *hittistes* (literally 'wall-hangers') have the patience neither for the internecine binarisms that partition political goods along FFS/RCD lines nor for the invocations of an imaginary, supranational 'Tamazgha' that presumably exists from the Canary Islands to the Siwa oasis in Egypt. Each of these local, national, and transnational levels outlines a different rendition of Kabyle politics, each defining its own martyrs and its own patriots.

NOTES

My thanks to Genevieve Bell and Jane Goodman, who read and provided feedback on various drafts and earlier versions of this article.

1. Berber speakers make up an estimated 25 per cent of Algeria's population. Other major concentrations of berberophones are found in the Aurès mountains, in the Tassili/Ahaggar of the far south, and in the Mzab of the central Algerian pre-Sahara. Berberophone communities also exist elsewhere in the Sahara (Gourara, Ngousa, Ghat) and in the Dahra/Chenoua area on the coast to the west of Algiers, between Cherchel and Tenes.
2. Salem Chaker, *Berbères aujourd'hui*. Second Edition (Paris: Harmattan 1998) p.36.

3. Mohammed Harbi, 'Nationalisme algérien et identité berbère', *Peuples Méditerranéens* 11 (April–June 1980) p.33.
4. See Omar Carlier, 'Note sur la crise berbériste de 1949', *Annuaire de l'Afrique du Nord* XXIII (1984) pp.347–71. For a more nuanced discussion of the place of Berber identity in the Algerian national narrative, see James McDougall, 'Myth and Counter-Myth: "the Berber" as National Signifier in Algerian Historiographies', *Radical History Review* 86, (forthcoming).
5. The most significant attacks on Mammeri were Mostefa Lacheraf, '*La Colline oubliée* ou les consciences anachroniques', *Le Jeune Musulman* (13 February 1953) and Mohammed Sahli, 'La colline du reniement', *Le Jeune Musulman* (2 January 1953); on this affair, see Colonna, this volume. Abbane Ramdane, a brilliant and controversial figure, was the political architect of the interior FLN in 1955–56, and the prime mover in the Soummam congress. He was murdered by his military colleagues in December 1957 – a death announced in the FLN's organ *El Moudjahid* (the following May) as having occurred 'in the field of honour', and only generally known to have been at the hands of the FLN itself much later. Krim Belkacem was one of the historic founder-leaders of the FLN, one of the earliest Kabyle *maquisards* and later Foreign Minister for the wartime Algerian Provisional Government. Implicated in Ramdane's death, he went into exile after 1965 and was himself murdered in Frankfurt in 1970. On the internecine violence in the upper echelons of the FLN, see also Benjamin Stora, *La gangrène et l'oubli* (Paris: La Découverte 1991) pp.156–71; 'Ceux qui ont levé le glaive', *Le Nouvel Observateur* (10–16 May 2001) pp.40–1.
6. See Frantz Fanon, *The Wretched of the Earth* (New York: Grove Press 1963) p.89.
7. While I do not have the space to pursue this point, there is a fascinating gendering of nationalist ideology as masculine. While women were certainly incorporated as active participants in the war of national liberation, the post-war discourse on martyrdom has historically relegated women's roles to the domestic sphere of mourning/memorialising their fallen male 'brothers'. On the role of women in the national liberation struggle, see Djamila Amrane, *Les femmes algériennes dans la guerre* (Paris: Plon 1991); Frantz Fanon, 'Algeria Unveiled', in his *A Dying Colonialism* (New York: Grove Press 1965) pp.35–67. (For instructively comparable developments in Morocco, see Kozma, this volume). For recent examples of women's public mourning (in this case following the 1998 assassination of Lounès Matoub), see Malika Matoub, *Matoub Lounès, mon frère* (Paris: Albin Michel 1999); Nadia Matoub, *Pour l'amour d'un rebelle* (Paris: Robert Laffont 2000). For an attempt to create a counter-discourse of female Algerian patriotism, see Louisa Hanoune, *Une autre voix pour l'Algérie* (Paris: La Découverte 1996); Khalida Messaoudi, *Une algérienne debout* (Paris: Flammarion 1995). For a critique of the 'new man' ideology in the spheres of culture and language, see Mohamed Benrabah, *Langue et pouvoir en Algérie. Histoire d'un traumatisme linguistique* (Paris: Séguier, 1999); for an influential statement of the ideology itself, by a notable Minister (at different times) of both Education and Culture, see Ahmed Taleb Ibrahimi, *De la Décolonisation à la Révolution Culturelle, 1962–1972* (Algiers: SNED 1973).
8. Malek Bennabi, *Les conditions de la renaissance. Problèmes d'une civilisation* (Algiers: Mosquée des Etudiants de l'Université d'Alger 1948); Mohamed Sadek Benyahia, 'Les mutations psychologiques dans la révolution algérienne', *Révolution africaine* 316 (1970) p.26. For a further discussion of the Algerian mythification of the war, see Stora (note 5) pp.161–72.
9. Ernest Renan, 'What is a Nation?', in Homi Bhabha (ed.), *Nation and Narration* (London: Routledge 1990) p.11. In addition to the Berberist/Arab nationalist struggle, the official representation of the war erased the memory of those 200,000 Algerian Muslims estimated killed during the bloody internal civil war between forces of the FLN's National Liberation Army (ALN) and the rival nationalist militia, the Algerian National Movement (MNA) of Messali Hadj, as well as the massacres of *harkis* – Algerian Muslims recruited as supplementary counter-insurgency troops for the French war effort – by the ALN. For statistics on wartime losses, see Stora (note 5) p.183. For the complexities of the case of the *harkis*, see Mohand Hamoumou, 'Les *harkis*, un trou de mémoire franco-algérien', *Esprit*

(May 1990) pp.25–45.

10. *Amazigh*, pl. *imazighen*, is today the generally current Berber name for Berberophones throughout North Africa and in the diaspora. The Berberophone dialects are collectively called *Tamazight* and 'the Berber land' (on which see further *infra*) is referred to as *Tamazgha*. 'Amazigh' can also be a personal name. On its etymology, see Salem Chaker, 'Amazi' (Amazigh), "le/un Berbère" ', in *Encyclopédie Berbère* (Aix-en-Provence: Edisud, several volumes, 1987–), Vol. IV, pp.562–68 (Editor's note).

11. Lounès Matoub, *Rebelle* (Paris: Stock 1995) pp.27–35; A. Cheminy Shamy, *Orgueilleuse Kabylie. La vie et la guerre* (Paris: Harmattan 1995).

12. University courses in Berber linguistics (in place since the colonial period) were eliminated, the public and literary use of Berber was outlawed, and a disproportionate number of Islamic institutes were established in Berberophone areas. For analyses of Algeria's post-independence linguistic struggles and Arabisation policies, see Gilbert Grandguillaume, *Arabisation et politique linguistique au Maghreb* (Paris: Maisonneuve et Larose 1983); Anne-Emanuelle Berger (ed.), *Algeria in Others' Languages* (Ithaca: Cornell University Press 2002).

13. Chaker (note 2) p.67.

14. Karima Direche-Slimani, *Histoire de l'émigration kabyle en France au XXe siècle. Réalités culturelles et réappropriations identitaires*. Thèse de doctorat. (Aix-en-Provence: Université de Provence 1992) p.118.

15. Salem Chaker, 'Berbérité et émigration kabyle', *Peuples Méditerranéens* 31–32 (1985) p.222.

16. For more complete discussions of the impact of the Berber Spring and its relationship to the 'minority' politics of 'Berberism', see Chaker (note 2) pp.51–64; Bruce Maddy-Weitzman, 'The Berber Question in Algeria: Nationalism in the Making?', in Ofra Bengio and Gabriel Ben-Dor (eds.), *Minorities and the State in the Arab World* (Boulder: Lynne Rienner 1999) pp.31–52; Bruce Maddy-Weitzman, 'Contested Identities: Berbers, "Berberism" and the State in North Africa', *The Journal of North African Studies* 6/3 (2001) pp.23–47; Mordechai Nisam, *Minorities in the Middle East. A History of Struggle and Self-Expression* (Jefferson, NC: McFarland 1991) pp.45–62. For an alternative interpretation, stressing the socio-economic bases of Kabyle dissent at the time of the Berber Spring and offering a critique of the notion of a 'Berber question', see Hugh Roberts, 'Towards an Understanding of the Kabyle Question in Contemporary Algeria', *The Maghreb Review* 5/5–6 (September–December 1980) pp.115–124.

17. The term 'Beur' has two possible origins: first, a syllabic inversion of *arabe* according to the vernacular linguistic form *verlan*; second, an abbreviation of *'Berbères d'Europe'*. The former interpretation is more widely accepted in the scholarly literature. Since the 1980s, the term Beur, and its corresponding ideology of hybridity, has been largely disavowed by Franco-Maghribis. For an extended discussion of the Beur Movement, see Farid Aïchoune (ed.), *La Beur Génération* (Paris: Arcantère 1985); Alec Hargreaves, *Immigration, 'Race' and Ethnicity in Contemporary France* (New York: Routledge 1995); Adil Jazouli, *L'action collective des jeunes maghrébins de France* (Paris: CIEMI/Harmattan 1986). For a comparison of the Beur Movement and the Berber cultural movement, see Paul Silverstein, 'Realizing Myth: Berbers in France and Algeria', *Middle East Report* 200 (Summer 1996) pp.11–15.

18. See Radio-Beur, *Octobre à Alger* (Paris: Seuil 1988).

19. A legendary female Berber chieftain supposed to have led Berber resistance to the Arab conquest in the 7th century.

20. The principal mountain range forming the geographical heartland of Kabylia.

21. Created in October 1987, and later absorbed into the increasingly commercial Radio Beur/Beur FM, Radio Tiwizi's name derives from the collective labour (*tiwizi*) that seasonally marks Kabyle village life.

22. In 1991, a large number of these associations were confederated into the *Fédération des Associations Culturelles Amazighes de France* (FACAF) under the aegis of the ACB and the Algerian Rally for Culture and Democracy (RCD) political party.

23. For informed discussions of the civil war in its political and economic dimensions, see William B. Quandt, *Between Ballots and Bullets* (Washington: Brookings Institution Press 1998); Martin Stone, *The Agony of Algeria* (New York: Columbia University Press 1997); Benjamin Stora, *La guerre invisible. Algérie, années 90* (Rabat: Centre Tarik Ibn Zyad 2001).

24. For one intellectual's own reflection on this violence, see Djaout's own, passionate last work, *Le Dernier Été de la Raison* (Paris: Seuil 1999), which he was writing just before his murder and which was published posthumously (Editor's Note).

25. On the (highly controversial, and ultimately doomed) Sant'Egidio conclave and the declaration that resulted, see Hugh Roberts, 'Algeria's Ruinous Impasse and the Honourable Way Out', *International Affairs* 71/2 (1995) pp.247–267 (Editor's note).

26. Pamphlet entitled '20 avril 1995: 15 ans de lutte ininterrompue' by the RCD-Immigration. The 'eternal Jugurtha' recalls the Numidian King of the 2nd century BCE, who (after rendering distinguished service to Rome) ultimately came into conflict with the empire and fought the war remembered under his name (thanks to the Roman historian Sallust). He would later become an emblem of struggle for liberty, notably through the nationalist pamphlet of Mohamed Chérif Sahli, *Le Message de Yougourtha* (Algiers: Imprimerie Générale 1947), and he symbolised an 'African personality' for the Kabyle poet Jean Amrouche, 'L'Éternel Jugurtha. Propositions sur le Génie Africain', *L'Arche* (an important but ephemeral Algiers literary review), (February 1946) pp.58–70. See also Tassadit Yacine, 'La revendication berbère', *Intersignes* 10 (July–December 1995) p.102.

27. José Garçon, La dérive sanglante des milices en Algérie, *Libération*, 15 April 1998.

28. On Kabyle *lessfuf*, see Mohand Khellil, *La Kabylie ou l'Ancêtre sacrifié* (Paris: Harmattan 1984) pp.33–4. For the anthropological literature on dual classification systems, see Claude Lévi-Strauss, 'Do Dual Organizations Exist?', *Structural Anthropology* (New York: Basic Books 1963) pp.132–66. For right-hand/left-hand dualism in Berber societies, see David Hart, 'Right and Left in the Atlas Mountains: Dual Symbolic Classifications Among the Moroccan Berbers', *The Journal of North African Studies* 4/3 (1999) pp.30–44.

29. Extended police round-ups (*rafles*) of suspected Islamist militants occurred after the 1995 bombings, preceding the 1998 World Cup, and, more recently, immediately following the 11 September 2001 attacks. In addition, heavily immigrant-populated *banlieues* (suburban areas of high-density, low-income housing) have become increasingly subject to police and military surveillance. In February 1999, socialist prime minister Lionel Jospin activated 13,000 riot police (CRS) and 17,000 military gendarmes to patrol several hundred such areas deemed 'sensitive urban zones' (*zones urbaines sensibles*). Patricia Tourancheau, 'Police de proximité cherche effectifs', *Libération*, 13–14 Februay 1999.

30. This exercise of double nationality was remarked as 'scandalous' by Farid Smahi, president of the integrationist group, *Arabisme et Francité*, who warned that it threatened to transform immigrant France into a series of miniature Gaza Strips. Farid Smahi, 'Plaidoyer contre la bi-nationalité', *Le Figaro*, 20 October 1995.

31. Not to be confused with its Palestinian namesake (*Harakat al-muqawama al-islamiyya*, the Islamic Resistance Movement), *shaykh* Mahfoud Nahnah's Algerian Hamas (originally the *Haraka li'l-mujtama' al-islami*, Movement for an Islamic Society) has more recently renamed itself *Harakat mujtama' al-silm*, the Movement of a Society of Peace, or MSP (*Mouvement de la Société de la Paix*) (Editor's note).

32. The RCD/ACB thus situated itself in the camp of the radical secularists against the legality of the headscarf in the French school system. For an articulation of this position, see Messaoudi (note 7). (The wearing of marks of religious distinction is a major tabu in France's politics of education; a major row erupted in the mid-1980s over whether Muslim girls should be permitted to wear headscarves – *foulards* – in school, a dispute which continued to run through the 1990s).

33. The 'Kabyle Myth' refers to a set of colonial discourses about the relative assimilability of 'Berbers' to French norms. See Charles-Robert Ageron, 'La France a-t-elle eu une politique kabyle?', *Revue Historique* 223–4 (1960) pp.311–52; Patricia M.E. Lorcin, *Imperial Identities* (London: I.B. Tauris 1995); Paul A. Silverstein, 'The Kabyle Myth: The

Production of Ethnicity in Colonial Algeria', in Brian Keith Axel (ed.), *From the Margins: Historical Anthropology and Its Futures* (Durham, NC: Duke University Press 2002) pp.122–55.

34. For a more detailed analysis of the relationship of sport to Amazigh consciousness, see Paul Silverstein, 'Stadium Politics: Sport, Islam and Amazigh Consciousness in France and North Africa', in Tara Magdalinski and Timothy Chandler (eds.), *With God on Their Side: Sport in the Service of Religion* (London: Routledge 2002) pp.37–70.

35. 'Final Declaration of the 2nd World Amazigh Congress', cited in Maddy-Weitzman, 'Contested Identities' (note 16) p.43.

36. Congrès Mondial Amazighe (Tamazgha), 'Halte aux manoeuvres anti-amazighes des usurpateurs de notre organisation' (21 July 2002), www.tamurt-imazighen.com/tamazgha/ [Accessed on 5 Sept. 2002].

37. Ironically, the CMA's internal history thus almost parallels that of the PPA/MTLD in 1953 (Editor's note).

38. For a more complete analysis of Matoub's assassination, see Zighen Aym, 'Tamazight Lost Its Popular Singer and Activist', *The Amazigh Voice* 7/3 (Fall 1998) pp.5–6; Paul A. Silverstein, '"The Rebel is Dead, Long Live the Martyr!" Kabyle Mobilisation and the Assassination of Lounès Matoub', *Middle East Report* 28/3 (1998) pp.3–4.

39. Indeed, one of his last major concerts was during Tafsut 1996 at the Palais du Congrès in Paris. During the concert, Matoub welcomed onstage one by one virtually the entire royalty of the expatriate community of Kabyle cultural producers in France.

40. 'Maquisard de la chanson', the title given by the Kabyle author Kateb Yacine to Matoub's generation of political folk singers.

41. Matoub (note 11) p.16,40–3.

42. *Le Monde*, 31 May 1996.

43. *Le Monde*, 6 June 1996.

44. William B. Quandt (note 23) p.64. Boudiaf, a prime mover in the founding of the FLN in 1954 and one of the last surviving *chefs historiques* of the War of Independence, returned from exile in 1992 and promised the reform and restoration of the state – he was shot dead by one of his bodyguard during a visit to Annaba in June of the same year. For a discussion of conspiracy theory as a salient epistemological modality during the civil war, see Paul A. Silverstein, 'An Excess of Truth: Violence, Conspiracy Theory, and the Algerian Civil War', *Anthropological Quarterly* 75/4 (Autumn 2002) pp.641–72.

45. Originally signed on 16 January 1991 by President Chadli Benjedid and designed to go into effect on 5 July 1994, the law was frozen by his successor Mohamed Boudiaf just prior to the latter's assassination.

46. 'I call for resistance... It is not only with words that one must stop terrorism, but with arms.' Matoub (note 11) p.279.

47. For a more complete analysis of Guermah's death and the ensuing insurrection, see Farid Aïchoune and René Backman, 'Algérie: l'explosion kabyle', *Le Nouvel Observateur*, 10–16 May 2001, pp.34–41; Paul Silverstein, '"No Pardon": Rage and Revolt in Kabylia', *Middle East Insight* 16/4 (2001) pp.61–65.

48. Hacène Ouandjeli, 'Erreurs coupables', *Liberté*, 24 May 2001.

49. Aïchoune and Backman (note 47) p.37.

50. *Le Quotidien d'Oran*, 1 May 2001.

51. *Coordination des aarouch, daïras et communes*, CADC.

Moroccan Women's Narratives of Liberation: A Passive Revolution?

LIAT KOZMA

Beginning in the early 1980s, Moroccan feminist authors started rewriting Moroccan national history as part of their struggle for equality. They challenged women's exclusion from dominant historiographies of the national struggle for independence, introduced women into this historiography and represented national heroines as feminist ones. At the beginning of the 1990s, when some of their demands for equality in law and in practice had been met, their historiography was also incorporated into the hegemonic narrative. Against the background of this social and political context, how ought we to understand feminist historiography in Morocco? How do we understand the incorporation of women into dominant historiography?

Several scholars have pointed to the gendered nature of national discourse and national historiography. Deniz Kandiyoti, for example, has shown the ambiguous role women play in national discourse in the Middle East, as agents of modernisation on the one hand and as bearers of tradition and national authenticity on the other.[1] Partha Chatterjee, in his research on Indian nationalism's discourse on women, analysed its ambiguous interaction with the discursive system of colonialism. Colonial administrators equated national 'backwardness' with the 'backwardness' of women, and South Asian nationalist intellectuals thus presented the liberation of women as part of the struggle for independence and nation building. At the same time, these male intellectuals perceived feminist ideas as European, identified them with colonial rule and saw them as contradictory to cultural authenticity. While women were ascribed the role of bearers of tradition and national authenticity, men were allowed to adopt a Western model of modernisation. Similar perspectives were adopted by Arab/Muslim intellectuals such as Qasim Amin in British-colonised Egypt and Tahar Haddad in French-colonised Tunisia.[2] This scholarly focus on colonial and local dominant discourses, however useful to our understanding of modern nationalism in colonial and post colonial societies, ascribes agency only to colonialist administrators and an indigenous male elite, not to indigenous women, nor to non-elite actors, whether men or women.

112

Recently, research which has focused on Western societies has highlighted the use of historiography by feminist academics and activists. Women's movements encouraged and led the writing of women's history, before, concurrently and in tension with academic historiography initiated by founders of women's studies in the universities.[3] Feminist activists demanded historiography that would provide heroines and historical examples, prove that women are capable of political activity, explain the roots of women's oppression and inspire political and feminist activism.[4] The main weakness of these works, however, is that they present both national and feminist historiographies as static, ahistorical and isolated from each other. They ignore the dialogue and the constant struggle in historiographic discourse, the constant dynamic that leads to historical and historiographic change.

In this article, I examine the historiographic struggle that has taken place over Moroccan women's participation in the national struggle for independence. I present this as a dynamic tension between dominant national historiography, which is used to justify discrimination against women in Morocco, and feminist historiography, which integrates women into the struggle for independence, attempting to legitimise and justify social change and to present feminism as an authentic part of Moroccan culture. Tension and dialogue between these versions of the past have changed the dominant national historiography, and led to the incorporation of women into dominant narratives. At the same time, the criticism embedded in feminist historiography has been numbed, neutralised by its incorporation into the dominant national narrative, which remains a vehicle of elite and patriarchal norms focused on the role and position of the monarchy.

My argument is based on the following premises. First, as Hayden White argued so long ago, historiography is based on an arbitrary selection of past events and their integration or emplotment into a narrative. Our perception of past events is thus constantly changing, as we integrate them into different wholes and different narratives. The emplotment the historian chooses and his or her ideology would determine, to a large extent, the narrative he or she creates. This choice is often moral or aesthetic, argues White, not necessarily epistemological. The professional historian is thus not necessarily more reliable than others, and oral history is not a priori more or less authentic than other versions of the past.[5]

This premise allows us, firstly, to present dominant and feminist historiographies as constructions, as different choices of narrative strategy to describe the same events. It warns us against the essentialist dichotomy between a masculine historiography and a feminine one, the former necessarily oppressive while the latter would be necessarily liberating, uncovering 'the' authentic voice of women. Furthermore, it enables us to see

113

historiography as a social, rather than merely an academic, process. As a first principle, it thus allows analysis of a wide, if not comprehensive, array of historiographic versions as operating within overlapping discursive fields.

Second, a historical narrative, as we all know, is the product of an interaction between the reality a historian is writing about and his or her own lived reality. This fact reminds us that we must consider both national and feminist historiographies examined here in the context of political realities in Morocco in the 1980s and the 1990s, and in the context of transformations in the lives of women as a social and political group. Following Scott, I examine a case in which it is the feminist movement which allows the visibility of women as an historical category.[6]

These two premises lead me to a third, which sees historiographic change as an outcome of hegemonic struggle. Following Antonio Gramsci, Raymond Williams defined hegemony as a system of social understandings which naturalises a certain social order – in our case, patriarchal power relations between men and women – and turns it into a part of our 'common sense'. Certain practices would be thus constructed as legitimate, while others will be presented as unthinkable, or unsayable. Hegemony defines what will be seen as common sense, and what will be seen as nonsense.[7]

In a hegemonic system there is an inherent tension and a constant struggle. Social groups which experience a gap between their own perceptions of their lived reality and its hegemonic representation would try to expose the social mechanisms which underlie the dominant social order and to present an alternative interpretation or world view. One of the alternatives in this system, but not the only one, is the 'emergent', which embodies new and diverse meanings, values and relations. The emergent is usually related to the emergence of a new social structure, a new class, or a new class consciousness. Social change, claim Williams and Gramsci, occurs through 'passive revolution'. Dominant groups try to incorporate groups which demand social change, in order to preserve their domination, to weaken these groups and to neutralise the threat they pose. In this process, and in spite of themselves, they bring about historical change.[8]

Historiography plays an important role in this process. Dominant groups use selective versions of the past to justify existing power relations. They choose what will be presented as 'archaic' and what will be presented as 'historical continuity'. Counter-hegemonic groups, claims Williams, use historiography to challenge the 'naturalness' of the prevailing social order and offer alternative understandings of the past. This is also a struggle about legitimacy to talk about the past: who can testify about past events, who shall represent them, who has the authority to narrate them. When the emergent group manages to expose the mechanisms that make hegemonic power seem natural, it threatens it.[9]

Moroccan feminist historiography, I argue, was the product of an emergent group of educated middle class women who used historiography to justify feminist social change. Changes in women's status in Morocco, beginning in the late 1970s, led to the emergence of a stratum of educated women, who experienced a gap between their own self-view, their skills and education, on the one hand, and the reigning discrimination against them in the Personal Status Code, in the job market, and in their exclusion from national politics, on the other. Particularly central to the feminist agenda in Morocco are the Personal Status Code and the exclusion of women from decision-making positions. The Personal Status Code (*mudawwanat al-ahwal al-shakhsiyya*) is based on the prescriptions of the Maliki school, one of the four schools of Islamic law, the one historically dominant in North Africa and also the strictest on women's status. According to the law, codified in 1958, two years after Morocco's independence, a woman is legally considered a minor throughout her life. Her legal guardian is to sign her marriage contract; the law further requires her father's or husband's consent before she can conduct any financial transactions, work outside the home or obtain a passport. Men have a monopoly over divorce and are allowed to marry up to four women.[10] Women were not represented in Morocco's national political arena until 1993.

Feminist historiography explicitly saw it as its goal to challenge this exclusion. In the introduction to their book *Femmes et Politique*, published on the eve of the 1993 elections, journalists Narjis Rarheye and Latifa Akharbach argued that their goal was to find precedents for women's participation in politics and to show that there is no contradiction between women and politics; hence to show that women can participate in political activism and even be elected to parliament:

> Of the Moroccans who are now 20 to 30 years of age, most of whom are going to vote for the first time in these coming elections, how many know about women's presence in the resistance movement, or about their activism since independence, within the political parties? The history that was written is masculine, and the present offers very little occasion for women to transcend their anonymity.[11]

These demands for social change were perceived in dominant discourse as importations of Western ideology and thus as contradictory to Morocco's cultural heritage. In national historiography, practices of discrimination against women were presented as being in continuity with history and tradition, as 'heritage'. In response, feminist thinkers tried to appropriate the struggle for national independence and to include women in the narratives of this crucial historical period. Through feminist historiography they tried to present women's participation in national politics as an integral part of Moroccan national heritage, and discrimination against them as a deviation from it. They presented women's absence from dominant versions of the past as a false construction, as a deliberate attempt to remove feminist demands from the national agenda, against which they set out to construct their own narrative.

The Palace eventually tried to incorporate this feminist writing and activism in Morocco and hence made a bid to weaken and neutralise it. The dominant narrative changed, and so did the feminist one. At the same time, the demands of women's movements to amend women's legal subordination were appropriated by the King. By appropriating women's demands to his own agenda, the King effectively prevented any radical reform in the status of Moroccan women. Before discussing this historiographic struggle itself, however, we must first consider the background to it – the emergence of a Moroccan national historiography, beginning in the 1960s, against a previously dominant colonial one. This historiography shaped the framework for the later emergence of a counter-hegemonic, feminist historiography.

Hegemonic Moroccan Historiography

More than any other event in modern Moroccan history, the struggle for national independence is used to justify the contemporary political order, and especially the status of the monarchy and the political system over which it presides. In the centre of the dominant historiography of nationalism is the figure of Sultan (later King) Muhammad V, who turned himself into the emblem of an anti-colonial liberation struggle which subsequently came to be known as 'the revolution of the King and the people' (*thawrat al-malik wa'l-sha'b*). The deportation of the sultan into exile by the French protectorate authorities on 20 August 1953 further strengthened his status, and the date is still commemorated as a national holiday in Morocco. The King's participation in the national struggle is noted as one of the cores of the monarchy's legitimacy, alongside the King's religious status as the Commander of the Faithful (*amir al-mu'minin*), his *baraka* (charisma), his ancestry as a member of the 'Alawi dynasty (Morocco's ruling dynasty since 1664), and his family's *sharifi* status as descendants of the Prophet Muhammad.[12]

Beginning in the 1960s, Moroccan historians wrote works that would serve as an antithesis to French colonial narratives and thus 'decolonise history', paraphrasing Algerian historian Mohamed Chérif Sahli.[13] Their declared goal was to confiscate Moroccan historiography from French authors, monopolising it, and change the historical narrative itself. While French colonial historiography was used to justify colonial domination, Moroccan historiography written in the 1960s and 1970s stressed its Arab and independent nature. Colonial historiography presented Morocco as a backward country, 'a sleeping beauty' awaiting French occupation to rescue it from stagnation and marginality. In colonial historiography, it was Islam that condemned Morocco to backwardness, and the colonial mission was to salvage it. Moroccan historians, on the other hand, argued for Islamic continuity in Morocco, and presented French colonialism as a painful rupture in Moroccan history. While French historiography presented historical antagonism between Berber and Arab communities, in an attempt to align the Berbers with the French and exclude the Arabs, Moroccan historiography presented an historical alliance between these two ethnic communities.[14]

This Moroccan historiography itself had its own gaps, and thus its own counter-histories. As Burke has argued, nationalist historiography ascribed agency in the struggle for independence mainly to the male elite. Peasants, women and minorities were not included in this narrative, or were described as brave, but lacking any political importance. Moroccans who co-operated with the colonial authorities, Moroccan soldiers who served in the French army and French colonists were excluded from this narrative as well. The interests of the elite were presented as the general interest, and ethnic, tribal, gender and class conflicts within the national movement were also excluded. In this dominant version of the past, independence guaranteed economic and social justice for all. Class struggle, or feminist struggle, are thus presented as redundant.[15]

The Emergence of Feminist Historiography

Women became thinkable as subjects of historical research in Morocco only in the 1980s, with the emergence of an economic and political group of educated, middle class women. This emergence in turn was an outcome of transformations in women's education, their presence in the labour market, and, concurrently, their emergence as holders of some economic, cultural and political power. Thus, for example, women's high school attendance increased from 10 per cent in 1971 to 16 per cent in 1982 and to 24 per cent in 1990, while the percentage of women in the universities increased from 1.2 per cent in 1971 to 2.7 per cent in 1982 and to 6.4 per cent in 1991. At the same time, labour market participation of women at the ages of 24–35 increased from 14.2 per cent in 1971 to 27.6 per cent in 1982 and then to 36.6 per cent in 1990. The marked increase in women's education and labour market participation was accompanied by a rise in the average age of first marriages and decreasing birth rates. Thus, for example, the average age of first marriage in Moroccan cities sharply increased from 17.5 in 1960, to 20.9 in 1970, to 23.2 in 1982 and then to 25 in 1992. At the same time, the average number of children per woman declined from 7.4 in 1973 to 5.9 in 1979, to 4 in 1989 and then to 3.4 in 1992.[16] Women married later and produced smaller families than had their mothers. These transformations created a group of young, educated, single women, who were both producers and consumers of feminist writings. These women experienced a growing gap between their skills and education on the one hand, and their inferior legal status, their exclusion from politics, and their subordination in education and in the labour market, on the other.[17]

This transformation created new frameworks for women's writing and for writing about women. Women left the political parties, founded independent organisations and edited independent magazines like *8 mars* and *Nisa' al-Maghrib*; independent journalists left the commercial press and founded *Kalima* magazine; scholars educated in foreign universities wrote their dissertations about women, returned to Morocco and founded women's studies centres.[18] Women became visible in history, and women's history became a tool in a political struggle.

The authors of the texts I will examine were part of this generation, of this emergent group, and used platforms created from the 1980s onwards – feminist magazines and a feminist publishing house. The authors are journalists, novelists and academics. Most of them were born in the 1950s, pursued higher education in the 1970s and 1980s, and took part in the creation of these new frameworks for feminist writing. The story of women's participation in the national struggle for independence was not written by its participants themselves, but by another generation of women; at times, even their own daughters.

In Morocco, as in other societies, feminism is presented as a foreign element. It is associated with sexual liberalism and with the dismantling of family values, as an 'anti-men' ideology.[19] This position, grounded in dominant historiographies as well as in religio-ethical and cultural-authenticist discourses, is used to delegitimise feminist demands for equality, and feminist thinkers thus ascribe considerable importance to counter-histories in legitimising their demands. When hegemonic narratives present patriarchy and the exclusion of women as a natural historical continuity, and feminism as an unnatural historical rupture, a deviation from 'the heritage', feminist authors present feminism as itself ingrained in this same national heritage. They try to present an indigenous genealogy of feminism and trace famous women in history and in folklore.

In his article 'Feminism in Morocco,' published in *Lamalif* magazine, Abdessamad Dialmy, one of Morocco's leading feminist thinkers, defined historiography as one of the missions of the feminist intellectual. Using Gramsci's concept of the 'organic intellectual', Dialmy saw the discovery of continuity, of 'traditional' origins for ideological modernity, as one of the goals of Moroccan feminists, and urged feminist intellectuals to write national history in a way that would illustrate the national nature of feminism in the Maghrib.[20]

Locating Women in the National Past

How do feminist authors see the role ascribed to women in dominant historiography? To which sites of history and memory do they refer? How do they analyse the role of historiography in perpetuating the *status quo*? These authors, I suggest, recognise that dominant nationalist ideology renders women invisible in history; they point to the role of historiography in perpetuating patriarchal domination. They refuse to accept the authority of the historian who argues, like the anonymous one quoted by Salwa al-Shaykh Fulus, that 'women never participated in anything, and never did anything'.[21] Fulus wrote her article in response to one by *al-Alam* editor Abd al-Karim Ghulab, 'Do we judge men, or do we judge history?' in which he discussed the historian's right to judge historical figures. Ghulab takes it for granted, claims Fulus, that men 'make political history, through war, government or politics'. Fulus presents this kind of historical judgement as biased and hence problematic: the Moroccan woman is judged by a historian of the opposite gender; he underestimates her contribution, does not see her as part of history, and sees, instead, the writing of her story as a defilement of her honour.[22] Journalist Touria Hadraoui, in an article published in the feminist magazine *Kalima*, argues that while many women put their hearts and souls into the struggle, 'paradoxically, none of them was saved from oblivion and none managed to cross the barrier of silence. Is it because our memory is more sensitive and more loyal to the harmony of masculine names, or is there an intention to erase the feminine reality from everyday life?'[23]

Feminist thinkers altogether condemn women's absence from dominant narratives and from hegemonic sites of memory (in Pierre Nora's sense of the term[24]), but different authors locate this absence in different places. *Kalima* journalist Touria Hadraoui locates it in street names, and argues that naming streets after female veterans 'could have served as a modest rehabilitation for these extraordinary individuals who gave so much to their country'.[25] Fulus examined lists compiled by the Higher Commission of Veterans of the Struggle and Members of the Liberation Army, which she defined as an institution which is supposed to 'honour the martyrs and serve those who are still living'. 'The names of women in all the official lists and tables submitted to me can be counted on one's fingers,' she observes, and 'at the same time, I am certain that the memory of many Moroccans is loaded with other names, names that oblivion could not erase.'[26] Sites of memory such as these lists have symbolic, but also practical importance. Official recognition is often accompanied by financial benefits and government positions. Malika al-Asimi argues:

> I could easily find many hypocrites and traitors who did not even participate in the struggle, now in high positions, swaggering with their decorations ... I did not find among them even a single female fighter donning any decoration following national independence. I did not find even one female *muqaddam*, nor any female activist, listed among recipients of special government pensions. Their activism was not recognised in history and they were not given any pension ... This way, historical justice was denied to women.[27]

Asma Benadada locates women's absence from national memory in history books about the struggle. She lists works written in, and outside of, Morocco which do not mention women's participation in the national struggle for independence, or which give it only a passing reference. 'How do we account for these authors' silence about women's participation in the struggle against colonialism?' she wonders. 'Can we say that Moroccan historiography is "masculine", history written only by men and for men?'[28] Editors of *8 mars* magazine also see history books as sites of collective memory. They argue that 'as usual when women are concerned, books written about the national struggle do not dedicate even one page to women. The history of women's struggle has not yet been written. Its heroines live, and might even die, without having a word written about them. The female public, which participated in the struggle and fulfilled all the simple tasks so vital to its success, has not been registered in collective memory, except on rare occasions.'[29]

These authors offer an alternative history. Like authors of dominant historiographies, they selectively emplot past events into narratives. They present women as historical agents and provide heroines and historical examples. They use the same events, the same texts and the same cultural codes as the dominant national historiography, but they find, instead of women's invisibility, subordination and silence, their active participation and contribution. Of all the meanings in past events, they choose those which oppose the dominant ideology. They too do not simply tell the story 'as it really was'. They choose certain events as worth narrating, they create an 'historical event' from events that were not previously considered as such. They isolate an event or a person from their original context and give it, her or him, a new one endowed with a new meaning. They define as 'feminist' events and engagements that were not necessarily experienced as such. They look for a feminine experience, a feminine consciousness or a collective feminine activism. They look for evidence of a continuity of feminist consciousness, even if one did not necessarily exist in the Morocco of the

1950s. These authors do not attempt to challenge the core of the dominant historiography, but to appropriate it. They do not challenge the centrality of the struggle for national independence in the existing 'natural' social order – they only want a larger part in it.

Women's participation in the struggle is therefore described as a political, and specifically feminist, act. Journalist Touria Hadraoui claims in a 1987 article published in *Kalima*: 'At the time of the resistance, women did not spare any effort in the struggle against the coloniser. For these women, suffocated by rigid patriarchy, ... the struggle for independence became a catalyst for their growing to a consciousness of their rights.'[30] According to Malika al-Asimi, 'the woman took off her veil, gathered all her energies, and engaged in education and work outside her home, in order to consolidate the legitimacy of her demands for liberation and the fulfilment of her human rights.'[31] In their book, referred to earlier, Akharbach and Rerhaye describe Rqia Lamrania, a 77-year-old grandmother and a former participant in the struggle, as an indigenous feminist. Unlike the divas of women's liberation movements, claim Akharbach and Rarhaye, Lamrania is an example of feminism 'anchored in our culture. Feminism the way we like it'.[32]

These authors stress the importance of *feminine* activism – it was their presence as women which contributed to the success of the struggle. They redefine 'political activism' and 'historical protagonists', and hence who is worthy of inclusion in the historical narrative. Women, in their narratives, smuggled weapons, documents, messages, pamphlets and money; they supplied logistical support, threw stones and hot water at soldiers, assisted in uncovering collaborators, raised donations for schools and for the families of victims; they participated in demonstrations and provided literacy training. Women initiated consciousness-raising meetings and organised attendance at meetings of the party, concealed warriors and attended the sick and wounded. Women's ululation ('*you-yous*'), for example, becomes in this history a myth of women's political power and political activism. Somewhat paradoxically, by outlawing ululation the French authorities had turned it into a subversive political act. Zakya Daoud, for example, sees it as 'women's way to encourage men to the battle, when they could not participate in it themselves'.[33] The '*you-you*' became a synonym for women's political activism. The word appeared, for example, in the title of an article written by Fatima Mernissi on the eve of the 1983 election, in which she argued that politicians are interested in women's votes, but not in promoting women's status.[34] Similarly, Hadraoui's historiographic article is entitled 'The Hour of the *You-You*'.[35]

Another prevalent theme is the claim that women manipulated French soldiers' stereotypes about the status of the Moroccan woman. Women used their bodies, a shopping bag, a purse or a diaper to hide weapons, money or messages. Muhammad Khalil BouKharid claimed, in an article entitled 'A warrior's testimony' in *8 mars* magazine: 'The Moroccan woman used the fact that the colonialist found it unlikely that she would perform the kind of activities she was in fact performing. For this reason, she was less subject to searches than were men.'[36] Asma Benadada interviewed a woman called Aisha, who claimed that 'the French soldiers did not suspect Moroccan women, because most of them stayed at home, did not work or study. The French soldiers thus found it inconceivable that they would perform this kind of action. The women counted on this assumption.'[37]

In some of the these narratives, the period of the struggle is described as one which enabled change in gender roles. Several examples can be found in Leila Abouzeid's novella *The Year of the Elephant*: a man escapes the French army dressed as a woman; a woman carrying a male prisoner's garb; a woman travelling around Morocco while her husband is confined in prison.[38] Historian Najah al-Marini describes her relative Hajja Fatima Zunaybariyya and her husband Mustafa Kindil, *'alim* and *faqih*, as equal participants in the struggle. Before she left for her missions, narrates Marini of her childhood memories, Kindil used to tease his wife: 'I am Fatima Zunaybariyya and you are Mustafa Kindil.'[39]

This narrative of women's participation in the national struggle is a tragic one. Women did take part in the struggle and achieved temporary victories, argue feminist authors, but with independence lost most of them. National independence is associated with the defeat of women. They describe women's exclusion from national politics, as well as the passing of the Personal Status Code, as direct outcomes of national independence, as the breaking of a promise. 'At the dawn of Moroccan independence,' writes feminist and sociologist Fatima Mernissi, 'nationalist leaders, who had undergone torture in prison so that equality and democracy could reign, designed the future of the Moroccan family without consulting the central element of that family – women.'[40] Asimi describes those women as 'buzzing bees, ... who were expelled from the queen's wedding feast after they finished building the palace'.[41] Journalist Touria Hadraoui sees the period of the struggle as one in which women realised their greatest achievements. 'One may ask', she continues, 'whether they did not regress thereafter'.[42] Zakya Daoud interviewed Sadiyya Douraidi, who used to plant home-made bombs in front of collaborators' residences, but who, before her death, felt that at independence she had 'missed an opportunity that will never return'. After independence, her sons became political prisoners, and one of them died as a result of a hunger strike. This woman, who struggled for Morocco's independence, had now to struggle against state oppression and became the 'Mother Courage' of the struggle of the families of political prisoners.[43]

Where does this alternative memory stem from? These authors often use private memory – interviews with women who participated in the struggle, as in Benadada's work or in interviews featured in *8 mars*, or childhood memories and memories of female relatives who participated in the struggle, such as those in Abouzeid's novella, Marini's article and Asimi's work. Like the biographies and autobiographies of veterans of the struggle, published in Morocco in the 1970s and 1980s, these narratives present themselves as offering an authentic version of past events. While the dominant narrative is criticised for its silence in respect of women, and their absence from its pages, these other narratives 'cross the barrier of silence'.[44] While dominant versions of the past exclude women, women's versions supposedly present a true and authentic version of the past. The feminist historians are endowed with a reformative role: voicing the voiceless and making the faces of women at last visible in history. Rqia Lamarnia's story, for example, 'lifts the veil from the faces of many others, who shared a similar destiny, but were condemned to oblivion'.[45] Novelist Leila Abouzeid presents her work as a poetic, but nonetheless authentic, unmediated, version of the past. In the introduction to the English translation of her book *The Year of the Elephant*, she writes: 'The main events and characters throughout [the book] are real. They have surprised or moved me in real life, and I wanted by their reconstitution in this book to provide the same feelings to the reader . . . I have not created these stories. I have simply told them as they are.'[46] As a scholar, Benadada sees oral testimony as the only way to rewrite dominant masculine history and to reach the historical truth. Benadada sees it as the researcher's task to try to 'salvage part of Moroccan history from oblivion. This will become possible only through the writing of historical facts, facts that can be found only in the memory of male and female warriors who experienced these events and who are still among the living.'[47]

But how authentic is this recourse to oral sources and to private memory? Moroccan historian Abdallah Laroui has criticised the naive assumption that every event has a reliable oral version, that all the historian has to do is to find and reconstruct. Oral history, argues Laroui, is not isolated from written history, and might even be directly derived from it.[48] It also cannot be assumed that oral history is itself somehow created outside of history, is not influenced by it, and is not mediated by cultural or social norms. The assumption of a straightforward recovery of truth through such accounts also ignores power relations between authors and their subjects, and educational, generational and class gaps between them.[49]

Tensions within Feminist Narratives

Feminist historiography is not homogenous. Tensions and struggles within it may reflect different political ideologies and different social perceptions. These tensions are manifested, for example, in the representation of Malika al-Fasi, the cousin of national leader Allal al-Fasi, and wife of the future Minister of Education, Muhammad al-Fasi. Malika Al-Fasi was, first and foremost, the only woman to sign the independence charter, and for this reason she is mentioned in passing in standard history books and became a heroine of feminist historiography. At the same time, different authors disagree as to the role she should play in feminist historiography, and as to whether this role exists only at the expense of other women, who are excluded from dominant historiography by class, not only gender, divisions.

Touria Hadraoui argues that many women participated in the struggle, 'headed by Malika al-Fasi, who signed the independence charter. As a young woman, she participated in the national movement, demanded women's rights to education and worked to ameliorate women's conditions.'[50] Zakya Daoud describes al-Fasi, dressed in a simple *jellaba*, carrying messages to Sultan Muhammad V, establishing the connection between the Palace and the national movement.[51] To Akharbach and Rarheye, al-Fasi is a proof that women can change the course of history. She is a symbol of women's militancy in particular as well as a symbol of the struggle more broadly. Like other women in feminist narratives, she is presented as a specifically feminist heroine who demanded women's rights and women's education. Short articles she wrote in the nationalist press during the struggle, demanding women's education and enfranchisement and condemning child marriage, make her a women's rights activist. The fact that her home became a meeting place for party activists, and her close relationship with her husband make her, to Rarhaye and Akharbach, a militant political activist. Like the story of other women, however, hers too is a tragic one. Unlike the men who signed the independence charter, including her own husband, she never received any public position. She never demanded any, nor was she offered one.[52]

To other feminist thinkers, on the other hand, Malika al-Fasi's exceptionalism was her status as a woman who enjoyed privileges available to few others at the time. She was a member of a well-to-do family in Fez, affiliated to the urban, patrician leadership of the nationalist movement. In her writing she condemned the exclusion of women from higher education, but it was her own class status which had allowed her to receive an education unavailable to the great majority of Moroccan women. Fatima El Kennaoui, in a recent lecture on feminist movements, commented on the focus on Malika al-Fasi as *representing* her generation. To Kennaoui, there is a paradox in a feminist historiography which focuses on the exceptional cases of urban, élite women who had access to education, while most of the country's women were illiterate: 'She wrote many articles, but how many of her generation could read them?'[53] Similarly, when in an interview I asked novelist Leila Abouzeid whether she believed people should know who Malika al-Fasi was, she responded: 'Who was she and what did she do? All she did was have access to education and happen to be Allal al-Fasi's cousin. There were many women, however, who did not share these privileges. Who is mentioned in history books? Women who were related to leaders, rich women who had access to education, not others.'[54]

Incorporation and Appropriation

At the beginning of the 1990s, women's political and legal status began to be transformed. In 1993, for the first time in Moroccan history, the Personal Status Code (*mudawwana*) was reformed following a huge campaign by petition that collected one million signatures. That same year, two women were elected to parliament. As the political system started to incorporate women, dominant historiography began incorporating the feminist one. The partial recognition of feminist demands, however, served only to weaken the Moroccan feminist movement. When King Hassan II agreed to change the Personal Status Code he did so by presenting himself as the initiator of the reform, and the interests of women and those of the throne as identical – the women's movement, as an independent expression of women themselves, was presented as redundant.

Feminist historiography underwent a similar process. Dominant historiography came to include women, but merely as auxiliary partners in the national struggle. Their inclusion in the struggle was justified through their inclusion in the private sphere rather then as active in the public sphere, and their presence in history was portrayed as unchanging. Their history was presented as one of non-conflictual alliance between the Moroccan monarchy and Moroccan women.

The High Commission of Veterans of the Struggle and the Liberation Army recognised women's participation in a conference entitled 'The Moroccan Woman and The Resistance Struggle' held on 8 March 1991, international women's day, in co-operation with the Ministry of Traditional Artisanship and Social Affairs. The declared aim of the conference was 'to honour womanhood in general and the female warrior in particular, in recognition of the active role she played in the struggle for the liberation of her country and for its territorial unity'. Scholars and veterans discussed women's role in the struggle. After a delay of 35 years, female veterans could receive veteran status, which meant state pensions and long-awaited formal recognition. The Commission decided to allocate part of its budget to research into and documentation of women's participation in the struggle.[55]

The new recognition of women's participation in national history, however, did not incorporate the criticism embedded in feminist historiographies. On 7 March 1992, activists of the Union of Feminine Action (Union de l'Action Féminine, UAF) initiated a 'one million signatures' campaign in support of the demand for a comprehensive reform of the Personal Status Code, including the abolition of polygamy, the abolition of the male guardianship of an adult woman, and judicial supervision of the divorce process. On 20 August 1992, five months later, the anniversary of the struggle for national independence, the King responded to this initiative. As the commander of the faithful, authorised to interpret the words of the Prophet, he asked women and women's organisations to write to him directly in order to begin a dialogue that would change the Personal Status Code, after consultation with the *'ulama*. In the same speech, he asked Moroccan women 'not to confuse that which is related to your religion, and that which is related to the mundane world and to politics', and argued that it would be a mistake to present the demand for a change in the *mudawwana* as a political demand.[56] He thus achieved a double goal. By appropriating women's demands, he legitimised them, but also neutralised the threat they posed. Although the UAF activists managed to collect one million signatures in support of their demands, only a few of these demands were actually adopted into law, and feminist activists defined the reform as insufficient. Even if the law provided some protection from the arbitrary will of the husband, this was not supported by any mechanisms of enforcement.[57]

> On this occasion of the anniversary of the Revolution of the King and the People, we cannot mention the Moroccan people without a special gesture towards the Moroccan woman, the Moroccan wife, the Moroccan mother and the Moroccan daughter, because I am aware of the burden and responsibility she took upon herself in this revolution, and of her role in its success.[58]

This quote from the King's speech opened the brochure *The Moroccan Woman* published the same year. Feminist activists, who had hitherto attacked the iniquities of women's status from outside the system, were now conscripted to defend it from within a government publication.[59] The introduction to this brochure presents Moroccan women as the preservers of cultural authenticity. It is a text that exemplifies the double role of woman in national discourse, as 'the guardian of Moroccan cultural values at home and the proponent of modernity outside her house'. Her role in the national body is defined through her biological roles, as 'a mother and a sister who, through the miracle of childbirth, personifies the miracle of creation, and can give birth to national awakening.' As such, feminist struggle is redundant for her. She is not 'troubled by false debates', and understands that 'her trumps reside in her "difference"', and that, as a result, her objective is less her equality *with* men, but rather her equality *before* the law'.[60]

Both the introduction to *The Moroccan Woman* and the King's speech which prefaces it incorporate women into national historiography, but subordinate them to the national narrative. They present a non-conflictual relationship between national ideology and the lived reality of Moroccan women. Women's issues are presented as familial, not political. The woman is a wife, a daughter, a sister or a mother. Her role in society is thus defined through her reproductive role in the family, and in relation to men. *The Moroccan Woman* further reminds the reader that she is not, or rather should not be, deceived by feminist slogans, but is (that is, should/must be) confident in the role prescribed for her.

Fatima Zahra Tamouh, a history professor at Mohammed V University in Rabat and a member of the left-wing Union of Feminine Action, wrote one of the articles in the brochure, entitled 'A rich feminine past'. In her article, as in the King's speech, Moroccan women are presented as a nameless and faceless mass and as generic, passive and reactive people, who are present in history, but never as agents who initiate historical processes. She presents, as does the King's speech, a non-conflictual relationship between women and power, between women and history writing, and between the spokespersons of Islam and the reality of women's lives. She writes: 'The Moroccan women were always present, and managed to mark with their presence decisive periods in the history of their country. They embraced the national cause to the maximum of their limits and will continue, no doubt, to *support* the currents of history.'[61]

Once incorporated into dominant historiography, women's participation in the struggle for independence is presented as a proof of the postcolonial regime's support of women's liberation. The tragic ending is replaced by a romantic one. In the new narrative presented by the hegemonic historiography, women have always been present in national memory, and there has never been any conflict between women's interests and patriarchal domination. Since the Palace is presented as the supporter of women's rights, the feminist movement is presented as redundant.

Conclusion

Theorising historical narrative as an arbitrary selection of past events enabled us to see Moroccan historiography as being in a state of constant negotiation

– first, between colonial and indigenous versions of the past and later, between national and feminist ones. These struggles can (indeed, must) be seen in the context of political developments. Feminist struggle rendered women visible in history, and feminist historiography helped justify a feminist agenda for social change, as opposed to the dominant historiography, which presented patriarchy and women's exclusion as a historical continuity, a part of the 'natural' order of things.

As we have seen, dominant historiography is not stable. When educated middle class women emerged as a political group, the Palace tried to incorporate and neutralise them. During the 1990s, women's status was changed in several respects, and an emergent feminist historiography was incorporated into the dominant, nationalist one. Feminist authors and activists were integrated into state institutions, and women were given formal platforms on which to present their historiography. The narrative they present from these platforms, however, is a harmonious one which abjures the conflict between feminist activism and a social order still dominated by patriarchy, and the palace at its centre. At the same time, the fact that women can now use official platforms to present women's participation in the public sphere as part of the nation's historical continuity, as part of the natural order, is a fact that now stems from their incorporated position within the workings of hegemony.

NOTES

An earlier version of this article was published in Hebrew, '"I am Fatma Zunayburia and you are Mustaafa Kindil": Writing Feminist History and National Historiography in Morocco', *Jama'a*, 6 (2000).

1. Deniz Kandiyoti, 'Identity and its Discontents: Women and the Nation', *Millennium: Journal of International Studies* 20 (1991) pp.429–43.
2. Partha Chatterjee, 'Colonialism, Nationalism, and Colonized Women: the Contest in India', *American Ethnologist* 16 (1989) pp.622–32. See, on Qasim Amin: Leila Ahmed, *Women and Gender in Islam: Historical Roots of a Modern Debate* (New Haven: Yale University Press 1992) pp.161–63; and on Tahar Haddad: Noureddine Sraieb, 'Islam, réformisme et condition feminine en Tunisie: Tahar Haddad (1898–1935)', *Clio: Histoire, Femmes et Sociétés* 9 (1999) pp.80–3.
3. Karen Offen, Ruth Roach Pierson and Jane Randel, 'Introduction' in Offen, Pierson and Randel (eds.), *Writing Women's History: International Perspectives* (Bloomington IN: Indiana University Press 1991) pp.xii–xvii.
4. Joan Scott, 'Women's history' in Peter Burke (ed.), *New Perspectives on Historical Writing* (Philadelphia: Pennsylvania University Press 1992) p.42.
5. Hayden V. White, *Metahistory: The Historical Imagination in Nineteenth-Century Europe* (Baltimore: John Hopkins University Press 1973).
6. Scott (note 4) pp.53–4.
7. Raymond Williams, *Marxism and Literature* (Oxford: Oxford University Press 1977) p.116.
8. Ibid. pp.124–5.
9. Ibid. p.116.
10. Zaynab Maadi, *Al-Mar'a bayn al-thaqafi wa-l-qadasi (surat al-mar'a fi-l-qanun)*

(Casablanca: Editions le Fennec 1992) pp.38–42. The background of feminist activism in neighbouring Tunisia and Algeria was significantly different, as the respective governments chose to codify a more egalitarian law in the aftermath of national independence in the Tunisian case, while codifying a relatively conservative one, 20 years later, in the Algerian case. For a detailed historical comparison see Mounira M. Charrad, *States and Women's Rights: The Making of Postcolonial Tunisia, Algeria, and Morocco* (Berkeley: University of California Press 2001).

11. Latifa Akharbach and Narjis Rerhaye, 'Introduction', in L. Akharbach and N. Rerhaye, *Femmes et politique* (Casablanca: Éditions le Fennec 1992) p.14.

12. John P. Entelis, *Culture and Counterculture in Moroccan Politics* (Boulder: Westview Press 1989) p.14.

13. Mohamed C. Sahli, *Décoloniser l'histoire. Introduction à l'histoire du Maghrib* (Paris: Maspero 1965).

14. Amina Aouchar Ihrai, 'Décoloniser l'histoire', *Lamalif* 96 (April 1978) pp.38–43; Abdelmajid Hannoum, 'Mythology and Memory in Modern North Africa: the Story of the Kahina', *Studia Islamica* 85 (1997) pp.103–8; Abdallah Laroui, *The History of the Maghrib*, trans. Ralph Manheim (Princeton: Princeton University Press 1977) pp.3–7; Muhammad Mazin, 'Manhaj kitabat al-ta'rikh al-qawmi, ishkaliyyat ta'rikh al-maghrib al-arabi', *Anwal* 9 Jan. 1988 pp.5–7.

15. Edmund Burke III, 'Theorizing the Histories of Colonialism and Nationalism in the Arab Maghrib', *Arab Studies Quarterly* 20 (Spring 1998) pp.5–9. See also Driss Maghraoui, 'Colonial Soldiers: between Selective Memory and Collective Memory', *Arab Studies Quarterly* 20 (Spring 1998) pp.21–41, and Gershovich (this volume).

16. Youssef Courbage, 'Economic and Political Issues of Fertility Transition in the Arab World – Answers and Questions', *Population and Environment: A Journal of Interdisciplinary Studies* 20/4 (March 1999) pp.362–3; Youssef Courbage, 'Demographic Change in the Arab World: the Impact of Migration, Education and Taxes in Egypt and Morocco', *Middle East Report* (Sept.–Oct. 1994) pp.20–2; Georges Sabagh, 'The Challenge of Population Growth in Morocco', *Middle East Report* (March–April 1993) pp.31,33.

17. Zakya Daoud, *Féminisme et politique au Maghrib: soixante ans de lutte* (Paris: Maisonneuve et Larose 1994) pp.273–5,280–3,296–8.

18. Abdessamad Dialmy, 'La Marocaine et le féminisme', paper presented to the international conference *Feminist Movements: Origins and Orientations* (Fez, 13–15 May 1999) p.4.

19. Elizabeth Fernea, *In Search of Islamic Feminism: One Woman's Global Journey* (New York: Doubleday 1998) p.13; for a comparative perspective, see, for example in Egypt: Margot Badran, 'Gender Activism: Feminists and Islamists in Egypt', in Valentine M. Moghadam (ed.), *Identity Politics and Women: Cultural Reassertions and Feminisms in International Perspectives* (Boulder: Westview Press 1994) pp.203,206; in Pakistan: Fauzia Gardezi, 'Islam, Feminism, and Women's Movement in Pakistan: 1981–1991', *South Asia Bulletin* 10/2 (1990) p.19; in Hungary: Fiona Flew with Barbara Bagilhole, Jean Carabine, Natalie Fenton, Celia Kitzinger, Ruth Listen and Sue Wilkinson, 'Introduction: Local Feminisms, Global Futures', *Women's Studies International Forum* 22/4 (1999) p.397. See also Amrita Basu, 'Introduction', in Amrita Basu (ed.), *The Challenge of Local Feminisms: Women's Movements in Global Perspective* (Boulder: Westview Press 1995) pp.6–7.

20. Abdessamad Dialmy, 'Le féminisme au Maroc', *Lamalif* 162 (Jan. 1985) p.23.

21. Salwa al-Shaykh Fulus, 'Ala hamish maqal al-ustadh Abd al-Karim Ghulab, 'Nuhakim al-rijal am al-ta'rikh' – al-mar'a al-maghribiyya, ay ta'rikh?' *al-Alam* 5 Jan.1993.

22. Ibid.

23. Touria Hadraoui, 'L'Heure des "you-you"', *Kalima* 18 (Sept. 1987) p.24.

24. Pierre Nora (ed.), *Les Lieux de mémoire* (Paris: Editions Gallimard 1984).

25. Hadraroui (note 23) p.25.

26. Fulus (note 21).

27. Malika Al-Asimi, *Al-mar'a wa-ishkaliyyat al-dimuqratiyya, qira'a fi al-waqi' wāl-khitab* (Casablanca: Afriqiyat al-sharq 1991) pp.71–2.

28. Asma Benadada, 'Ba'd Tajliyat al-mubadarat al-nisa'iyya min khilal musharakat mar'a

muqawima', Aicha Belarbi (ed.), *Initiatives Féminines* (Casablanca: Editions le Fennec 1999) p.33.

29. '8 mars fi liqaa ma' al-muqawima Khaduj al-Zaragtuni: a'taz bi-kawni rafaqtu 29 akhi li-yanfudha 'amaliyatuhu al-fida'iyya al-ula', *8 mars* 7 (1986) pp.14,31.

30. Hadraoui (note 23) p.24.

31. Asimi (note 27) p.80.

32. 'Rqia Lamrania: une femme dans la résistance', in Akharbach and Rarheye (note 11) p.35.

33. Daoud (note 17) p.241.

34. Fatima Mernissi, 'Yu... Yu... Yu...', *Anwal* 10 March 1983, p.6.

35. Hadraoui (note 23) pp.24–25.

36. Muhammad Khalil BouKharid. 'Shahadat Muqawim', *8 mars* 7 (1986), p.31.

37. Benadada (note 28) p.36.

38. Leila Abouzeid, *The Year of the Elephant: A Moroccan Woman's Journey Toward Independence*, transl. Barbara Parmenter (Austin: University of Texas Press 1989).

39. Naja al-Marini, 'al-hajja fatima zunaybariyya: min raidat al-haraka al-nisa iyya al-salawiyya', *al-Alam* 22 March 1994 p.8.

40. Fatima Mernissi, *Doing Daily Battle: Interviews with Moroccan Women* (New Brunswick: Rutgers University Press 1989) p.2.

41. Asimi (note 27) p.70.

42. Hadraoui (note 23) p.24.

43. Daoud (note 17) p.254.

44. Hadraoui (note 23) p.24.

45. 'Rqia Lamrania' in Akharbach and Rerhaye (note 11) p.36.

46. Abouzeid (note 38) pp.ix–x.

47. Benadada (note 28) p.33.

48. Abdallah Laroui, 'Histoire idéologique, histoire critique' in his *Esquisses historiques* (Casablanca: Centre Culturel Arabe 1993) pp.8–9.

49. Ruth Roach Pierson, 'Experience, difference, dominance and voice in the writing of Canadian women's history', in Offen *et al.* (note 3) pp.91–2.

50. Hadraoui (note 23) p.26.

51. Daoud (note 17) p.251.

52. 'Malika Al Fassi: l'intellectuelle du Mouvement National', in Akharbach and Rerhaye (note 11) pp.17–18, 25–26.

53. Fatima El Kennaoui, 'Feminist Movements in Morocco', paper presented to the international conference on *Feminist Movements: Origins and Orientations,*Fez, 13–15 May 1999.

54. Interview with Leila Abouzeid, Fez, 14 May 1999.

55. 'Al-Yawm al-alami li-l-mar'a: nadwat al-mar'a al-maghribiyya wa-l-muqawama', *Majalal al-muqawama wa-jaysh al-tahrir* 27 (1991) pp.8–14.

56. 'Jalalat al-malik fi khitab dhikrat 20 ghusht, 'ard mashru' muraja'at al-dustur 'ala al-sha'b', *al-Alam* 22 Aug. 1992 p.1.

57. Farida Benani, 'Kiraa awaliyya fi mashru' ta'dil mudawwanat al-ahwal al-shakhsiyya', in *Journées d'étude sur le thème: Femme et Politique,* Rabat 4–5 Oct. 1993 (Rabat: al-Ma'arif al-Jadida1993) pp.215–46.

58. 'Jalalat al-Malik' (note 56).

59. Among the authors were Noufisa Sbai, today the chair of the Association of the Young Women in the Maghrib (Association Femme Jeunesse dans l'Environnement Maghrébin); Amina Lamrini, President of the Democratic Asociation of Moroccan Women (Association Démocratique des Femmes Marocaines, ADFM) and journalists Fatima Belarbi and Narjis Rarheye.

60. 'La femme marocaine: ambiguité et ambivalence', Ministère des Affaires Etrangères et de la Coopération, *La Femme Marocaine* 1992 p.1.

61. Fatima Zahra Tamouh, 'Au riche passé au féminin', *La Femme Marocaine* pp.2–4 (emphasis added).

Citizens and Subjects in the Bank: Corporate Visions of Modern Art and Moroccan Identity

KATARZYNA PIEPRZAK

The official publication on Moroccan museums disseminated by the Moroccan National Tourist Board in association with the Ministry of Culture is a glossy and attractive pamphlet. On the cover is a Roman mosaic (Figure 1) in which a partly clothed woman reclines suggestively while another partially represented figure wafts soft winds towards her. This visual image of ancient luxury is a fitting choice for the introduction to the text.

On opening the booklet, the reader is greeted with a photograph of old keys and the following text:

FIGURE 1
COVER OF THE MOROCCAN MUSEUMS PUBLICATION

Source: Moroccan Tourist Board, Moroccan Museums (Rabat: Moroccan Tourist Board and Moroccan Ministry of Culture 1994).

131

Inhabited since prehistoric times, with a culture that goes back thirty centuries, at the crossroads of Roman, Berber and Arab civilisations, Morocco is rich in museums overflowing with treasures. These magical places are entirely devoted to admiration. The touch of a master transforms the humblest objects into masterpieces. Carpets, pottery, garments or arms, here everything is a work of art. [... A] visit to the museums of Morocco is not merely a means of understanding more about a different culture, nor merely an introduction to part of humanity's heritage; it is in fact an opportunity to experience a total enchantment of the spirit and the senses.[1]

The keys juxtaposed with the text invite the reader to open the magical doors of Moroccan patrimony and explore the architecture which houses national treasures from centuries past. The sumptuous photographs of museum courtyards and interiors reflect the architectural preoccupation of the text. The Museum of Moroccan Arts in Tangiers is described as an 'imposing silhouette' that 'dominates the Tangier Kasbah', 'a worthy setting for works of art from all over Morocco'.[2] The ethnographic museum in Chefchaouen is introduced as 'a haven of peace in a magnificent Andalusian garden',[3] the Oudaya Museum in Rabat, 'an opulent lodge',[4] the Dar Si Said Museum in Marrakesh, 'a sumptuous palace housing the very quintessence of Moroccan art'.[5] The pamphlet proclaims of such architecture of beauty and pleasure that 'Moroccan museums are very often monuments in their own right. Even empty, they would be well worth a visit.'[6] The preoccupation of the pamphlet with architecture as opposed to museum content reveals the symbolic role of the museum. As monuments, Moroccan museums function as a stage for the performance of Moroccan culture; they are infrastructures through which and upon which narratives of Moroccan history and art are created. These narratives are firmly lodged in the idea of a Moroccanness that is deeply rooted in a shared Roman, Berber and Arab past, a past tied to Europe and the West, but culturally distinct. By the display of objects from centuries past, the museums secure the heart of Moroccan cultural identity in a rich tradition of artisan production and set the terms by which to understand the Moroccan nation itself.

Theories on the museum as a site of representation for the nation have been widely expressed by historians and anthropologists alike.[7] In *The Birth of the Museum*, Tony Bennett explores how the origins of the museum in nineteenth-century Europe are inextricably tied to definitions and formulations of national identity. He writes that the museum functioned as a 'technology' of culture which served to construct modern images and modern audiences for a national culture.[8] The concept of the museum was imbued with an ideology of progress: the museum was to represent the democratisation of knowledge, the transfer of art from private to state hands and ultimately the construction of a patrimony that narrated the history of the nation and its citizens, placing art and culture in a teleology of scientific progress and imperial ambition. In this narration of the nation, not only art, but the entire world was brought into the museum and ordered according to local paradigms. As Ivan Karp and Steven Lavine write: 'Decisions about how cultures are presented reflect deeper judgements of power and authority, and can, indeed, resolve themselves into claims about what a nation is or ought to be as well as how citizens should relate to one another.'[9]

In her survey of late twentieth-century museums in Africa, *Les états africains et leurs musées: La mise en scène de la nation*, Anne Gaugue treats the museum as a stage upon which nationalist narratives of nationhood are presented through emphasised and silenced histories: 'In the large majority of newly independent states, the museum is conceived as a tool for the dissemination of the idea of the nation [...] Exhibitions that concern historical periods prior to the formation of national territory are constructed to represent the ancient character of the nation by emphasising historical links that exist between the people that live today on this territory.'[10] In the case of Moroccan museums, while the Moroccan Tourist Office proclaims Moroccan identity to be located at the interstice of a historical Roman, Berber and Arab past, the actual objects on display create a narrative that favours the Merenid period (thirteenth to fifteenth centuries) of Moroccan history, extols an urban Arab cultural heritage and suppresses minority cultures such as Moroccan Jews.[11] The national museums in Morocco silence certain populations and histories in order to formulate a seamless cultural identity that is based in the past. And the question of the past is the key here. While the Batha Museum in Fez holds early twentieth-century miniatures, this is as close to contemporary culture as the museums get.[12] To the great dismay of a modernist cultural elite, the Moroccan state has never fully recognised the place of contemporary art in the nation's cultural identity. The staging of the nation is directed towards a glorious past, not an uncertain future.

Since the early years after independence in 1956, Moroccan artists and intellectuals have called for the creation of a museum that would be devoted to modern Moroccan art, an architecture that would not only speak to the Moroccan past, but to the new history of the nation. In the 1960 catalogue *Jeune Peinture Marocaine*, published by the Ministry of National Education, the Moroccan state made the following rather vague promise: 'We hope that in a relatively near future we will take on the organisation of a museum consecrated to the work of our modern artists.'[13] But no concrete plans were made. In her article on 'The Cultural Legacy of Power in Morocco', Rahma Bourqia argues that the Moroccan state deploys the symbols and language of modernity in strategic doses in order to maintain a balance between its legitimacy, based in heritage, and its desire to modernise. The result, according to Bourqia, is a devaluation of that very language.[14]

The empty promise of a modern art museum resulted in a litany of complaints and demands from Moroccan artists and intellectuals alike throughout the 1960s and 1970s, starting with the seminal meeting of painters in the press in August 1965. Bemoaning the lack of a modern art museum, on 4 August 1965 the painter André Elbaz wrote in the Moroccan newspaper *L'Opinion*:

> A country without a museum is a country in which the artist, genius that he may be, finishes by finding himself alone in his room between four walls, obliged to invent a language. [...] Cherkaoui and I have often found ourselves face to face with incomprehension and lack of encouragement each time that we have wanted to work on the creation of a modern art museum in Morocco. We are only asking for good faith, for some administrators, that one votes a budget and most of all that one gives us a building. And we promise you that we will create and organise a museum of modern art.[15]

Elbaz, in conjunction with Morocco's most famous painter, Ahmed Cherkaoui, promised to take essentially all responsibility out of the state's hands if only they could have a space and some funding. Eight days later, the writer Abdellatif Bennis responded in support of Elbaz declaring the museum project to be a crucial one for the development of the country.[16] And the following day, a young Moroccan painter named Mohammed Bellal joined the conversation, exclaiming:

> The Ministry of Tourism deploys all its efforts for the construction of tourist centers and sea-side resorts. But what percentage of Moroccan nationals benefit from these structures? To follow the idea of Mr Elbaz, could we begin, and this would be a first step, with the creation of a meeting place for those unknown artists and for that public that does not know them: a museum! A museum for artists, what a school! But also a museum where the public will undertake their education.[17]

A museum authenticates not only its objects, but also the culture around it.[18] For Bellal, the museum would legitimise the work of modern artists and modern culture through the presence of modern art and an educated art public. The next day, Ahmed Cherkaoui joined the conversation, listing numerous ways in which the state could encourage and promote Moroccan arts. He concluded that above all, the state must create a museum: 'this would be in the interest of the entire country'.[19]

When the two weeks of exchange on the future of Moroccan arts came to a close, there was still no published response from the Moroccan state. In 1966, in an essay entitled 'Reflections on Art and the Artist', the writer 'C.E.Y.' exclaimed that the state should finally create a museum: 'It is as indispensable as a bank vault.'[20] Ironically, 22 years later, it would be a Moroccan bank that answered this call.

In this article, I examine the rhetoric around the creation of a contemporary art gallery within arguably the largest private-sector bank in Morocco, Wafabank.[21] In proclaiming itself a modern citizen with duties to the modern arts of Morocco, the bank constructs an image of Western modernity for both itself and its clients, using art to narrate and attest to Morocco's inclusion in a global community with shared values. Through an analysis of the discourse surrounding the opening of the gallery and a reading of its exhibition practices, I explore how the bank negotiates its identity between global citizen and local subject, promoting values of modernity while simultaneously embracing Moroccan political and social structures that often contradict them. Unlike the national museums, the bank gallery does not present a glorious vision of the past, but rather through art it narrates a contemporary and often schizophrenic late twentieth-century Morocco.

Talking about Modern Citizens and Subjects

In 1988 the Moroccan Minister of Culture, photographer turned politician, Mohammed Benaissa wrote in praise of Moroccan painting, declaring that it had finally 'reached a level of remarkable maturity', that 'it produces great works and sits by the side of other traditions and cultural sectors that have contributed to enrich the civilisational diversity of Morocco.'[22] By the late 1980s and 1990s, members of the cultural elite of the 1960s and 1970s had entered political structures of power: in the 1980s, Benaissa was Minister of Culture, and by the late 1990s he was replaced by Aachari, a poet, who chose among his aides in the cabinet the visual artists Aissa Iken and Ahmed Jarid. With their elevation to positions of power in the state, these artists finally held the political authority to legitimise painting as part of Morocco's artistic heritage and create cultural infrastructures to support the fine arts. However, Benaissa's sincere thanks for the work of Moroccan artists over the 30 years that had passed since Moroccan independence came not at the opening of a long-awaited state-run museum for Morocco's contemporary arts. Instead, his remarks were delivered on the occasion of the opening of the 'Wafabank Space', a gallery and foundation located within Wafabank's headquarters in Casablanca:

I am overwhelmed with happiness to see pictorial art occupy once again the avant-garde in the promotion of a new type of patronage in Morocco, through this important project that is the inauguration of an art gallery in the heart of the Wafabank, and through the creation of a foundation. Without a doubt, this exemplary event will incite other institutions and national enterprises from the private sector to afford more attention to the fulfilment and development of Moroccan Man through his culture, and will support his efforts towards socio-economic development. This action will be only the re-enactment of a noble tradition of patronage that throughout our history has permitted the enrichment and preservation of our patrimony.[23]

Benaissa affirmed that through modern culture, Moroccan socio-economic modernity could be supported and developed. This rhetoric of culture as a tool of development was not a new one. As Claude Daniel Ardouin writes in his essay on 'Culture, Museums and Development in Africa', throughout the latter half of the twentieth century the terms *culture* and *development* were almost talismanic in the way in which African states used and abused them to immediately signify 'ambiguous notions of modernisation and progress'.[24] Benaissa's use of the terms 'development', 'culture' and 'the Moroccan Man' spoke to a nebulous project of modernity; however, this time the terms were not evoked in order to signify state efforts to modernise, but rather to highlight the entry of a financial institution into the cultural project.

As a man of the state, Benaissa praised the initiative of Wafabank and legitimised the entry of a private-sector institution into cultural policy. This was performed through a rhetoric of authenticity – Wafabank was re-enacting an authentically Moroccan practice: 'The initiative of Wafabank comes in time to re-invigorate a civilisational practice that is authentically Moroccan, that we hope to see enriched thanks to the different institutions and enterprises of the private sector.'[25] The labelling of artistic patronage as a distinctly Moroccan institution was a strategic move for the state; Benaissa played to the patriotism of large and wealthy corporations. By encouraging the participation of private-sector institutions in a realm of culture that was primarily controlled by the state, the Ministry could stretch its budget and delay the construction of a modern art museum, looking instead to the private sector to continue the development of modern state architecture. As Ahmed Aydoun writes in the periodical *Le Temps du Maroc*: 'We are witnessing a paradoxical situation in which everyone is speaking about culture (politicians, administrators, intellectuals, artists, international organisations...) but always in avoidance of the necessary financial effort to accompany these ideas.'[26] Aydoun lists the budgets allocated to the Ministry of Culture since 1968 in order to show the fluctuations in the funding received by the Ministry over the years, emphasising its instability: 1968–72, 2.8 million dirhams, 1973–77, 33.5 million, 1978–80, 7.3 million, and 1981–85, 63.4 million. By identifying patronage as something distinctly Moroccan, Benaissa reminded the bank that even though it was a private-sector institution, it was to work for a national culture under the auspices of the state:

> In effect, culture cannot be the responsibility of a sole administration, so large is its size. Enriching the culture and the patrimony of a nation is a civilisational project in that it renders the participation of all cultural institutions important and essential – whether it be an art gallery, a library or a museum – in the conjunction of efforts and regrouping of possibilities for the execution of the High Directives of His Majesty the King Hassan II, Protector of Culture and Arts, in order that the diversity of our country should continue to thrive, marking and reflecting the genius of Moroccan civilisation both here and abroad.[27]

The Minister touched on all the key points in Moroccan cultural policy. First of all, culture was a 'civilisational project' for the entire nation. Secondly, the state in its limited financial capacity could not do everything; the private sector was just as responsible for the development of culture. This did not mean that the state was not concerned with the arts and that it would not remain its prime benefactor; Benaissa was sure to identify the King as not only the 'Commander of the Faithful', but also the 'Protector of Culture and Arts'. Finally, Moroccan cultural policy was to emphasise the genius of Moroccan civilisation both in Morocco, and perhaps most importantly abroad. By means of an 'authentically' Moroccan system of patronage working in tandem with the state, Benaissa argued that all these points of cultural policy could be achieved.

Whilst the institution of patronage may have been well established in Moroccan culture, it was by no means something distinctly or purely Moroccan, as described by Benaissa.[28] Patronage relationships between business and art have been traced to as early as 70–8 BCE, to the Etruscan financier Gaius Maecenas (from whom the French and German terms for patronage, *mécénat* and *Mäzenatentum* are derived[29]). In the case of *corporate* art patronage, art historians have traced its origins to the 1940s and 1950s in the United States. Marjory Jacobson writes:

> The shift from the fortuitous predilection of the individual capitalist to the more seasoned relationship between capitalism and art patronage as a serious substructure of civilisation is a late twentieth century prodigy. […] In a new guise of enlightened self interest, it has become 'the business of business' to support this cultural imperative.[30]

In the United States, the Rockefellers exemplified this transition from a system of individual or family support of the arts to corporate patronage. After the death of his mother, Abby Rockefeller, co-founder of and major collector for the Museum of Modern Art in New York, David Rockefeller decided to continue Rockefeller support of contemporary art through his financial institution, the Chase Manhattan bank. In 1948, he formed an Art Advisory Committee, composed of Museum of Modern Art directors and curators, who joined him and one other bank member in their deliberations on the acquisition of art. By 1959, the art collection was launched with impressive holdings of abstract expressionist art. In looking back on this venture, David Rockefeller wrote in 1984:

> The Chase art program attracted much attention and gathered momentum. While there were many who were critical of it, an increasing number of both staff members and customers became fascinated by it, even though they did not like everything we bought. Little by little, other banks and corporations in this country and abroad were encouraged to start art programs of their own. Today, relatively few major banks and corporations are without an art program of one kind or another. I believe that Chase can take pride in having established a trend that has beautified the work places of businesses everywhere and, at the same time, has given important encouragement to contemporary artists.[31]

However, art in the bank did much more than just beautify the workplace and encourage contemporary artists. It redefined the image of the bank, from a dark panelled, dimly lit, conservative organisation with portraits of men in waistcoats hanging on the walls, to that of a business at the cutting edge, vibrant, dynamic, and full of living art. Most importantly, the trend redefined the relationship between the financial sector and cultural production as more and more corporations invested in art. By the 1980s, it was widely recognised that a mature and successful financial organisation in a liberal capitalist democracy had a responsibility, if not a duty, to support culture.[32]

While the state presented Wafabank's involvement in the arts as an authentically Moroccan commitment to art in Morocco, Wafabank was just as interested in the development of its own image as a modern financial institution. It was not due to a sentimental idea of Moroccan subjecthood that Wafabank had opted to become a patron of the arts; the very nature and success of its institution as an international bank required that it participate in this global trend.

The first Wafabank publication *La Peinture marocaine au rendez-vous de l'histoire* [Moroccan Painting in a Meeting with History], a beautiful and glossy illustrated catalogue, emphasised the bank's commitment to the living arts in Morocco. While the title claimed that Moroccan painting had a date with history, the underlying message was that *through art* it was the bank which would establish its place in the history of modern capitalism. Modern art was a means by which the bank could distinguish itself and pledge its allegiance to a global financial community. The book was not for sale, but rather was distributed by the bank to both its Moroccan and foreign investors as a public relations project to show how, like other international banks, it understood the importance of culture.[33]

In the preface to the book, Wafabank vice-president Abdelhak Bennani[34] made clear that the opening of the Wafabank gallery was part and parcel of Morocco's progress into the modern world, but he also situated the opening in a larger global context:

> Intimately persuaded that this strong entry of enterprises into the field of culture is one of the societal phenomena that will bring the most hope for our own society, we have created the Wafabank foundation and have installed in the heart of our corporate headquarters a high-profile space for Art with the ambition of becoming a crossroads of creation and diffusion at the disposal of the City. This only distances us in appearance from our basic activity, the creation of wealth, the production of goods and services; the economic and cultural sectors are and have been thus profoundly linked over all time, mutually feeding each other. Thus our steps follow this rhythm: one step in the direction of the market and another in the direction of the City, with one sole objective, to respond to needs and force forward progress.[35]

The bank invested, just as much as did the state and the cultural elite, in cultural education and its utility in the drive to progress precisely because it was just as concerned as they were to be itself invested with the concept of Western modernity. Like Benaissa's comments that linked culture and socio-economic development under the aegis of a plan for progress, Bennani's remarks emphasised that the gallery 'only distances us in appearance' from the creation of wealth. For Bennani and the bank, culture and economics are inextricably linked in the modernisation of Morocco. As discussed above, this understanding arose not only from modernisation discourses, but also from the very model and duties of a bank that had been defined in the West. Art in the Moroccan bank thus had a double significance: it linked cultural and socio-economic modernisation efforts in Morocco through the agency of the bank, and it lent prestige to the bank in its public relations with the West.

In providing an essay on the history of Moroccan art for the Wafabank publication, the Moroccan writer and critic Edmond Amram El Maleh was less hasty in his praise of the Wafabank initiative, intimating that perhaps the Moroccan public and its artists had not yet received the institution they so desired:

It is appropriate to congratulate without further ado the initiative taken by Wafabank in opening a gallery in the very heart of its corporate headquarters. I was tempted to say, in a humorous vein, that Moroccan painters finally have their bank, something infinitely enviable, but that in this unexpected 'hold-up', [English in the original] they find themselves taken as happy 'hostages'. This is a way of saying that patronage is an initiative that one must hope will develop and diversify itself, in the way that the examples of Europe and the United States have shown.[36]

The inauguration of corporate patronage implied competition for funding, and El Maleh's comments betray an anxiety that the determination of the value of art would leave the hands of a small artistic group and cultural elite, that aesthetic judgement would be relocated into the hands of the banks. He feared that artists would have to change their work (its content, its form, its size) in order to fit into a corporate world. The autonomy of the artistic field would be compromised by something other – and perhaps more powerful – than the state. The bank's involvement in the fine arts was described by El Maleh as unexpected and sudden. The idea of holding artists as happy hostages further intimated that this development was out of the artist's control, even though El Maleh writes that his metaphor was just 'a way of saying that patronage is an initiative that one must hope will develop'. This last comment, that patronage in Morocco should develop and diversify in ways similar to what was happening in Europe and the United States in the 1980s, expresses the fear that corporate patronage in Morocco would, like the language of modernity itself, be devalued into a gesture to the West, that the bank, not unlike the state, would use the Moroccan arts purely for its own political ends.

A year later, however, on publication by Wafabank of the first competition results awarded by jury, El Maleh's tone had changed from caution to celebration and encouragement:

It is appropriate to congratulate, in all objectivity, the recent initiatives taken by the Wafabank foundation in the framework of its cultural politics inaugurated by the creation of the Wafabank Space. A sign of new times, the bank is no longer a safety vault, a cash counter, a complex financial machine that is only interested in money. From now on, it will play a role that can hardly be negligible in social and cultural development, while still exercising its other functions. Thus is the thing understood: it is a practice that is more and more current in the USA and Europe, notably in France these last years. Large corporations and banks multiply their initiatives in favour of the arts and literature in diverse domains and forms – exhibitions, prizes, fellowships. Our country could not remain behind in this movement.[37]

Wafabank was living up to its promises to artists, and the first competition had been a great success. The bank had effectively taken over the organisation of the contemporary art field, producing exhibitions, competitions and publications that on certain levels of importance overshadowed artist-organised biennial exhibitions and publications. The bank was able to convene juries for its yearly competitions whose members were drawn from an international cultural elite. In 1989, the distinguished jury consisted of the Artistic Director of the Institut du Monde Arabe in Paris, the painter Farid Belkahia, the writer Mohammed Berrada, and the critic El Maleh. Lahbib M'Seffer, Wafabank Director of Human and Material Resources, director of the art programme, (and also, in a testimony to the rise of artists to positions of political and economic power in contemporary Morocco, a successful landscape painter) explained how the bank always chose at least one jury member from foreign/Western institutions in order to allow judgement of art to proceed according to global standards of contemporary art.[38]

The discursive tension between the support of the Moroccan arts for patriotic reasons and the promotion of the bank's own image in global public relations can be read from the way the bank navigates between its images of Moroccan and international identities through a rhetoric of citizenship and populism. When I interviewed Lahbib M'Seffer in May 2000, he stated that in the 1980s, the Wafabank redefined its identity and started to consider itself a citizen with certain duties to its country. 'We considered that at a certain moment it would be necessary for banks to play the role of citizens. We even wrote this into our charter because we see ourselves both as an economic force in the country and as a citizen. It is absolutely necessary that we play our role on a national level, especially as the state can't do everything.'[39] As a citizen, M'Seffer argued, the bank had a duty to support the arts and guarantee access to them for the entire population. Recently, on the Wafabank website, M'Seffer restated this goal: 'We are working for the development of transparency, rigour, professionalism and modernity. Innovation, creativity, integrity and citizenship are equally part of a system of values that has always been the force of our organisation.'[40] The repeated use of the word *citizen* by a bank director is especially interesting and provocative in the current political climate in Morocco, for the movement from monarchical subject to national citizen has entered into debate in Moroccan society.

Negotiating Global and Local Subjectivity

In the 1994 short story *Youssef fi butn ummhu* [Youssef in his Mother's Womb], Moroccan writer and journalist Idriss Al-Khoury recounts a mother's conversation with her unborn son. While the entire family prepares for his arrival with great celebration, preparing food, washing elegant dishes, filling the house with delicious fragrances, Youssef, quietly sitting in his mother's womb, decides that he would rather not be born. The family and his mother wait impatiently for his arrival, but no sign of birth is imminent. Finally the mother asks her child why he must tarry so long:

> When will you come out? – When I see fit. – But the matter is not in your hands. – Then when God wants me to. – I want you to right now. – But I am afraid. – Of what? – Of the world and of my unknown future. – There will be a place for you in this world, a place for you to sit in school. – I doubt that, I fear that I will be one of the outcasts. – No, they will welcome you, they now have new classes open all over. – And if the reporters on television made a mistake? – No, there is not much of a chance of that. – Let me sleep.[41]

Youssef's concern about his future and the world into which he is to be born articulates itself through the possibilities of education and advancement. What is the point of being born when there is no chance of self-fulfilment, no chance of an education and no chance of a job? Youssef would rather remain in the warm and cavernous womb of his mother than go out into his dark and dismal future. His mother tries to assure him that all will be well, that there is a place in the world for him; however, Youssef is never quite convinced, and in the closing lines of the story, as he is being born, he asks himself the following question: 'Shall I stay? Will there be a place for me in school, a bed for me in the hospital, a seat for me in an office?'[42] Upon entering the world, young Youssef can only imagine leaving it. Al-Khoury's story points to the stark reality of Moroccan life in the 1990s. While intellectuals and politicians forecast hope of a modern democratic society that would conform to global standards of modernity, reality presented a grim future of unemployment, lack of education, orchestrated elections and a growing number of adolescents committing suicide.[43]

Ann Elizabeth Mayer argues in her article 'Moroccans – Citizens or Subjects? A People at the Crossroads' that in the early 1990s the monarchy and its critics had a 'sharply diverging vision of the future of the Moroccan polity, differing greatly in their views as to the optimal balance between the monarch's prerogatives and the rights of his subjects, who increasingly seem to think of themselves as citizens of Morocco rather than as King Hassan's subjects.'[44] It might be argued that in contemporary Morocco this turn in identification from subject to citizen has further intensified with the reformist tendencies of Mohammed VI who appears to be heading the country in the direction of a true constitutional monarchy. In an interview, Prime Minister Abderrahman Youssoufi described his meeting with Mohammed VI: 'At our first working meeting the King said, "You must know I'm a democrat." That's reassuring.'[45] In his first speech from the throne, Mohammed VI was even clearer when he said, 'We are devoted to constitutional monarchy, a multi-party system, economic liberalism, regionalisation and decentralisation, the construction of a state committed to the rule of law, the safeguarding of human rights and individual and collective freedoms, and the preservation of security and stability for all.'[46] In short, everything that would constitute a modern nation.

However for the Moroccan majority, promises of a modern life of self-fulfilment, freedom and wealth remained exactly that – promises. Marvine Howe writes that in the 1990s, 'Morocco would at last seem firmly on the road to becoming a modern progressive democracy – an aspiration of both left-wing and conservative nationalists since independence in 1956.'[47] However 'seem' is the operative word here, for as Howe concludes in her analysis, 'How long will the Moroccan people, spearheaded by a new, buoyant civil society, be satisfied with symbols and promises, before demanding real changes in their lives?'[48]

While Mayer and Howe discuss the legal significance of the terms citizen and subject in Morocco, I would like to take a moment to consider the cultural implications of the two terms. By moving from a model of the subject whereby the state and the King control and dictate culture, the concept of citizenship implies democratic participation in law, society and ultimately culture. In part, the arts would be transferred to the control of private citizens and state institutions who, bound by a democratic duty, would preserve national patrimony. This is what M'Seffer implied in his comments: the Wafabank gallery was ideally a modern democratic institution, open to all Moroccans. Unlike the state-run museums that pander to tourists more than to a Moroccan public, the Wafabank space, a private-sector space, would – ironically – be the first truly democratic and modern cultural institution in Morocco.

M'Seffer stated that 'in Morocco, there are no museums'.[49] In other words, there are no real public institutions that would, as Carol Duncan claims in 'Art Museums and the Ritual of Citizenship', become a link between the state and its citizenry, participating in a ritual affirmation of the social contract between the two.[50] Until the state opens a national art museum that can perform such a ritual affirmation and preserve national patrimony for all Moroccans, Wafabank sees itself as the protector of the contemporary arts. Is this a direct challenge to the King as 'Protector of Arts and Culture' by an institution that sees itself not as a subject, but as a citizen? On a certain theoretical level, the institution's rhetoric reflects a greater allegiance to international standards of modernity than to the political reality of the country. However, on a practical level, M'Seffer was quick to dispel any threat to the state by saying that as soon as a national museum is opened in Morocco, Wafabank will donate its entire collection of artwork to the state. When I asked if this would happen in the year 2002, as per the Ministry of Culture's architectural plans and projections, M'Seffer was highly doubtful.[51] He knows that the bank's collection is far from being given away at this point in time.[52]

The adoption of the term *citizen* shows Wafabank's participation in another world order, that of international capitalism and the liberal democracy that feeds it. The bank in its existence in two worlds, that of the Kingdom of Morocco and that of an international free-market economy, is in a position to be both subject and citizen. Let us finally step into the gallery and see how this negotiation takes place through exhibition space.

The gallery is located in the lobby of the Wafabank's corporate headquarters in the centre of Casablanca. This is the Casablanca of international finance with wide avenues and high-rise buildings, and the Wafabank building fits into this image with about 30 storeys of reflective glass.[53] On entering the building, to the right of the lobby are bank cashiers and consultant desks; the centre of the lobby houses elevator banks and a security desk; to the left of the elevators is the gallery. There is no door to enter the gallery, but the space is monitored by security guards at the entrance. In order that I might take photographs, Lahbib M'Seffer called down to the security guard to grant me permission; for security reasons I was not allowed to take photographs of anything but the gallery. This close monitoring and control of the bank space reveals to what extent the bank sees itself as the promoter of security on all levels of interaction with its clients. Their money, their personal safety, and even 'their' artwork is assured. However, this concern for security also builds walls between art and its audience, accentuating the fact that the art is not so much for a general public, as it is for a small clientele.

The physical space of the gallery reflects the rest of the building: the floors are marble and the paintings well-lit (Figure 2.) The paintings that are on display are representative of the short but rich history of Moroccan painting and included are works by artists such as Melehi, Chaibia and Tallal. The majority of canvases are not labelled, pointing perhaps less to the importance of individual works, than to their recognised modernity. Primarily abstract, these paintings speak a language of modern art that may be difficult to understand, but which is easy to recognise. As one enters, this space radiates its identity as a modern art gallery.

FIGURE 2
WAFABANK GALLERY INTERIOR

The first painting that faces the viewer (Figure 3) is by Hussein Tallal, an academic artist who refused any identity politics for his art and considered himself an international artist above all else. Tallal's mother Chaibia Tallal is one of Morocco's most celebrated unschooled painters, manipulating and playing with symbols of everyday Moroccan life using broad strokes and bright colours. However, Tallal has rejected this vocabulary, stating in 1967: 'I *am* a Moroccan – thus I have no need to paint a mosque or a fantasia to prove it. It is not a nationality or an origin that tells me what to paint. And anyway, I think that Delacroix has already painted everything about Morocco and that there is nothing else to add.'[54] The representation of Morocco as structured through a tourist vocabulary largely derived from a nineteenth-century Orientalist vocabulary did not interest Tallal. Rather, like other members of the cultural elite in the 1960s and 70s, Tallal has argued for autonomy in art.[55]

In the Wafabank gallery, his large scale pictorial representation of two clown-like figures in blue, red and white, one with exposed breasts, seems a peculiar choice for the first painting to greet the visitor. There are no explicit references to Arab, Berber or Islamic culture within the work that would identify it as distinctly Moroccan. However, it is this very aspect of the painting that most closely reflects the desired image of the bank: like the painting, the bank can accept and refuse definition. Both painting and bank can

FIGURE 3
WAFABANK GALLERY INTERIOR WITH TALLAL PAINTING AND PORTRAIT OF
HASSAN II

dissimulate their identity and deterritorialise their image from its Moroccan origins into the explicit cosmopolitanism of an international institution.

And yet, what keeps both the bank and the painting with one foot on Moroccan soil is the portrait photograph of the King that hangs directly above Tallal's canvas. The juxtaposition of a portrait of the late King Hassan II and photographs of his two sons directly above the painting could be read as provocative and potentially subversive; is the King being directly compared with Tallal's clowns? However, rather than associate the figures in the images through direct analogy, I would see the association between the painting and the photographs in the symbolism of the space in which they are placed.

The most important dynamic in the space is the marked separation between the white walls of the gallery and the darker wooden panels on which hangs the portrait of the King. The white cube method of display in modern art has been described by Pam Meecham and Julie Sheldon as an attempt to create a pure space, free of ideology, in which paintings can be displayed on their own merit and with their own messages:

> The presentation of modern art in puritanically regulated white-walled rooms, with strategically placed spotlights and humidity monitors is a familiar part of any visit to the modern art gallery – across the globe. [...] The modern art gallery, without the same obligations to present

146

identity-forming national collections or to serve the redemptive functions of many nineteenth-century philantrophic collections, seemed [...] to provide an ideology-free space.[56]

However, as Meecham and Sheldon continue to argue, while these gallery spaces in their inception were not overtly implicated in discourses of imperialism, social engineering and anthropology, by the very basis of their rejection of dominant discourses, they have never been free of ideology. The whiteness of the Wafabank space attests to the desire to create an ideology-free space *per* international conventions for the display of modern art, to construct an autonomous sphere for art, but by its very nature, it too is not free of ideology. The whiteness attests to modernity.[57]

The King is placed outside this space, but in close proximity to it. In Morocco, the presence of a portrait photograph of the King serves as a stamp of approval to anything in its proximity, for the image of the King, not unlike his actual physical presence, lends a certain *baraka* or blessing to those around it. As Susan Ossman writes in *Picturing Casablanca: Portraits of Power in a Modern City*:

> The quality of *baraka* [grace] had always been attributed to saints, wise men and sultans. [...] With the advent of the camera, *baraka* was represented with increased frequency through photographs and film. Today, photographs of the King are mandatory in public places. In homes too, people often display pictures of authority figures: the King, fathers, sons.[58]

Rahma Bourqia provides an important caveat to this definition, stating that 'although *baraka* is diffused in words, things and places, it is transmitted through the process of polar attraction whereby all forms of it converge around the sacred object'.[59] In this modern art gallery, it is not art, but rather the photograph of royalty, that is the 'sacred object'. The elevation of the King's image above all works of art, above the claims of an ideologically free space, shows how the King, in an elevated benevolence, has given the art, the gallery, and Wafabank his blessing and the gift of state legitimacy. Ironically, the presence of the King and the state outside the white cube grants art its autonomous sphere 'detached' from politics and religion. As I mentioned previously, Carol Duncan argues that in a Western state-run art museum, the work of art itself serves as the medium through which the relationship between state and citizen is articulated and affirmed.[60] Through art, its display and its preservation, a museum performs its duty to the citizen to safeguard national treasures. In the Wafabank case, it is not the art or the gallery that links the citizen to the state; rather, the relationship between citizen and state is mediated through the King. Through the photograph of the King, itself a representation by modern technology, the contractual relationship between state, private sector and public is affirmed. The paintings in the gallery reflect a certain modernity, but it should not be forgotten that their power as symbols of such, rests in part if not wholly with the state's benevolence and desire to modernise. The placement of the King's image in the gallery, and not just in the banking area of the building, which would fulfil the mandatory aspect of displaying the King in a business setting, performs an allegiance to the King as the 'Protector of the Arts' and Morocco's leader down the road to modernity. The King is not just an antiquated figure from a feudal past; he has a place in the modern future of Morocco. Thus while Wafabank sees itself as a citizen in its commitment to the arts as an autonomous institution, it does not stray too far from its position as the King's subject.

If this site is one of enactment of a ritual of imagined citizenship and subjectivity, then we should turn to the question of the gallery's public. The bank considers this space to be public even though it is within a high-security institution. How does this translate into reality? Who is the gallery's public? Lahbib M'Seffer is very proud of the bank's community outreach programmes and in his description of these actions, his rhetoric becomes almost populist in nature.[61] First of all, when the bank is invited to sponsor an exhibition abroad, as it recently has done in both France and Spain, it insists that its participation is contingent on the exhibition travelling to Morocco. Furthermore, the bank will not publish any exhibition materials unless the exhibition has come to their space. This has led to several free exhibitions of high quality in the Wafabank space such as exhibitions on Picasso, neo-figurative Mexican art, and contemporary British Sculpture, to name a few.[62] According to M'Seffer, these exhibitions, as well as the results of the annual painting competition, have openings that attract 700 to 800 people. When asked about the make-up of the crowd, M'Seffer described the public as journalists, cultural figures, government officials and lovers of art. This description does not sound too unlike descriptions of gallery openings in the 1960s' press: openings attended by a modernist cultural elite. How does the Wafabank really go beyond the cultural elite and the bourgeoisie in its creation of a public? M'Seffer claims that those people who come into the bank to perform financial transactions all benefit from the gallery: 'When a transaction lasts 20 minutes, instead of waiting, clients wander into the gallery and sometimes even become impassioned by what they see.'[63] But who is this client with 20 minute transactions? Surely not the average Moroccan who lives near or below the poverty line. The implication of this in light of the bank's professed commitment to Morocco and its culture as a *citizen* among citizens is problematic. Does this mean that only those with 'money in the bank' can become citizens entitled to their country's artistic patrimony? Does this mean that those who are not permitted to enter the space of the bank will remain forever subjects? In order to attest to its participation in the values of modernity, the bank has espoused a rhetoric of democratising and developing modern art for Moroccan citizens. However, in order for its rhetoric to have meaning, the bank has essentially delimited the meaning of 'citizen' to 'client of the bank'. Thus, like any other modern institution, it is able to ensure that all 'citizens' have free access to the latest artistic creations in the country.

For the bank's fellow citizens, a restricted public of Moroccan bourgeois and international investors, images of modernity as present in the art serve to give these viewers greater confidence in the economic future of *their* modern Morocco and in the economic prospects of the Wafabank. The model of corporate patronage in the bank is based on models in Europe and the West, and the presence of modern, Western-style artwork serves to convince and placate the bank's public that their financial institution is similar to those in the West. The bank thus incarnates a post-modern problematic. Rather than being haunted by questions of hegemony, it accepts that Moroccan history, like global history, is moving in different directions and at different speeds. As Néstor Garcia Canclini writes in *Hybrid Cultures: Strategies for Entering and Leaving Modernity*: 'In this period, when history is moving in many directions, any conclusion is marked with uncertainty. More cultivated types of knowledge lead to more precarious decisions about how to enter or leave modernity, where to invest, and how to relate culture to power.'[64] While, rhetorically, Wafabank pledges an allegiance to the development of Morocco through culture, in practice it services a small group of people who move in the same circles. To this restricted, 'modern' public, the bank can affirm the values of modernity.

Banking on the Future

The success of Wafabank's strategy of art in public relations can be read in the willingness and extent of other financial institutions in Morocco to present art exhibitions in their lobbies. For example, the Caisse de Dépot et de Gestion (CDG) in Rabat publishes exhibition pamphlets to accompany its exhibits. Unlike the Wafabank, which does not sell any of its pieces, the CDG has price tags on all of its art, and the art is not cheap. In April and May 2000, CDG hosted an exhibition of the work of Bouchta Al-Hayani. Whilst the cover of the pamphlet shows one of Al-Hayani's paintings (Figure 4), the first page of the publication is a photograph of CDG's modern corporate building (Figure 5).[65] The photograph echoes the colours of Al-Hayani's work, dark purples, yellows and reds, and the scale of the photograph is identical to the scale of the painting on the cover. This juxtaposition of images begs the

FIGURE 4
COVER OF AL HAYANI EXHIBIT BROCHURE

BOUCHTA EL HAYANI
EXPOSE

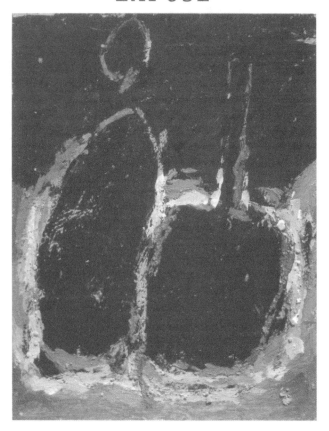

Galerie d'art CDG

27 avril - 11 mai 2000

Source: Caisse de Depot et de Gestion, *Bouchta El Hayani Expose* (Rabat: Galerie d'art CDG 2000).

150

FIGURE 5
CAISSE DE DEPOT ET DE GESTION CORPORATE BUILDING

Source: Caisse de Depot et de Gastion, *Bouchta El Hayani Expose* (Rabat: Galerie d'art CDG 2000).

viewer to make a mental comparison between the two, linking their modernity. In the tradition of Wafabank juries, the short texts that surround Al-Hayani's work in the 16-page publication come from a slice of the Moroccan cultural elite, (novelist Mohamed Loakira, theorist and writer Abdelkebir Khatibi, and novelist and social activist Abdelhak Serhane) as well as Western scholars (Francophone literature expert Marc Gontard and art historian Lydia Harambourg). This textual insertion provides a valorisation of both Al-Hayani's work and the CDG's interest in it. By describing Al-Hayani as an important painter who is on the cutting edge of artistic production, the bank secures its own modern image in Morocco, and among an international community of finance, convincing and assuring its clientele in the process.

Banks across Morocco are creating spaces for art that symbolise and narrate the acquisition of wealth and their participation in a global community with shared modern values. While by rich examples of artistic production from

151

centuries past, state-run museums narrate a cultural identity for Morocco that is based in history, by modern art, Moroccan bank galleries are creating narratives that look to the future. In articulating the reasons for opening a gallery within its corporate headquarters, Wafabank invoked a discourse not only about the place of contemporary painting in Morocco, but also about the cultural identity of a kingdom poised to be a nation. Negotiating between its image as an international citizen and a loyal subject, Wafabank has developed strategies by which it is possible to imagine and stage both. In between these identities, we may find Moroccan artists and their art. In Edmond Amram El Maleh's words, they are still 'happy hostages', though it is uncertain for how long.[66]

NOTES

1. Moroccan National Tourist Board, *Morocco: Museums* (Rabat: Moroccan National Tourist Board and the Moroccan Ministry of Culture 1994) p.3.
2. Ibid. p.4.
3. Ibid. p.6.
4. Ibid. p.12.
5. Ibid. p.18.
6. Ibid. p.1.
7. See Tim Barringer and Tom Flynn (eds.), *Colonialism and the Object: Empire, Material Culture and the Museum* (London: Routledge 1998); Tony Bennett, *The Birth of the Museum: History, Theory, Politics* (London: Routledge 1995); Carol Duncan, *Civilising Rituals: Inside Public Art Museums* (London: Routledge 1995); Anne Gaugue, *Les états africains et leurs musées: La mise en scène de la nation* (Paris: L'Harmattan 1997); Ivan Karp and Steven Lavine (eds.), *Exhibiting Cultures: The Poetics and Politics of Museum Display* (Washington DC: Smithsonian Institution 1991); and Stephen Weil, *A Cabinet of Curiosities: Inquiries into Museums and Their Prospects* (Washington, DC: Smithsonian Institution 1995).
8. Bennett (note 7) discusses this concept in depth in 'Museums and Progress: Narrative, Ideology, Performance' in which he considers 'the different ways in which, in the late nineteenth and early twentieth-century formation, museums, fairs and exhibitions functioned as technologies of progress. […] Indeed, it was quite common at the time for museums and the like to be referred to as "machines for progress". 'ch.7 p.10.
9. Ivan Karp and Steven Lavine (note 7), 'Introduction: Museums and Multiculturalism' p.ix.
10. Anne Gaugue (note 7) pp.28, 35.
11. See Katarzyna Pieprzak, 'Whose Patrimony is it Anyway? The Quarrel between Ali Baba's Cave and the National Museums of Morocco', *Yearbook of Comparative and General Literature* No.49 (2001) pp.155–75, for a deeper analysis of this dynamic.
12. While the Oudaya Museum in Rabat has held exhibits of contemporary art, these are never integrated into the dominant timeline of Moroccan art and are displayed in a room adjacent to the main exhibition space.
13. Ministère de l'Education Nationale: Service des monuments historiques des arts et du folklore, *Jeune Peinture Marocaine* (Rabat: Ministry of Education 1960) p.5.
14. Rahma Bourqia, 'The Cultural Legacy of Power in Morocco', in Bourqia and Miller (eds.), *In the Shadow of the Sultan: Culture, Power, and Politics in Morocco* (Cambridge MA: Harvard University Press 1999) p.251.
15. Andre Elbaz, 'Jeune Peintres où sommes-nous?' *L'Opinion* (4 Aug. 1965) p.4.
16. Abdellatif Bennis, 'L'Ecole marocaine doit affronter toutes les competitions internationales', *L'Opinion* (12 Aug. 1965) p.4.

17. Mohammed Bellal, 'Qui lèvera le rideau?' *L'Opinion* (13 Aug. 1965) p.4.
18. This dynamic is described in Ning Wang, *Tourism and Modernity: A Sociological Study* (New York: Permagon 2000).
19. Abdellatif Bennis, 'Cherkaoui révèle: Le Maroc, invité n'ira pas à la Biennale de Sao Paulo'. *L'Opinion* (14 Aug. 1965) p.4.
20. C.E.Y., 'Reflections sur l'art et l'artiste', *Lamalif* 7 (Nov. 1966) p.44.
21. In 2000 the Wafabank had 189 branches in Morocco, two international agencies and 26 international representatives. The group is active in insurance, property, mortgages, banking, and investment in the Moroccan stock market. For more detailed information on the Wafabank financial group including stock performance, annual reports, presence and interests, see the Wafabank website: www.wafaonline.com.
22. Mohammed Benaissa, 'Dédicace', *La Peinture marocaine au rendez-vous de l'histoire* (Casablanca: Editions Espace Wafabank 1988) p.ii.
23. Ibid. p.ii.
24. Claude Daniel Ardouin, 'Culture, Museums and Development in Africa', in Salah M. Hassan and Philip Altbach (eds.), *The Muse of Modernity: Essays on Culture as Development in Africa* (Trenton NJ: Africa World Press Inc. 1996) p.182.
25. Mohammed Benaissa, 'Dedicace' (note 22) p.ii.
26. Ahmed Adyoun, 'L'enjeu culturel', *Le Temps du Maroc* 168 (15–21 Jan. 1999) www.tempsdumaroc.press.ma/hebdomadaire/1999/1521janv168/cult3.htm
27. Mohammed Benaissa, 'Dedicace' (note 22) p.iii.
28. For further reading on the history of art patronage in Morocco, see Phillipe Piguet, 'Le Maroc entre culture et mécénat', *L'Oeil* 481 (July/Aug.1996) pp.72–81.
29. Mary Jacobson, *Art and Business: New Strategies for Corporate Collecting* (London: Thames and Hudson 1993) p.10.
30. Ibid.
31. David Rockefeller in the foreword to Marshall Lee (ed.), *Art at Work: The Chase Manhattan Collection* (New York: E.P. Dutton Inc. 1984) p.12.
32. Marjory Jacobson (note 29) p.10.
33. Lahbib M'Seffer, interview with author, tape recording, Wafabank Casablanca, 26 May 2000.
34. Since 1988, Bennani has been promoted to President of Wafabank. He is prominently featured in the Wafabank website: www.wafaonline.com.
35. Abdelhak Bennani, 'Prologue', *La Peinture marocaine au rendez-vous de l'histoire* (Casablanca: Editions Espace Wafabank, 1988) p.v.
36. Edmond Amram El Maleh, 'La Peinture marocaine: tradition et modernité', *La Peinture marocaine au rendez-vous de l'histoire* (Casablanca: Editions Espace Wafabank 1988) p.17.
37. Edmond Amram El Maleh, 'Préface', *Première rencontre de la jeune peinture marocaine* (Casablanca: Editions Fondation Wafabank 1989) p.1.
38. Lahbib M'Seffer (note 33).
39. Ibid.
40. LahbibM'Seffer, www.wafaonline.com/common/impr_comprendre.asp?> 31 May 2002.
41. Idriss Al-Khoury, *Youssef fi butn ummhu* (Rabat: Dar Nashar Al-Mu'arifa 1994) p.20.
42. Ibid. p.21.
43. See Henry Munson Jr., 'The Elections of 1993 and Democratisation in Morocco', in Bourqia and Miller (note 14) pp.259–281; Susan E. Waltz, 'Interpreting Political Reform in Morocco', in Bourqia and Miller (note 14) pp.282–305; and Marvine Howe, 'Morocco's Democratic Experience', *World Policy Journal* 17 (Spring 2000) pp.65–70.
44. Ann Elizabeth Mayer, 'Moroccans – Citizens or Subjects? A People at the Crossroads', *International Law and Politics* Vol.26:63 (1993) p.65.
45. Marvine Howe (note 43) pp.67–8.
46. Ibid. p.67.
47. Ibid. p.70.
48. Ibid.
49. M'Seffer (note 33).

50. Carol Duncan , 'Art Museums and the Ritual of Citizenship', in Ivan Karp and Steven Lavine (note 7) pp.88–103.
51. In my 11 May 2000 interview with Ahmed Jarid at the Ministry of Culture in Rabat, Jarid discussed the opening of a large scale national museum in Rabat that would include exhibits of modern Moroccan art. He showed me architectural plans for the museum building and projected that they would hopefully get off the ground in 2001.
52. M'Seffer, interview by author.
53. For an analysis of Casablanca as a 'modern' city see Susan Ossman, *Picturing Casablanca: Portraits of Power in a Modern City* (Berkeley: University of California Press 1994).
54. Cited in Zakya Daoud, 'Le monde fantastique de Tallal', *Lamalif* 16 (Nov. 1967) p.40.
55. For an in depth discussion of 1960s and 1970s discourse on Moroccan art by its activist artists see Katarzyna Pieprzak, 'De-Monumentalising Modernity: The Writing of the Moroccan Arts', in 'Which Way to the Modern Art Museum? Cultural Discourse on Art and Modernity in Post-Colonial Morocco' (Ph.D. diss, University of Michigan 2001), ch.2.
56. Pam Meecham and Julie Sheldon, *Modern Art: A Critical Introduction* (London: Routledge 2000) pp.198–9.
57. For further discussion of the function of the white cube, see Brian O'Doherty, *Inside the White Cube: The Ideology of the Gallery Space* (Berkeley: University of California Press 1999).
58. Susan Ossman (note 53) p.11.
59. Rahma Bourqia (note 14) p.247.
60. Carol Duncan (note 50) pp.88–103.
61. Lahbib M'Seffer (note 33).
62. See www.wafaonline.com for a list of visiting exhibits at the Wafabank gallery.
63. M'Seffer (note 33).
64. Néstor Garcia Canclini, *Hybrid Cultures: Strategies for Entering and Leaving Modernity*, transl. Chiappari and Lopez (Minneapolis: University of Minesota Press 1995) p.266.
65. Caisse de Dépôt et de Gestion, Bouchta El Hayani Exposé (Rabat : Galérie d'art CDG 2000).
66. Edmond Amram El Maleh (note 36).

The Nation's 'Unknowing Other': Three Intellectuals and the Culture(s) of Being Algerian, or the Impossibility of Subaltern Studies in Algeria

FANNY COLONNA

I will take as my starting point an apparently minor event – the declaration (in November 2000) of ineligibility of final-year *licence* (Bachelor's degree) dissertations in local history and anthropology in the Department of Berber Language and Culture at the University of Tizi Ouzou, an institution created only in 1991 and whose own history is one of a long and difficult struggle for existence. This administrative measure, which sparked a student strike, offers a point of entry for reflection on an enduring cultural fact of contemporary Algeria: the deep-seated refusal to recognise as legitimate (indeed, the *de facto* prohibition of) any consideration of, and research on, the local, the particular, the 'singular'. The Tizi Ouzou strike did not attain its objective. It lasted for several weeks and further destabilised an already fragile academic department; in so doing, it revealed itself as only one symptom among many of the country's malaise in 2001, a malaise which was not specifically 'Kabyle' but properly *national*. It was a preliminary sign of the violent and – in every sense of the word – costly troubles that shook the country in the spring and summer of that year and which persisted into 2002, evidenced in particular by Kabylia's boycott of the legislative elections in June.

The decision to single out at the outset of this article an event so apparently minuscule aims to pinpoint *ab initio* the extent to which the twin (and equally imaginary) 'realities' of Nation and Culture are conjoined in Algeria – as those who have closely followed the country's recent social movements will have understood – and the extent to which, too, the fact of speaking of culture and cultural production (and cultural *producers*) is, in this case, to walk straight into a minefield. Finally, not the least of my reasons for wishing to draw attention to this event is, since one of the concerns of this collection of articles is to speak of 'voices from below', that the voice, precisely, of the students of a peripheral department of a provincial university (which nonetheless bears the name, emblematic in Algeria, of *Université Mouloud Mammeri*) merits, to my mind, at least as much attention as would some prestigious text.

After all, these students are, in several respects, a sample of those most concerned – the rising generation. Jacques Rancière, a philosopher and historian whose work has for 30 years been devoted entirely to the questions which concern us here, writes that 'we can speak of a democratic historicity *when everyone, or anyone, is susceptible of being an historical subject*', by which he means a producer of an historical discourse, writing further on of 'this type of historicity which is tied to the fact that *everyone – and anyone – makes* history'.[1] This fact, at least to my mind, is precisely one of those which we must address.

Subaltern Studies in Algeria? From Disinterest in Popular Insurgency to the 'Culturalist Turn'

As an entry into this subject, I shall limit myself to the observation of a few general landmarks which can orient us with respect to what is, even if we consider only the period since 1962, an extremely complex intellectual history. To trace even rapidly the peculiar context of Algeria in relation to the now international debate initiated by *Subaltern Studies* – a salutary exercise even if somewhat arbitrary, since such an intellectual movement or 'collective' has never existed as such, or indeed as *anything*, in Algeria, and this is one of the points I wish to document: that everyone preaches to his own parish, so to speak – would require a discussion of considerable proportions. We should have to consider the infinitesimal attention accorded to the popular insurgencies of the nineteenth century, a subject of study frankly frowned upon; go back over the historiography of the first 20 years of independence – which concentrated almost exclusively on the history of the National Movement in the twentieth century, and did so within a very 'official' framework, singling out the political parties and their forerunners, and the nationalist press. The 'primitive rebels' have had very little share in all this, save – and this is a particular case in any event – the insurrection of 8 May 1945. (I am here concerned only with research carried out in Algeria itself, bearing in mind that there has been progressively less and less research done outside, and fewer strong links in Algeria with research carried out abroad.) We should have to speak, too, of the effects of the radical 'arabisation' of the social sciences beginning in the academic year 1981–82; of the fate of successive and vain attempts to create research groups – often from among the same individuals – focusing on the local or the 'fragmentary' (the Centre for Research in Archaeology, Prehistory and Ethnography in Algiers, the

CDSH and its successors in Oran, finally the Department of Berber Language and Culture at Tizi Ouzou – all three real *parcours du combattant*! [struggles against the odds]). In brief, those authors who have taken as their object of study the role of dominated and marginalised groups in the anticolonial struggle have been very rare.

There thus exists nothing, or very little, to compare with the 'first phase' of South Asian Subaltern Studies, that concerned with peasant insurgencies etc., even while certain specialists on the nineteenth century have, in fact, interested themselves in the *Senatus Consultes* (*i.e.* the colonial legislation regarding rural land registration and its entry into the market) and their effects.[2] Very quickly, in fact, research agendas were set in the realm of culture, on much surer ground and in a highly subjective approach that we might term 'realist' or 'naturalistic', each documenting 'his' own domain. In a sense, we entered a 'postmodern phase *avant la lettre*',[3] save that it had, and still has, no theoretical base, either on the part of those engaged in such work or on the part of their critics – except in terms of reciprocal, politicised anathematisation. Hence the lack of a comparative perspective engaging with work that has been done elsewhere. All of this bears witness to the absence of autonomy of intellectual (and in particular, academic) production in the face of the political.

To all of the above one could doubtless object; one could name certain exceptions, certain signs of optimism. The global situation in Algeria, in contrast to other countries – even Tunisia or Morocco – appears to me nonetheless to be as I have described. Up to a point, the contribution of contemporary literature might appear to compensate for this void in the cultural–intellectual output of the academy, but even so, this is much less true of Algeria than it is, for example, in Egypt.

And yet, for lack of anything better, what *has* been done is far from negligible, and it is to that that we must now turn.

Three Prominent Algerian Intellectuals and their 'Patrimony': Mostefa Lacheraf, Mouloud Mammeri and Abu 'l-Qasim Sa'adallah

Posing the question of 'voices from below' through the work of three major intellectuals seems to me a useful shortcut in a situation where the academic field barely permits itself to pose any kind of question outside the officially imposed 'frame' (in the cinematic sense), and where those rare works which do allow themselves such latitude remain completely unknown to university students who are unable to overcome the barrier of *de facto* self-censorship. Why these three? The principal reason for choosing these authors is that, in contrast to the very rare, unfinished or invisible academic works dealing with culture(s), the work of all three is *highly legitimate*, for reasons that vary with each case but which all have to do with a certain notoriety which extends well beyond Algeria itself. Despite their very different profiles – and very different relationships with the régime – these authors have in common that, over the long term, they have all devoted considerable energy to making known figures and works of a localised, anonymous or personalised nature, whether in French, Berber or Arabic. One could say that among other objectives – since they have also been, respectively, a constitutional theorist of the régime and diplomat (Lacheraf), a novelist and linguist (Mammeri), and official *salafi* historian (Sa'adallah) – they have had a curiously common aim. Their works, despite their great personal differences (for they are hardly fond of one another and have on occasion engaged in stormy public disputes) and different objectives, thus concur in the demonstration of an 'Algerianness' more 'thickly' constituted, more tangible than that proclaimed and prescribed by the discourse of the state, and that not only by the collection and publication of primary material but also by means of dense reflection on the questions of nation, society, history and culture, particularly in the case of Lacheraf. Moreover, they are approximately the same age, share the same experience of Algerian history – colonisation, war, post-independence society – which, even when they seem to have more in common (Lacheraf and Mammeri), *they each interpret in a different code.*

Names and Places – Lacheraf

Mostefa Lacheraf was born in 1917 in Sidi Aissa, in the steppe south of Algiers, into a literate family: his father was a magistrate in the Muslim civil court. Lacheraf received a solid bilingual education, first in the local Qur'anic school *(kuttab)* and then at the French *lycée* in Algiers and at the *Tha'âlibiyya,* a higher-level colonial school for Muslim Algerians (*médersa* in Algerian parlance) dispensing an excellent standard of instruction. Finally he studied in Paris, at the (highly prestigious) *lycée* Louis le Grand, and at the Sorbonne. A militant in the PPA *(Parti du Peuple Algérien,* Algerian People's Party) at the age of 22, he continued thereafter to hold important party functions. He joined the FLN in 1954 and, with an originality of thought particular to him, carried out political missions, and engaged in information work and doctrinal elaboration during the revolution. It can be said without exaggeration that he is, if not the only, nonetheless one of the very rare, intellectuals of the FLN.

He was arrested in 1956 when the French authorities hijacked the Moroccan royal jet carrying an FLN delegation from Rabat to Tunis, and spent much of the war in prison alongside Boudiaf, Ben Bella and others. Having escaped from captivity in 1961, he participated in the drafting of the Tripoli charter and took charge of its defence before the National Council of the

Revolution, in 1962. Editor-in-chief of the single state daily, *El Moudjahid*, in 1962, he then went as Ambassador to Latin America, an experience that had a lasting effect, making a cosmopolitan of him, before returning to political life in Algiers at the request of Boumedienne. Fifteen years after the elaboration of the Tripoli platform, he contributed significantly to the National Charter of 1976, Boumedienne's 'political testament' – and a text which hardly strikes one for its attention to 'voices from below'.[4] A brief and unhappy spell as Minister of National Education (1978), where he attempted to promote bilingualism, ended with his resignation in the face of a closing of ranks by the *Badisiyya salafi*-reformists.[5] Thereafter once more ambassador in Latin America, he returned to Algeria in 1986, where he wrote regularly and furiously in the state-owned, and then in the independent, press, retaining warm but private contacts with numerous intellectuals of every persuasion.

Even so long (too long) a biographical note is inadequate to the complexity of this personality. He is the author of numerous unpublished literary texts, and also of several crucial works, of which the two most important are *L'Algérie, nation et société*,[6] published in 1965, and most recently *Des Noms et des Lieux. Mémoires d'une Algérie oubliée*,[7] which appeared in 1998. He has also remained, if not a doctrinaire, at least a theoretician of FLN hegemony. It must nevertheless be remarked that these two books, at least, probably constitute the strongest, the best documented and the most solidly thought-out programme that any Algerian has produced on the question of culture. All the more so in that the second of these texts has finally made good on the promises of the first, ceasing at last to say 'what must be done' and actually doing it – that is, speaking of the concrete, of *people*, and thus of himself, of his experience as a *socially and historically situated person* and not merely as a political voice. Everything in these works, beginning in 1964–65, (since the earlier book ends with a text published in 1964 by *Les Temps modernes* and which is a model of penetrative understanding) on localised Algerian societies, their capacity for 'self-direction', their consciousness of ends and means; on 'spoken languages which are more than dialects', on the 'disconcerting totality of individual cases' which constitutes village culture; and on this very culture, which, under colonialism, 'retrenches and which only, henceforward, religious tradition, itself vulnerable, appears to defend'– all this speaks all too eloquently to researchers who have gone to study these societies at first hand. It would surely have more than satisfied an Indian subalternist like Ranajit Guha.[8] As for his last book – and we must hope that he will not long break his stride on so good a road[9] – what postmodernist would be left unmoved by its sense of affect, the evocation of childhood in the steppe, of the society of women, of objects and places (what he calls 'the staircases of my childhood' – and it is

159

true that in Arab houses, these really are places, objects, as Syrian and Tunisian filmmakers have been able to show), the whole interlaced with invective against the *'qawmiyyin'*, the 'Ba'thist' nationalists held to have derailed and illegitimately appropriated the representation of the nation.

The Forgotten Uplands – Mammeri

Killed in an absurd road accident in 1989, Mouloud Mammeri was also born in 1917, at Taourirt Mimoun in the Djurdjura massif (Kabylia), which forms the backdrop to his very remarkable, and very scandalous, first novel *La Colline Oubliée* (1952, film in 1994).[10] His family included poets (his father was an *amusnaw*, a Kabyle tribal elder-philosopher-sage) and a famous painter. He pursued secondary education *'à la française'* in Rabat, Algiers and Paris, at the Louis le Grand *lycée*'s preparatory class for the Ecole Normale Supérieure. With the outbreak of war, he was mobilised in 1939 and again in 1942 – between the two terms of service he wrote his master's thesis under the supervision of the eminent Hellenist, Louis Gernet, a privilege he shared with Camus and Berque, among others – and participated in campaigns in Italy, France, and Germany (an experience he recounted in *Le Sommeil du Juste*[11]). A teacher of French at Médéa, then in Algiers, his non-conformism and imagination won him the adoration of his students both European and Algerian.

In 1957, with the Battle of Algiers,[12] he went into self-imposed exile in Morocco, where, among other things, he found the inspiration for his novel *L'Opium et le Bâton*, which was filmed in 1967. After 1962, he taught ethnology at the University of Algiers, as well as a very popular extra-curricular course in Berber language, offered in defiance of the academic authorities. It was around this time that his problems began. In 1968 he nonetheless ran a centre for the study of prehistory, an institution inherited from the French period,[13] where he developed without difficulty – since volunteers to join were legion – a section for research in cultural anthropology. In this capacity he organised a number of field studies which were to inform his work on Berber linguistics, and also initiated, with a whole team of colleagues, a passion for *'recherches rapprochées'* (close-range, detailed fieldwork), undertaken in such 'peripheral' spaces as the Hoggar, at Timimoun in the Western Erg and in the Aurès. (It is to this institutional context that I owe, myself, the possibility of carrying out the long research which gave rise to the publication of *Les Versets de l'Invincibilité*.[14])

An internationally recognised writer, Mammeri travelled the world, visiting, in particular, the USSR, which had a strong influence on him. In 1980 and 1981, his own responsibility (only indirect) and above all that of the young researchers at his institute, the CRAPE, (entirely direct) in the events that came to be called the 'Berber Spring', and the effervescence which followed, resulted in his eviction from the directorship of the Centre.

Thereafter, he divided his time between Algiers, his village in the Djurdjura and Paris, where he created a review which still exists, *Awal*.[15]

Having no connection whatsoever to the régime, being a touch dilettante, and in no way doctrinaire – even regarding the 'Berber question' – Mammeri constantly, even before independence, experienced uncomfortable brushes with the nationalists and their scribblers. Calmly persuaded of the importance of his cultural heritage, he promoted it in two equally subversive registers: through both his novels and his work on linguistics. In 1976, he published the first Berber (*tamazight* dialect) grammar to be written in Berber, and from this date onwards he was also responsible for the appearance of a certain corpus of poetry of great value, by Kabyle authors (*Les Isefra de Si Mohand*, *Poèmes kabyles anciens*[16]) or drawn from an anonymous Zenatid tradition (*L'Ahallil de Gourara*[17]). He also wrote, in Berber, an important work on the poet and saint *shaykh* Mohand u-Lhocine.[18] In short, he demolished, with ease and without any real demonstrative intent, all those hollow, reiterated assumptions about *berbérité* as an archaic, immobile, self-reproducing peasant culture. His introduction to *Poèmes kabyles anciens* shows in irrefutable fashion just how a tribal tradition can also be a learned one.

Having come thus far, and before moving on to Abu 'l-Qasim Sa'adallah, about whom we have far fewer biographical elements, it is important to note the elitist character – both as regards family origins and educational trajectory – of the two spokesman for 'voices from below' whom we have now met. Both are clearly representative of a position which the *Subaltern Studies* scholars have usefully identified and analysed, that is of elites constituting themselves as the representatives of marginalised groups. What is of most concern here, however, is *their relationship with nationalism and nationalists* – a position not without ambiguity in the case of Lacheraf who is otherwise so remarkably lucid. Equally important is the link that both of these individuals demonstrate, between a Parisian education, received as *colonisés*, and the relationship to his own culture that each thereafter developed – a particularity that Sa'adallah, as we shall see, does not share.

A Cultural History of Authenticity: Sa'adallah

Abu 'l-Qasim Sa'adallah was born in 1927 at Guemmar in the Suf, an oasis complex in the south Constantinois (in eastern Algeria). He studied the Qur'an at the local *kuttab* and probably completed his early education in scriptural knowledge (*'ilm*) at the independent school created by a local *'alim*, a man from a maraboutic family converted to *salafi* ideas, 'Abd al-Aziz ben al-Hachemi ben Ibrahim. The Suf was, with Laghouat and the Aurès mountains, one of the rare peripheral areas of Algeria to come into early contact with, and propagate, the new ideas of *salafi* reformism and its Arab–Islamic *nahda* (renaissance).[19] In 1947, thanks to the financial support of Ben Badis' reformist Association of *'Ulama* (AUMA[20]), Sa'adallah enrolled at the Zaytuna in Tunis, where he studied for seven years. Back in Algeria, he taught in the reformists' independent schools, at El Harrach near Algiers, then at Aïn Beïda. In 1955, he went with a scholarship from the AUMA to Cairo, where in 1959 he obtained a degree in Arabic Letters and Islamic Civilisation. In 1962, funded by an FLN scholarship and a Fulbright grant, he went to the USA and gained a PhD from the University of Minnesota in 1965 with a dissertation (in English) on 'The Rise of Algerian Nationalism, 1900–1930' which was first published in Arabic in Beirut and then translated into French, published in Algiers by the state publisher in 1983, and reprinted in 1985.[21] On his return he taught history at the University of Algiers, where he rapidly became (and long remained) head of the History Department, one of the first departments at the university to offer its courses exclusively in Arabic. He now teaches in Jordan, at the Ahl al-Bayt University; an influential but discreet personality, this is more or less all that is known about his trajectory.

A poet as well as a historian and, above all, an encyclopaedist, his poetic work as well as his first monographs on Algerian intellectuals have been published in Egypt or Lebanon; these texts are not easily accessible in Algeria,[22] where he is known for his academic role, highly influential among his students, (including those who do not share his ideological orientation), and for a number of virulent articles published in the official press. His *Cultural History of Algeria*, published in several volumes which began to appear in the 1970s, has attracted the most attention for its engagement in a programme of restoring a national cultural patrimony in the widest sense, exhuming regional authors entirely unknown until then[23] and actively participating in the cataloguing of *zawiya* libraries – a concern somewhat surprising in a *Badisi* reformist.

For, as he himself points out in the French Preface to the remarkable third edition of this veritable monument, *Ta'rikh al-Jazâ'ir al-thaqâfi*, published in Lebanon with an excellent index,[24] the Arabic-language education of Algerians was oriented towards equipping them for 'teaching in schools and preaching in mosques', towards 'the formation of men's characters, not the confection of texts'. It is in this quite exceptional singularity that he is interesting in the context of our present discussion; it is in this, too, that he distinguishes himself from other, more flamboyant, reformist personalities such as Tawfiq al-Madani or 'Abdallah Cheriet, both, and particularly the former, authors of books which are certainly not to be ignored but who, in contrast to Sa'adallah, departed relatively quickly from an academic role to take up more prominent functions and who, above all, never displayed the slightest interest in a local Algerian patrimony.[25] That said, it is difficult for the moment to say (and it cannot be observed in the catalogues of works in Arabic published in Algiers) whether or not this singular interest has been taken up by his students.[26]

Reading between the lines of his biography, it seems, too, that he belongs, in Bourdieu's terms, to the *'boursiers'* (scholarship winners) rather than to the *'héritiers'*, (heirs; recipients of accumulated capital, of whatever type), which fact, however one precisely understands the latter term, clearly differentiates him from our two preceding authors. This is true independently of the question of his education – one pursued on a track which, during the colonial period, was clearly in a relegated position relative to training in French. All the more important to ask oneself how he developed a concern for 'patrimony', perhaps (this is a hypothesis) in contact with a *milieu* – that of Cairo – which cheerfully despises Algerian cultural production in Arabic and would hardly suspect the existence of such a patrimony. One can read indirect traces of this in the Preface mentioned above. In any case, *Ta'rikh al-Jaza'ir al-thaqafi*, a work of much too considerable proportions to allow us to enter into its detail here, is certainly a major, and, in the circumstances, quasi-miraculous contribution to our subject.

Segmentarity at Work Where You Least Expect It

These men, of the same generation and comparable historical experience, all three connecting strong provincial attachments to a wide cosmopolitan experience gained in parts of the world with massive cultural strength and profoundly revolutionised, if not revolutionary, societies (Latin America, the USSR, Egypt in the 1950s/70s), and endowed with the same high idea of *'algérianité'* and of their own vocation to return to it its proper prestige, ought to have 'had offspring' – created schools, followings. Despite their convictions, talent, and undeniable charisma, however, it is clear, not only that they did not do so but that their works have not resulted in the visibility, even for the Algerian public, of *a shared patrimony*, a truly *Algerian* patrimony common to francophones, berberophones and arabophones. This is perhaps a difficult statement to prove, but it appears evident to most observers of Algeria, whether internal or external.

We saw above how the ideological *and institutional* context of the first decades after independence was opposed to any such development. We must recall the reason for this resistance, one sometimes implicit and sometimes proclaimed out loud, to any deviation from the official idea of the Nation and of the official history of its victory over the coloniser (a resistance against which Lacheraf has been perfectly lucid and highly polemical): nothing could be allowed to oppose itself to the *hegemony* of a highly defined social stratum, that minuscule, urban petite bourgeoisie, of middling education in Arabic or French but of relatively marked acculturation, which had furnished the *cadres* of the revolutionary movement which had achieved emancipation, the PPA/MTLD.[27] Nothing could be permitted to oppose its status of 'enlightened avant-garde', modernising and above all, *unifying*. Hence the fear of the *kuttab*, a vestigial archaism. Hence the fear of the fragmentary, the local, the particular, whether social or religious: the word 'tribe' is banned, [tribal] insurrections too, the word 'brotherhood' [*tariqa*] and equally Ibadism (the Algerian branch of kharijism, found in the Mzab) which keeps a very low profile, and of course vernacular languages, considered the worst rather than the best of things.[28] All fears which the reformists share wholeheartedly with the nationalists.

But that is not the whole story. 'The unknowing other', to borrow an expression from Rancière – s/he who finds him/herself 'on the side of sound and not that of speech'[29] – s/he whose defence nationalism (like scientism) can and must take up in the name of dignity *but not equality*, he who can be a 'brother' in alienation but *not a companion in the effort of thought,* nor in the assumption of Culture – is not only (as in the Qur'anic injunctions) 'the poor and the orphan', the 'dominated'; nor only the peasant or the *'zoufri'* (worker), but s/he who speaks 'the other' language and does not know mine, who has a geographical, historical, vernacular location other than mine. Above all, and following the extent to which one develops in political instruction and political consciousness, s/he – not who votes differently from me, since that is of no importance – but who identifies him/herself in a 'family' of the national movement other than mine, and therefore *in another representation of 'Us'*. These mechanisms of exclusion are powerfully present, including in those who, like our three pioneers, make themselves spokesmen of 'their own' constituency/locality. This observation is not new and goes back, in fact, to the proto-history of the Algerian cultural–nationalist field, but the situation has hardly changed since then.

Since most Algerians, as cultural producers and consumers, are, contrary to a received impression, at least bilingual and often trilingual, the key to these struggles lies not in linguistic divisions, but in assumed or ascribed 'identitarian' affiliations, in *the impossibility of thinking cultural personality outside of the political idiom* in the narrow sense; one could only be, in Algeria, a 'true Nationalist', a 'suspect Berberist', an 'atheistic Communist', a 'conservative Reformist', etc. I have shown elsewhere how, in the 1950s, an attested flowering of Algerian cultural and intellectual talent was sterilised by ideological splits which translated into a censorship against which no appeal could be made.[30] Lacheraf, for example, was at that time one of the severest and most closely followed critics of Mammeri's *La Colline Oubliée*, attacked for its supposed egotistical regionalism and isolationism;[31] a striking aspect of his 1998 memoir is the complete lack of any trace of self-criticism in Lacheraf who, at 75, allows himself to do precisely what he censured then in a young man of 20 who had the misfortune to be talented – to speak with emotion of the roots of his own attachment to his *terroir*. After independence, this situation only became more severe. In 1998, in the Preface *in French* to his *Ta'rikh al-Jaza'ir al-thaqafi,* Sa'adallah writes coldly:

> As for those Algerians who received a uniquely French education [and no doubt he means precisely our two other authors], they separated themselves, or almost, from their roots and their origins, losing all contact with Arabic documents and manuscripts, and even with their genealogical tables, all of them established in Arabic throughout the different periods of the country's history. *Such kinds of Algerians were therefore in no sense fit to write the cultural history of their country.*[32]

Observers of the Algerian scene might recall, too, that Sa'adallah was the author of an incendiary article, published in the widely read official weekly press (*El Moudjahid Culturel* in Arabic) in 1979, accusing Kateb Yacine, Mouloud Mammeri and others of 'corrupting Algerian youth' (a rather flattering accusation, since one was thereby placed in the company of Socrates). This accusation, against Kateb! – against one of the most clear-sighted of intellectuals regarding the cultural fracture of the country, and one of the most active in struggling against it, in every language! Kateb, who staged plays in a dialectal Arabic which he mastered only with difficulty, and not completely, and who called his youngest son Amazigh, a Berber term (indeed, now the generally used Berber term for 'Berber') imbued with dense symbolism.[33] Mammeri declined to reply, for he was not a man to throw anathemas, but neither was he neutral in these conflicts himself; his profound rejection of Arabic and, therewith, Islamic, heritage (while he was no non-believer) led him sometimes to extremes, to the extent of claiming that 'his' *shaykh* Mohand u-Lhocine was illiterate (implicitly, in Arabic) – he who was a dignitary of the Rahmaniyya order, the most strongly scripturary brotherhood in Algeria! In this respect, a text such as his dialogue with Bourdieu on oral poetry, published in *Actes de la recherche en sciences sociales* in 1978,[34] is at once particularly clear and stupefying, despite its elegance! This rejection has profoundly marked, and, given the personal aura of Mammeri, continues to mark, the Berber language movement, closing to it the possibility of understanding its own cultural continuity and its links to the rest of the world through Islam.

So one might think, as a first analysis, that the major victor of these 'fratricidal' struggles has, definitively, been Nationalism, or at least the

Unanimism which it has so consistently produced.[35] But not even this is so certain. For, in the absence of any common denominator between these different talents and works of self-expression, it may be that, by a wicked trick of the cunning of History, it is religion, that unthought constant of the national movement, and of the Republic and the society to which it gave birth, that remains the only meta-code which Algerians recognise themselves as having *in common*. Kateb Yacine suggested as much, very early on.[36] Despite certain ambiguities, a number of progressive and secularist intellectuals such as the communist Chebbah Mekki, or Mourad Bourboune, bear witness to the same observation.[37] Such a conclusion would make sense of *the paradoxical persistence of the 'Badisien' paradigm* ('Islam is my religion, Arabic is my language, Algeria is my fatherland') for defining *algérianité* in the discourse of the régime,[38] and might go some way towards explaining its diffusion as widely among the popular classes as among intellectual and political elites, its adoption in literate berberophone regions,[39] despite (or because of) its obsession with uniformity and consensus. It would also, and without in any sense positing a direct filiation between the two, make the diffusion of Islamism in the past 20 years appear less extraordinary. The large audience, for a long time minimised by the regime's censors, of an Islamist and clearly xenophobic (this being the least one might say) theoretician like Malek Bennabi might indicate the same.[40] Even today, despite appearances, agreement on religious adherence to Islam remains, at least once one moves beyond the country's most thoroughly modernised milieus, the most stable pivot of the system's legitimacy[41] – to the lasting detriment of Lacheraf.[42]

Return to '*a Forgotten Algeria*': a Self-Accepting 'Subject'?

Never so strongly as in writing this have I been struck by the very simple fact of the absence of *contradictory and democratic debate* between the positions which I have personified here by particular proper names, but which are certainly shared by others; of any such debate, whether direct or, failing that, by interposed texts. Lacheraf is a very demanding writer, difficult to read and obscure as his convictions are strong, but the introduction to *L'Algérie, Nation et Société*, and equally the final chapter of that book, strangely prophetic given its date (1964–65), his shots at the *qawmiyyin* in 1998, confronted with the reformist positions of Sa'adallah or those of Mammeri, ought at least to have nourished academic debate inside the country. But one has the impression that these texts have never been taken as anything other than *pro domo* self-defences – which they also are – and, indeed, how could it have been otherwise? When I remarked, to a young Algerian colleague, (someone perfectly informed regarding the question at the centre of this article and, since he lives in the USA, also capable of a greater critical distance than I am myself) on the absence of self-criticism in Lacheraf's work, his response was that people like him (Lacheraf), and the same is doubtless true of the others too, already have enough to do in self-defence without starting to beat themselves up on their own account. Self-defence against whom, or what? Against political reproof, no doubt, against excommunication (in writing as much, I have to tell myself that at the same time, Algeria was nonetheless not Albania...), but above all, I think, against themselves, caught in a reflex of self-censorship all the more powerful for being unconscious: never to give weapons to those one considers as the enemy.

And since we must escape from irresolvable hand-to-hand tussles with the-Nation-as-imagined, on the one side, and on the other, with all the trifling platitudes about 'identity',[43] what is required now is a *general theoretical debate*; recourse to a non-positivist social science, like that for which Jacques Rancière pleads, and to comparativism.[44] That would suppose a critique of our disciplines, 'compromised [as they are] with the great discursive systems of modernity.' It would imply the necessity of 'thinking [for example] history at the limit.'[45] It would not, on the other hand, be a question of inventing 'the subject', but of *restoring him/her there where s/he has always been*, in 'the local', in individual, familial, regional, religious singularity; in brief, in the private, the domestic, the affective – if not in opposition to, then *in the face of* the public, the national and the state. Such singularities escape the categorisations of both positive science and nationalist ideology, because they precede them and obey different logics of production. This *would* suppose a renunciation of totalisations, of syntheses and of any overarching, commanding view of 'culture', 'society', or 'religion', and *a fortiori* of 'the state' or 'Algeria' – which does not necessarily imply a return to monographs and encylopaedias. We would be able to accept work on *the fragmentary, the discontinuous,* and we would look for new kinds of writing – which, moreover, have already been at work, some for a considerable time.[46]

Conclusion

It remains the case, however, that the current situation – let us not delude ourselves – and especially the last ten years, that is, since Algeria has been living through a real war, is not merely one of a deficit of reflexivity or theorisation but simply of the survival of a few modest pathways that had been opened up in minuscule spaces. The failure of the student strike with which I began is precisely the sign, or a sign, of this crisis, since in a climate of such peril, 'culture from below' is hardly the primary concern, even of those who live such *subalternity* (one only has to see the growing number of suspended theses). As for the numerically huge intellectual diaspora, in France and elsewhere, it is far from playing to its full potential the role that others, for example that of India, do. That may be due to multiple factors, of which not the least is the social demand of the host countries; of exiled Algerian intellectuals, publishers ask for writing on the state, the army and the special forces, not their maternal culture.

It seems today more difficult than ever to answer, from inside Algeria, the question: what is being Algerian? And it is hardly paradoxical to note that the most serene replies come, *in spite of everything,* from exile (painters, film-makers, novelists), so much is it true that one is someone only through one's own history (which is what distinguishes a *personality* from the carry-all concept of 'identity').[47] On the other hand, such a history also cannot be thought without a distancing from oneself and a confrontation with others – a process which the dominant Unanimism forbids, knowing nothing of Otherness but its demonisation ('the West') or its obliteration (the 'local').

NOTES

1. Jacques Rancière, 'Les hommes comme animaux littéraires' (interview), *Mouvements* 3 (1999) pp.133–44.
2. Jacques Pouchepadass, 'Les Subaltern Studies ou la critique postcoloniale de la modernité', in Jackie Assayag (ed.), *Intellectuels en diaspora et théories nomades,* special issue of *L'Homme* 156 (2000) pp.161–82.
3. Ibid.
4. I have remarked elsewhere on the view of the peasantry to be found in the National Charter of 1976: see Fanny Colonna, *Les Versets de l'Invincibilité. Permanence et changements religieux dans l'Algérie contemporaine* (Paris: FNSP 1995) pp.27–8.
5. That is, those claiming the inheritance of the Islamic-modernist reform movement led in the interwar period by *shaykh* 'Abd al-Hamid Ben Badis (1889–1940).
6. Paris: Maspero 1965.
7. Algiers: Casbah éditions 1998.
8. Roland Lardinois, (ed.), *Miroir de l'Inde, Etudes indiennes en sciences sociales* (Paris: Editions de la Maison des Sciences de l'Homme 1988.)
9. In the summer of 2001, Lacheraf was busy working on the sequel to *Des Noms et des Lieux* (Editor's note).
10. Paris: Plon 1952.
11. Paris: Plon 1955.
12. The FLN's urban guerrilla campaign in the capital, repressed by the French military who took over police powers, sealed the Casbah and tortured suspects.
13. The *Centre de Recherches en Anthropologie, Préhistoire et Ethnologie* (CRAPE) of the University of Algiers inherited the prehistory and ethnology functions of earlier institutions, as well as the academic journal *Libyca* published before independence by the *Service des Antiquités* of the Government General, which had also run colonial Algeria's museums and archaeological investigations.
14. Colonna (note 4).
15. *Awal. Revue d'Études berbères.* (Paris: Publications de la Maison des Sciences de l'Homme).
16. Mouloud Mammeri, *Les Isefra, poèmes de Si-Mohand ou-Mhand* (Paris: Maspéro 1978) and *Poèmes kabyles anciens* (Paris: Maspéro 1980).

17. Mammeri, *L'Ahallil du Gourara* (Paris: Editions de la Maison des Sciences de l'Homme 1984).
18. Mammeri, *Inna-Yas Ccix Muhend (Cheikh Mohand a dit)* (Paris: Ceram 1990).
19. On the reformists and their relationship to rural Algeria, see Colonna, *Versets* (note 4).
20. *Jam'iyat al-'Ulama al-Muslimin al-Jaza'iriyyin/Association des Uléma Musulmans Algériens*, founded by Ben Badis in 1931.
21. Abou al Qacim Saadallah, 'The Rise of Algerian Nationalism, 1900–30' (PhD thesis, University of Minnesota 1965); *Al Haraka al wataniyya al jaza'iriyya* (Beirut: Dar al Adab 1969); *La montée du nationalisme en Algérie* (Algiers: ENAL 1983, 2nd edn. ENAL 1985).
22. On these inaccessible works of Sa'adallah, see the excellent dictionary by Achour Cheurfi, *Mémoire algérienne* (Algiers: Editions Dahlab 1996), which can also be profitably consulted under the entries for Mammeri and Lacheraf.
23. On these unknown authors, see also Cheurfi (note 22).
24. 9 vols., (Beirut: Dar al-Gharb al-Islami 1998).
25. Tawfiq al-Madani was born in 1899, in Tunis, to a family of Algerian émigrés. A journalist and historian, he was a high profile but somewhat heterodox personality in the reformist movement. Secretary General of the AUMA before 1954, he later (1956) became a spokesman for the FLN in Cairo and in other Arab and Muslim countries, and held positions in the first Provisional Government (1958) and the first independent Algerian cabinet (1962). Abdallah Cheriet was born in 1921, at La Meskiana (in the northern Aurès). He received a French education before attending the Zaytuna at Tunis, and later took a degree in philosophy at Damascus (1951). From 1956 to 1962 he was director of the Arabic-language edition of *El Moudjahid*, the FLN's official organ. The author of several works, first in French and then in Arabic, he took a doctorate in 1972, and taught political philosophy at the University of Algiers. (See entry in Cheurfi, note 22)
26. With the hope of throwing some light on this question, a round table has been planned, to be held at the Maison Méditerranéenne des Sciences de l'Homme in Aix-en-Provence in 2003, on current research into local history in Algeria, with papers being presented primarily by Algerian colleagues who have been trained in Arabic since the reform of social science teaching and research in the country, in 1981.
27. *Parti du Peuple Algérien* (founded in 1937 and banned in 1939, thereafter clandestine, the PPA was the successor of the first nationalist group, the *Étoile Nord-Africaine*, founded in 1926), and its legal cover, the *Mouvement pour la Triomphe des Libertés Démocratiques* (founded in 1946); this was the political formation whose militants included the founders of the FLN, and from whose factional split in 1953–54 the FLN was formed.
28. On this horror of the fragmentary, see Colonna (note 4), especially ch.9, pp.328ff.
29. See Rancière (note 1), and the same author's *La nuit des prolétaires, Archives du rêve ouvrier* (Paris: Fayard 1981. A paperback edition of this work was published in 1997).
30. Fanny Colonna, (ed.) *Aurès/Algérie 1954. Les fruits verts d'une révolution* (Paris: Autrement, *série Mémoires* 33, 1994).
31. Arezki Metref, 'Deux affaires de censure' (note 30) pp.138–62.
32. Sa'adallah (note 24) p.5, (to be found at the end of Vol. 9).
33. On the etymology of the word *amazigh*, pl. *imazighen*, now a commonly self-ascribed ethnonym among berberophone communities (and the Berber cultural movement in North Africa and in the diaspora), assumed to mean originally 'free man', see Salem Chaker, art. 'Amaziɣ' (Amazigh), 'le/un Berbère', *Encyclopédie Berbère* (Aix-en-Provence: Edisud 1985) vol. IV: 562–8.
34. Paris, Sept. 1978, No.23.
35. Fanny Colonna (ed.), *Algérie, la fin de l'Unanimisme. Débats et combats des années 80 et 90*, special issue of *Maghreb Mashreq*, 15, (1997) and particularly the Introduction.
36. Kateb Yacine, *Abdelkader et l'indépendance algérienne* (Algiers, author 1947, 2nd edn. 1983).
37. Chebbah Mekki (Mekki Chebbah) 1894–1988, co-founder and militant of the *Etoile Nord-Africaine*, and then of the Algerian Communist Party, was born in the southern Aurès and died in Algiers. After a spell as a worker in France during the 1920s and 1930s, he returned

to the Aurès where he engaged in local subversive activity. A prolific author of Arabic theatre, he also left behind him a short autobiography, written in dialectal Arabic, which was published in Algiers in 1989. Educated at the *kuttab,* an experience he never disowned, he was close to the Badisi reformists despite his adherence to Marxian ideas. Mourad Bourboune was born in 1938, at Jijel (on the Constantinois coast). He studied in Constantine, Tunis and Paris, and was a founder of the *Union des écrivains* in Algiers in 1963. He left the country after the *coup d'état* of 1965 and has since lived in France. A journalist, he is above all the author of novels written in a deliberately transgressive French *(Le mont des genêts, Le muezzin),* but has also published poetry, and has written screenplays for a number of major Algerian films.

38. Hocine Benkheira, *Revue maghrébine d'études politiques et religieuses* (Oran) 1 (1988). Similarly Lahouari Addi, *L'impasse du populisme. L'Algérie: Collectivité politique et Etat en construction* (Algiers: Entreprise nationale du Livre 1990).
39. See Colonna (note 4).
40. See Metref (note 31).
41. See Colonna (note 4) pp.355–64.
42. See Lacheraf, *Des noms et des lieux* (note 7).
43. For a severe critique of the notion of identity, see Jean-François Bayard, *L'illusion identitaire* (Paris: Fayard 1996).
44. Rancière (note 1).
45. Pouchepadas (note 2).
46. For example, Kevin Dwyer, *Moroccan Dialogues* (Baltimore: Johns Hopkins University Press 1982) or Smadar Lavie, *The Poetics of Military Occupation* (Chicago: Chicago University Press 1990).
47. For a consideration of the difference between *identity* and *personality,* see Laurent Thévenot,'L'action comme engagement', in J.M. Barbier (ed.), *L'analyse de la singularité de l'action* (Paris: PUF, 1999) and Marc Brévigliéri, 'L'usage et l'habiter. Contribution à une sociologie de la proximité' (Thèse de sociologie, EHESS, Paris, under the supervision of L. Thévenot.) Both contributions take their inspiration from the thought of Paul Ricoeur, in particular his latest work, *La Mémoire, l'Histoire, l'Oubli* (Paris: Seuil 2000). English readers might usefully also consult an earlier essay by Ricoeur, 'Life in Quest of Narrative', in David Wood (ed.), *On Paul Ricoeur. Narrative and Interpretation* (London: Routledge 1991).

Abstracts

**Algeria/Morocco: The Passions of the Past. Representations
of the Nation that Unite and Divide**
Benjamin Stora

Algeria and Morocco are the two largest countries, the two principal states of the
Maghrib. An Algero–Moroccan partnership has the greatest potential as the
motor of dynamic economic and political development for the whole region.
However, at the beginning of the twenty-first century, the development process,
its aspirations embodied in the Maghrib Arab Union, is blocked by the *impasse*
in Algero–Moroccan relations. This article examines how, beyond the crucial
Western Sahara dispute, other factors, differential contemporary relationships to
space and to history, influence this problematic relationship. Different
constructions of nationalism in the two cases are revealing, as is the relation of
each country to its national space. These two major states of North Africa,
similar and divided by so many things held in common, must seek in their recent
history the means of a *rapprochement*. However, it is not at the level of the state,
but at that of civil society that such a rapprochement is now taking place.

Ideologies of the Nation in Tunisian Cinema
Kmar Kchir-Bendana

This article offers an overview of the different ways in which Tunisian artists
have produced images of their society and nation, its recent and more distant
history, its regions and social problems, through the first 40 years of cinema
in independent Tunisia. Each discernible trend in political orientation, use of
language, aesthetic considerations, and characterisation is discussed against a
theoretical background which takes film as an aspect of cultural production in
which the imaginary relation of individuals to their real conditions of social
existence may become visible. The article also considers the location of
Tunisian cinema in the regional and world market, and the significance of the
'national' cinema as a category of expression and analysis.

**Stories on the Road from Fez to Marrakesh:
Oral History on the Margins of National Identity**
Moshe Gershovich

Post-colonial discourses tend sometimes to belittle or even ignore altogether
individuals and groups that collaborated with the colonial order. However,

171

their unique position between the colonised society and the colonising power merits attention. This article examines the collective profile of Moroccan veterans who served in the French army. It examines their backgrounds, career patterns, relations with their peers and commanders, as well as their reintegration within post-colonial Moroccan society. Through the use of oral history it gives representation to an otherwise silent group and it critically evaluates certain perceptions and stereotypes that prevailed on both sides of the Franco-Moroccan military symbiosis in the colonial era.

Echoes of National Liberation:
Turkey Viewed from the Maghrib in the 1920s
Odile Moreau

The distant aim towards whose fulfilment this article hopes to contribute is that of elucidating the emergence of ideas of the nation, and the structures of the 'nation' state, in North Africa, a process whose beginnings ought to be situated in the early 1920s. The more immediate goal is to investigate some of the ways in which North Africans saw, and responded to, the Turkish nationalist movement between 1919 and 1924, and the radical institutional transformations undertaken by the young Turkish republic in this brief and turbulent period. The paper suggests that, while the victory of Turkish nationalism against the European powers offered inspiration to North Africans, the abolition of the caliphate effectively removed one important link which had, until then, subsisted between the Maghrib (especially Tunis) and the Middle East.

Libya's Refugees, their Places of Exile, and the Shaping of their National Idea
Anna Baldinetti

This article focuses on the history of Libyan exiles during the colonial period, tracing the history of the Libyan refugee associations in Tunisia, Egypt and Syria and analysing their early political activities. It argues that the refugees' activities between 1911 and 1951 can be regarded as the first nucleus of Libyan nationalism. Exploring certain key issues and problems concerning the history of Libyan nationalism, the article also gives a brief overview of the historiography on colonial Libya more broadly, seeking to set the country within its broader historical framework in both the Maghrib and the Middle East.

Martyrs and Patriots: Ethnic, National and Transnational Dimensions of Kabyle Politics
Paul A. Silverstein

One of the many facets of the 1990s civil war in Algeria has been the renewed importance of regional dynamics within the Algerian nation-state. This essay focuses on this aspect of the conflict and the consequences it entails for the reinvention of Kabyle political subjectivity. Placing the current conflict – as it has been experienced in Kabylia and in the Kabyle diaspora – in a longer history of struggles for cultural, linguistic, and political representation, the article explores the tensions between the ethnic, national, and transnational dimensions of Kabyle politics. With a particular focus on the representation and enactment of Kabyle struggle in the diaspora, the study attempts to understand these dynamics through the changing image of the martyr-patriot as successively victimised by forces of colonialism, Islamism, and the independent Algerian state. It is argued that, while Kabyle politics has become progressively transnationalised, it nonetheless remains firmly ensconced in local-level concerns over the social and economic conditions of a future, post-war Algerian nation.

Moroccan Women's Narratives of Liberation: A Passive Revolution?
Liat Kozma

Feminist research often presents national and feminist historiographies as essential, static, ahistorical and isolated entities. The article examines Moroccan national historiography as a site of hegemonic struggle, in which various versions of the past continuously confront each other. First, feminist historiography is considered in the context of the political and social reality of the 1980s and the 1990s, a reality which enabled the visibility of women as historical subjects. Next it is shown how feminist thinkers used the struggle for national independence in the formation of an indigenous genealogy for Moroccan feminism, one which would legitimise their egalitarian ideology. Finally, it is examined how tension and dialogue between national and feminist historical narratives led to a transformation of national historiography and the incorporation of women within it; through this process, we can also see how the criticism embedded in feminist historiography was undermined by its inclusion in the dominant historiography.

Citizens and Subjects in the Bank:
Corporate Visions of Modern Art and Moroccan Identity
Katarzyna Pieprzak

This article examines the rhetoric around the creation of a contemporary art gallery within arguably the largest private-sector bank in Morocco, Wafabank. In proclaiming itself a modern citizen with duties to the modern arts of Morocco, the bank constructs an image of Western modernity for both itself and its clients, using art to narrate and attest to Morocco's inclusion in a global economic community with shared values. Through an analysis of the discourse surrounding the opening of the gallery and a reading of its exhibition practices, this article explores how the bank negotiates its identity between global citizen and local subject, promoting values of modernity while simultaneously embracing Moroccan political and social structures that often contradict them. Unlike the national museums, the bank gallery does not present a glorious vision of the past, but rather, through art, it narrates a contemporary and often schizophrenic late twentieth-century Morocco.

The Nation's 'Unknowing Other':
Three Intellectuals and the Culture(s) of Being Algerian, or the Impossibility of Subaltern Studies in Algeria
Fanny Colonna

This article examines the position of the humanities and social sciences in Algeria over the past 40 years, taking the work of the *Subaltern Studies* collective, and more generally the question of voices and modes of resistance 'from below', as a foil. The absence of any comparable development in Algeria is taken as a sign of the extremely powerful hold exercised by the political field, in ideological and institutional terms, over any and all expression of *'algérianité'*. Taking the paradoxical example of three major authors whose works reflect, each in his own way, much more complex conceptions of nationhood than that constructed in official discourse, it is contended that these figures nevertheless have not succeeded in producing – and have not sought to produce – an image of Algerian society, its past, its culture and its struggles, which could be held in common by all Algerians. Each is trapped in a chauvinistic vision of a country which he jealously cherishes, each rejecting the images advanced by the others, in a situation of permanent mutual ostracism which reflects the language question, itself a symptom of a deeper, older, and still unresolved socio-cultural and political fragmentation.

Notes on Contributors

Anna Baldinetti received her doctorate from the University of Siena in 1994. She now teaches African and Middle Eastern history at the Faculty of Political Sciences at the University of Perugia. Her research concerns the political history of Egypt and the Maghrib in the nineteenth and twentieth centuries. She is the author of *Orientalismo e colonialismo. La ricerca di consenso in Egitto all'impresa di Libia* (Rome: Istituto per l'Oriente, 1997).

Kmar Kchir-Bendana is a researcher at the Institut Supérieur de l'Histoire du Mouvement National (ISHMN) at the University of La Manouba, and a Research Associate at the Institut de Recherche sur le Maghreb Contemporain (IRMC), Tunis. She is a film devotee and also specialises in the cultural and intellectual history of Tunisia in the nineteenth and twentieth centuries.

Fanny Colonna is a sociologist and Directeur de Recherche Émérite at the CNRS (Laboratoire Méditerranéen de Sociologie, Aix-en-Provence). Born in Algeria in 1934 to a family which had migrated there in the nineteenth century, she was a student and then professor at the University of Algiers. Most notably the author of *Instituteurs algériens, 1883-1939* (Paris: FNSP, 1975) and of *Les Versets de l'Invincibilité: Permanence et changements religieux dans l'Algérie contemporaine* (Paris: FNSP, 1995), she is particularly concerned with intellectuals and local culture in Algeria and, more recently, in Egypt. She has lived in France since 1993.

Moshe Gershovich is an Associate Professor of History at the University of Nebraska at Omaha. He is the author of *French Military Rule in Morocco: Colonialism and its Consequences* (London and Portland, OR: Frank Cass, 2000). He received his doctorate from Harvard in 1995. His contribution is part of an oral history project concerning Moroccan veterans of the French Army.

Liat Kozma is a graduate student at the department of Middle Eastern Studies at New York University. She holds an MA in Middle Eastern Studies from Tel Aviv University, and is currently researching concepts of licit and illicit sexuality in late nineteenth century Egypt.

James McDougall is a Junior Research Fellow at the Middle East Centre of St Antony's College, Oxford, where he also completed his doctoral thesis. His research interests include the cultural and intellectual history of nationalism in the Middle East and North Africa, the history of French colonialism, and theories of historiography.

Odile Moreau studied Arabic and Turkish at the Institut National de Langues et Civilisations Orientales (INALCO), Paris. Her doctoral dissertation examined the military reforms of the late Ottoman empire. She is now a researcher at the Institut de Recherches sur le Maghreb Contemporain (IRMC), Tunis, where she coordinates an international research group on 'the Reform of the State in the Mediterranean Muslim World in the Nineteenth and Twentieth Centuries'.

Katarzyna Pieprzak received her Ph.D. in Comparative Literature from the University of Michigan in December 2001. Her research interests include globalisation and culture in North Africa and the narration of trauma in Algerian and Rwandan literature. She currently teaches at the City University of New York.

Paul A. Silverstein is Assistant Professor of Anthropology at Reed College (Portland, USA) and a member of the editorial committee of *Middle East Report*. He is currently finishing a book project, *Trans-Politics: Islam, Berberity and the French Nation-State,* and is co-editor (with Ussama Makdisi) of *Memory and Violence in the Middle East and North Africa* (forthcoming).

Benjamin Stora has recently been appointed to a chair in the History of the Maghrib at the Institut National de Langues et Civilisations Orientales (INALCO), Paris. Born in Algeria, he is a frequent commentator on North African affairs in the francophone media, and the author of *La Gangrène et l'Oubli: la Mémoire de la Guerre d'Algérie* (Paris: la Découverte, 1991) and of numerous other books and articles. His work has considered the social and political history of Algerian nationalism, Franco-Maghribi relations before and after decolonisation, Algerian immigration to France, and the current conflict in Algeria.

Index

Index

Other Titles of Interest

North Africa, Islam and the Mediterranean World

From the Almoravids to the Algerian War

Julia Clancy-Smith, *The University of Arizona* (Ed)

Long-regarded as the preserve of French scholars and Francophone audiences due to its significance to France's colonial empires, North Africa is increasingly recognised for its own singular importance as a crossroads region. Situated where Islamic, Mediterranean, African and European histories intersect, the Maghrib has long acted as a cultural conduit, mediator, and broker. From the medieval era, when the oasis of Sijilmasa in the Moroccan wilderness funnelled caravan loads of gold into international networks, through the sixteenth century when two superpowers, the Ottomans and the Spanish Hapsburgs, battled for mastery of the Mediterranean along the North African frontier, and well into the twentieth century which witnessed one of Africa's cruellest colonial wars unfold in 'French Algeria', the Maghrib has retained its uniqueness as a place where worlds meet.

Written by recognised specialists, the nine essays in this book ffer the latest research and thinking on North African history, and particularly on the region's complex relationship with adjoining cultures, regions and civilisations.

Contributors: *Julia Clancy-Smith, Amira K Bennison, James A Miller, Ronald A Messier, Mohamed El Mansour, Dalenda Larguèche, Abdelhamid Larguèche, Edmund Burke III, Jonathan G Katz* and *James D Le Sueur*

192 pages 2001
0 7146 5170 2 cloth
0 7146 8184 9 paper
A special issue of The Journal of North African Studies

FRANK CASS PUBLISHERS
Crown House, 47 Chase Side, Southgate, London N14 5BP
Tel: +44 (0)20 8920 2100 Fax: +44 (0)20 8447 8548 E-mail: info@frankcass.com
NORTH AMERICA
920 NE 58th Avenue Suite 300, Portland, OR 97213-3786 USA
Tel: 800 944 6190 Fax: 503 280 8832 E-mail: cass@isbs.com
Website: www.frankcass.com

French Military Rule in Morocco
Colonialism and its Consequences
Moshe Gershovich, *University of Nebraska, Omaha*

'Gershovich provides an admirably succinct summary of the
French side of the Rif War … an excellent introduction to the
French colonial peirod in Morocco.'

Middle East Journal

'careful, densely packed study of French military rule in
Morocco.'

Military History

This book presents a comprehensive analysis of French colonial
ideology and delineates the manner in which the French army sought to
conquer Morocco and control its inhabitants. It further examines the
manner in which France recruited and utilized Moroccan combatants,
highlighting their contribution to France's national security and imperial
expansion. In conclusion, the book explores the Franco-Moroccan
military symbiosis during the early years of Moroccan independence
and assesses the impact of French rule on the shaping of Morocco's
post-colonial national character.

256 pages maps 2000
0 7146 4949 X cloth
History and Society in the Islamic World

FRANK CASS PUBLISHERS
Crown House, 47 Chase Side, Southgate, London N14 5BP
Tel: +44 (0)20 8920 2100 Fax: +44 (0)20 8447 8548 E-mail: info@frankcass.com
NORTH AMERICA
920 NE 58th Avenue Suite 300, Portland, OR 97213-3786 USA
Tel: 800 944 6190 Fax: 503 280 8832 E-mail: cass@isbs.com
Website: www.frankcass.com

The Walled Arab City in Literature, Architure and History

The Living Medina in the Maghrib

Susan Slyomovics, *Massachusetts Institute of Technology* (Ed)

This book offers a multidisciplinary approach to the medina, the traditional walled Arab city of North Africa. The medina becomes a conrete
case study for comparative explorations of general questions about the
social use of urban space by opening up fields of research at the intersection of history, comparative cultural studies, architecture and
anthropology. Essays by American, European and North African
scholars demonstrate the variety of new sources and theoretical
approaches now being used in writing historical narratives framed
within the city space, shed light on recent studies by anthropologists
regarding social praxis within the urban context, and analyse the urban
experience of the medina and the Kasbah as they are represented in
visual and material culture.

Contributors: *Susan Slyomovics, James E. Housefield, Susan Gilson
Miller, Diana K Davis, Denys Frappier, Djilali Sari, Justin McGuinness and
Mia Fuller.*

176 pages 2001
0 7146 5177 X cloth
0 7146 8215 2 paper
A special issue of The Journal of North African Studies
History and Society in the Islamic World

FRANK CASS PUBLISHERS
Crown House, 47 Chase Side, Southgate, London N14 5BP
Tel: +44 (0)20 8920 2100 Fax: +44 (0)20 8447 8548 E-mail: info@frankcass.com
NORTH AMERICA
920 NE 58th Avenue Suite 300, Portland, OR 97213-3786 USA
Tel: 800 944 6190 Fax: 503 280 8832 E-mail: cass@isbs.com
Website: www.frankcass.com

Tribe and Society in Rural Morocco

David M Hart

This volume brings together a series of articles that examine different features of the precolonial, socio-economic and socio-political organization and customary law of various Berber-speaking tribal groups in Morocco.

Contents: Tribalism: The Backbone of the Moroccan Nation. Scratch a Moroccan, Find a Berber. Scission, Discontinuity and Reduplication of Agnatic Descent Groups in Precolonial Berber Societies in Morocco. The Role of Goliath in Moroccan Berber Genealogies. The Role and the Modalities of Trial by Collective Oath in the Berber-speaking Highlands of Morocco. Rural and Tribal Uprisings in Post-colonial Morocco, 1957–1960: An Overview and a Reappraisal. The Rif and the Rifians: Problems of Definition. Spanish Colonial Ethnography in the Rural and Tribal Northern Zone of Morocco, 1912–1956: An Overview and an Appraisal. Origins Myths, Autochthonous and 'Stranger' Elements in Lineage and Community Formation, and the Question of Onomastic Recurrences in the Moroccan Rif. Pre-colonial Rifian Communities outside the Moroccan Rif: Battiwa and Tangier. Comparative Land Tenure and Division of Irrigation Water in Two Moroccan Berber Societies: The Aith Waryaghar of the Rif and the Aith 'Atta of the Saghru and South Central Atlas.

224 pages 2000
0 7146 5016 1 cloth
0 7146 8073 7 paper
A special issue of The Journal of North African Studies
History and Society in the Islamic World

FRANK CASS PUBLISHERS
Crown House, 47 Chase Side, Southgate, London N14 5BP
Tel: +44 (0)20 8920 2100 Fax: +44 (0)20 8447 8548 E-mail: info@frankcass.com
NORTH AMERICA
920 NE 58th Avenue Suite 300, Portland, OR 97213-3786 USA
Tel: 800 944 6190 Fax: 503 280 8832 E-mail: cass@isbs.com
Website: www.frankcass.com
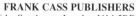